Market Tremors

Hari P. Krishnan · Ash Bennington

# Market Tremors

## Quantifying Structural Risks in Modern Financial Markets

palgrave
macmillan

Hari P. Krishnan
SCT Capital
New York, NY, USA

Ash Bennington
Real Vision TV
New York, NY, USA

ISBN 978-3-030-79252-7 ISBN 978-3-030-79253-4 (eBook)
https://doi.org/10.1007/978-3-030-79253-4



Cover credit: Tom Wang/shutterstock.com

This Palgrave Macmillan imprint is published by the registered company Springer Nature Switzerland AG
The registered company address is: Gewerbestrasse 11, 6330 Cham, Switzerland

# Acknowledgements

HPK and Ash Bennington would like to thank:

Stephan Sturm, for several insightful conversations in 2018 and 2019. Stephan introduced us to recent work on Mean Field Games and the application of dimensional analysis to price impact models.

Dan DiBartolomeo, for providing the crucial analogy between the price impact of forced liquidations and corporate takeovers.

Michael Howell, for numerous conversations about the impact of liquidity and positioning on market bubbles and crashes.

Jason Buck, Taylor Pearson and Jeff Malec, for their entrepreneurial spirit and thought leadership in the long volatility space. They added context to the more technical material in this book.

Randeep Gug, director of the CQF Institute, for providing a platform for presenting the main case studies in the book.

Tula Weis and Balaji Varadharaju for their prompt and high-quality editorial support.

Raoul Pal, Ed Harrison, Max Wiethe, Jack Farley, Tyler Neville, and the production crew at Real Vision, for providing a vehicle for long format interviews about various topics in the book.

Thanks also goes to (in alphabetical order): Stuart Barton, Ranjan Bhaduri, Nicholas Brown, Diego von Buch, John Burke, Brian Casselman, Kevin Coldiron, Christopher Cole, John Cummings, Nick Denbow, Vasant Dhar, Bob Doherty, Mark Finn, Jonathan Gane, Mike Green, Dan Grombacher, Jason Hill, Wayne Himelsein, Corey Hoffstein, Demetris Kofinas, Jon Marcus, Marty Mazorra, Nick Mazorra, Avery More, Chris Morser, Jon Marcus, Norbert Mitwollen, Stephen "SOG" O'Gallagher, R. M. Pathy, Joan Plensa, Sri Prakash, Patchara Santawisook, Mark Serafini, Kris Sidial and Tim Usher Jones for numerous interesting discussions regarding the book.

Ash Bennington would like to thank his family for their unwavering support: Adrienne Carchia, Carl Carchia and his late father Enrico Benigno.

Finally, HPK would like to give a special thanks to his immediate family: Kailash, Sudarshan, Lalitha, Rajee, Savitri, Raman and his late father Padmanaban. All have been helpful in their own special way.

# Contents


1 Introduction 1

2 Financial Networks in the Presence of a Dominant Agent 25

3 Exchange-Traded Products as a Source of Network Risk 61

4 The VIX "Volmaggedon", with Exchange-Traded Notes Destabilizing the Market 83

5 Liquidity Fissures in the Corporate Bond Markets 121

6 Market Makers, Stabilizing or Disruptive? 159

7 The Elephants in the Room: Banks and the "Almighty" Central Bank 201

8 Playing Defense and Attack in the Presence of a Dominant Agent 233

References 241

Index 245

# List of Figures


| | | |
|---|---|---|
| Fig. 1.1 | 30 year secular bear market for government yields (*Source* Bloomberg) | 6 |
| Fig. 1.2 | Historical time series of US corporate bond issuance (*Source* SIFMA) | 8 |
| Fig. 1.3 | Historical time series of US high yield debt issuance | 8 |
| Fig. 1.4 | Slightly cartoonish representation of the global financial network (*Courtesy* https://www.interaction-design.org) | 10 |
| Fig. 1.5 | Normal distributions assign virtually 0 probability to moves much larger than 3 standard deviations up or down (*Courtesy* https://www.geyerinstructional.com) | 16 |
| Fig. 2.1 | Histogram of daily returns for the INR/USD exchange rate (*Source* Yahoo! Finance) | 31 |
| Fig. 2.2 | Conditions where the Mean Field approximation makes sense (*Source* https://www.interaction-design.org/) | 35 |
| Fig. 2.3 | Representation of the financial network: dense core with massive number of interconnections (*Source* https://www.fincxus.uzh.ch/en/events/past-events/bigdatafinance-school.html) | 37 |
| Fig. 2.4 | Simulated distribution based on feedback from a Dominant Agent | 45 |
| Fig. 2.5 | An intraday jump caused by concentrated STOP SELL orders at a specific price | 47 |
| Fig. 2.6 | Parabolic growth of ETF assets, leading to flow-driven market dynamics (*Source* FRED [St. Louis Federal Reserve Database]) | 50 |

| | | |
|---|---|---|
| Fig. 2.7 | Counterparty exposures within the Australian Banking System (*Source* Mapping the Australian Banking System Network I RBA, https://www.rba.gov.au/publications/bulletin/2013/jun/6.html) | 54 |
| Fig. 2.8 | Extraordinary balance sheet expansion among the leading Central Banks (*Source* FRED [St. Louis Federal Reserve Database]) | 55 |
| Fig. 2.9 | Gold: an archetypal LJS bubble and crash in 1979 and 1980 (*Source* Bloomberg) | 57 |
| Fig. 2.10 | Mexican Peso rate: violent jumps do not require parabolic moves beforehand (*Source* Bloomberg) | 58 |
| Fig. 2.11 | Short volatility strategies tend to grind up before collapsing (*Source* Bloomberg) | 59 |
| Fig. 3.1 | Rapid growth of ETFs, with equities leading the way (*Source* Investment Company Institute) | 62 |
| Fig. 3.2 | Ignoring the price impact of investor flows, ETFs offer a cost advantage (*Source* Investment Company Institute) | 64 |
| Fig. 3.3 | Largest levered Exchange-Traded Products, as of March 2021. Tech dominated products in CAPS (*Source* ETF Database [etfdb.com]) | 75 |
| Fig. 3.4 | Surprising divergence in performance between levered and unlevered gold ETFs over longer horizons (*Source* Yahoo! Finance) | 77 |
| Fig. 4.1 | The Volpocalypse occurred nearly without warning in February 2018 (*Source* Bloomberg) | 84 |
| Fig. 4.2 | Intraday price moves for front month VIX futures on February 5, 2018 (*Source* Bloomberg) | 84 |
| Fig. 4.3 | Over daily intervals, front month VIX futures provide reliable exposure to the spot VIX (*Source* Bloomberg) | 86 |
| Fig. 4.4 | Remarkable impact of the spot VIX on a long equity portfolio (*Source* Yahoo! Finance) | 86 |
| Fig. 4.5 | In quiet markets, the VIX futures curve tends to be in severe contango (*Source* Bloomberg) | 88 |
| Fig. 4.6 | The front end of the VIX term structure is relatively responsive to changes in the spot VIX (*Source* Bloomberg) | 89 |
| Fig. 4.7 | Performance of rolling VIX futures benchmark in 2008 and early 2009 (*Source* Bloomberg) | 91 |
| Fig. 4.8 | Contango in quiet markets, backwardation after a risk event (*Source* Bloomberg) | 93 |
| Fig. 4.9 | Historical steepness at the short end of the VIX futures curve (*Source* Bloomberg) | 94 |
| Fig. 4.10 | Long VIX futures: roll costs overwhelm protection offered, when viewed over the long term (*Source* Bloomberg) | 96 |

Fig. 4.11 VIX futures erode any risk premium that the S&P 500 may offer (*Source* Bloomberg) 96
Fig. 4.12 Performance chasing leads to dangerously strong asset growth for inverse VIX ETNs in 2017 99
Fig. 4.13 Re-emphasizing intraday dynamics for VIX futures on February 5, 2018 (*Source* Bloomberg) 103
Fig. 4.14 Cost of executing a trade accounting for 20% of daily volume, based on constant of proportionality in square root impact function 110
Fig. 4.15 Curve fitting through historical trades in the order book is fraught with danger (simulated graph) 111
Fig. 4.16 Reasonable stability in the average takeover premium from one year to the next (*Source* FactSet) 113
Fig. 4.17 Inverse VIX ETN performance to February 2, 2018 (*Source* Bloomberg) 116
Fig. 4.18 If one sheep jumps off a cliff, others may follow (*Source* Bloomberg) 116
Fig. 4.19 Fragility of VIX ETN complex is actually *higher* when market volatility is low (parameterization based on FactSet data) 117
Fig. 4.20 Shorting VIX futures: disguised risk prior to the Volmageddon (*Source* Bloomberg) 118
Fig. 5.1 Comparison of premium/discount levels for a large cap equity and corporate bond ETF over time (*Source* Bloomberg) 125
Fig. 5.2 Realized volatility for the HYG ETF bounded below 12% from 2017 to 2019 (*Source* Bloomberg) 129
Fig. 5.3 HYG exhibited far less risk than the S&P 500 from 2017 to 2019. Realized risk giving the green light (*Source* Bloomberg) 129
Fig. 5.4 Large $$$ required to push the price of an equity or ETF by only a few percent 135
Fig. 5.5 Dealers focused on reducing balance sheet risk post-GFC (*Source* Federal Reserve Bank of New York) 137
Fig. 5.6 Dealer high yield exposure also on the downtrend (*Source* Federal Reserve Bank of New York) 138
Fig. 5.7 While dealers step out of the market, high yield supply increases (*Source* SIFMA) 139
Fig. 5.8 Typical flow-performance curve for equity mutual funds, based on historical data 143
Fig. 5.9 Convexity flipped for bond mutual funds 144
Fig. 5.10 The benchmark BND ETF largely consists of US government and highly rated corporate bonds (*Source* Vanguard) 151

Fig. 5.11 In quiet regimes, HYG has a modest beta to equities (*Source* Bloomberg) 151
Fig. 5.12 Jump in high yield spreads during the Covid-19 crisis (*Source* Bloomberg) 153
Fig. 5.13 Rolling 10 day average of high yield ETF flows, early 2020 (*Source* Bloomberg) 155
Fig. 5.14 As the VIX rises, HYG's link to the cash bond market becomes increasingly unstable (*Source* Bloomberg) 156
Fig. 5.15 Money flows back into HYG and JNK once Fed's intentions are digested by the market (*Source* Bloomberg) 156
Fig. 5.16 The alchemy of liquidity fails when investors require liquidity the most (*Source* Bloomberg) 157
Fig. 5.17 High yield mutual fund outflow expectations, based on the GJN paper methodology (*Source* Bloomberg) 157
Fig. 6.1 The S&P 500: positive trend interrupted by a sudden drop in 2020 (*Source* Yahoo! Finance) 160
Fig. 6.2 Cross-asset class volatility depressed in advance of the COVID-19 crisis (*Source* Bloomberg) 160
Fig. 6.3 Violent two-way action in S&P 500 during the February and March 2020 sell off (*Source* Yahoo! Finance) 161
Fig. 6.4 Nowcasts do not explain sharp reversals during the sell off (*Source* Federal Reserve Bank of Atlanta) 161
Fig. 6.5 Fairly smooth increase in spread of virus (*Source* ourworldindata.org) 163
Fig. 6.6 Payout of a collared position at maturity, beloved by many allocators 164
Fig. 6.7 Options market maker exposure given institutional demand for collars 166
Fig. 6.8 Conditional impact of market maker hedging, based on index level 169
Fig. 6.9 Using options open interest to infer where the various regions might be (*Source* CQG) 170
Fig. 6.10 Characterizing the forward distribution based on current index level relative to options open interest 172
Fig. 6.11 Near call strikes with high open interest, market makers act as a volatility dampener 173
Fig. 6.12 Historical time series for the GEX (*Source* squeezemetrics.com) 175
Fig. 6.13 Dealer exposure is not only level but volatility dependent 176
Fig. 6.14 High dispersion of 1 day forward returns when GEX is relatively low (*Source* squeezemetrics.com, Yahoo! Finance) 177
Fig. 6.15 Outsized returns tend to occur in sequence when the GEX is low (*Source* squeezemetrics.com, Yahoo! Finance) 178

Fig. 6.16 The scatter plot becomes noisier as we extend the forecast horizon (*Source* squeezemetrics.com, Yahoo! Finance) 178
Fig. 6.17 Over 15 day forward horizons, more structure is lost (*Source* squeezemetrics.com, Yahoo! Finance) 179
Fig. 6.18 When the GEX is low, the distribution of 1 day forward returns exhibits severe negative skewness (*Source* squeezemetrics.com, Yahoo! Finance) 181
Fig. 6.19 15 day forward distribution of S&P returns, scaled by VIX, when GEX is low (*Source* squeezemetrics.com, Yahoo! Finance) 182
Fig. 6.20 US 10 year constant maturity Treasury yield, December 2019 to March 2020 (*Source* FRED [St. Louis Federal Reserve Database]) 184
Fig. 6.21 Smoothed version of the GEX, January to June 2020 (*Source* squeezemetrics.com) 185
Fig. 6.22 Low GEX, high dispersion of 1 day returns (*Source* Yahoo! Finance) 186
Fig. 6.23 Payout profile of a short options straddle, close to maturity 187
Fig. 6.24 Payout profile of a LONG straddle, close to maturity 189
Fig. 6.25 Simulated distance between a stock and a nearby options strike as maturity approaches (*Source* https://citeseerx.ist.psu.edu/viewdoc/download?doi=10.1.1.146.143&rep=rep1&type=pdf, https://papers.ssrn.com/sol3/papers.cfm?abstract_id=458020) 192
Fig. 6.26 Call strikes attract a path that originally rises, put strikes create instability for paths that drift far below the initial price 195
Fig. 6.27 Simulation of lowest percentile 1 day return as maturity approaches 196
Fig. 6.28 Highest percentile 1 day return as maturity approaches, using the same set of simulated paths 197
Fig. 6.29 Dispersion of 1 day returns across simulations, as maturity approaches 197
Fig. 7.1 Fed assets since inception, using a log scale (*Source* Center for Financial Stability, FRED [St. Louis Federal Reserve Database]) 203
Fig. 7.2 Jumps occur in similar locations for commercial bank assets since 2000 (*Source* FRED) 204
Fig. 7.3 The discount rate lever is not particularly operational with rates near 0 (*Source* FRED) 206
Fig. 7.4 The Fed is always large, but becomes a Dominant Agent based on how it acts relative to the recent past (*Source* Center for Financial Stability) 208
Fig. 7.5 Times when the Fed has acted fairly strongly at the margins (*Source* Center for Financial Stability) 208

Fig. 7.6 The amount of physical currency in circulation increases quite predictably over time (*Source* FRED) 209
Fig. 7.7 Times when the Fed has acted very strongly at the margins 210
Fig. 7.8 The Fed's historical response to widening BAA credit spreads (*Source* FRED) 212
Fig. 7.9 6 month forward impact of Fed policy on BAA credit spreads (*Source* FRED) 213
Fig. 7.10 Quality of 3-factor forecasting model (*Source* FRED) 215
Fig. 7.11 Impact of Fed policy is cloudy in advance of the GFC (*Source* FRED) 216
Fig. 7.12 Components of the investment problem in a Strategic Asset Allocation framework 218
Fig. 7.13 The dollar quantity of equities has not been very sensitive to new issuance (*Source* FRED) 221
Fig. 7.14 The US credit supercycle since 1951 (*Source* FRED) 222
Fig. 7.15 The historical dollar supply of equities relative to (equities + bonds + cash) (*Source* FRED) 226
Fig. 7.16 Equity supply forecasting results, 10 year forward horizon (*Source* FRED) 227
Fig. 7.17 Shiller CAPE forecasting results, 10 year forward horizon (*Source* Online Data, Robert Shiller [http://www.econ.yale.edu/~shiller/data.htm]) 228
Fig. 7.18 Equity supply forecasting results, 5 year forward horizon (*Source* FRED) 228
Fig. 7.19 Relative deterioration in the power of Shiller CAPE, 5 year forecast horizon (*Source* Online Data, Robert Shiller [http://www.econ.yale.edu/~shiller/data.htm]) 229
Fig. 7.20 Equity supply indicator results, 2 year forecast horizon (*Source* FRED) 229
Fig. 7.21 Shiller CAPE forecasting results, 2 year forward horizon (*Source* Online Data, Robert Shiller [http://www.econ.yale.edu/~shiller/data.htm]) 230
Fig. 7.22 Summary of results (*Source* FRED, Robert Shiller [http://www.econ.yale.edu/~shiller/data.htm]) 230
Fig. 7.23 Historical time series for each indicator (*Source* FRED, Robert Shiller [http://www.econ.yale.edu/~shiller/data.htm]) 231

# List of Tables


| | | |
|---|---|---|
| Table 4.1 | Number of front month futures contracts needed to replicate a $-1X$ levered ETN per $1 billion of equity. Previous closing value: 15.62 | 102 |
| Table 4.2 | Number of front month futures contracts needed to replicate a $2X$ levered ETN. Previous closing value: 15.62. (REDUNDANT) | 102 |
| Table 5.1 | Possible states for a given fund in a given risk regime | 148 |
| Table 6.1 | Sample inputs for Eq. 6.1, given S&P options market maker positioning | 193 |
| Table 7.1 | Multivariate regression results | 214 |
| Table 7.2 | Regression results before the great financial crisis | 215 |

# 1

# Introduction

> People who count their chickens before they are hatched act very wisely because chickens run about so absurdly that it's impossible to count them accurately.
>
> —Oscar Wilde

As we look out across the spectrum of global markets in the middle of 2021, there are no visible signs of overt distress. In fact, we see the opposite: many markets appear "Zombified"—saddled with astronomical levels of public and private debt as yields remain pinned to the zero bound. Meanwhile, many veteran investors are bewildered by asset prices that no longer seem linked to traditional valuation metrics, such as price to book value. On a recurring basis, the high priests of finance try to justify the most recent rally on financial news networks to a growing legion of benumbed investors.

Against this surreal but seemingly benign financial backdrop, the authors of this book find themselves wrestling with several thorny questions: Are there circumstances where market volatility is persistently low, while a rising danger lurks beneath the surface? Can we identify structurally weak asset classes where a small price shock will spiral into a major sell off? If so, how can we defend against price meltdowns and liquidations before they actually occur?

As we will discover in the chapters that follow, the answer is a qualified "Yes!" There are many important situations where we can improve upon standard risk estimates, based on our knowledge of the major players in a given market and how they are likely to act. In service of that goal, this book is intended for readers who wish to understand and profit from situations


H. P. Krishnan and A. Bennington, *Market Tremors*,
https://doi.org/10.1007/978-3-030-79253-4_1

where risk is rising in the financial network while credit spreads and realized volatility remain low.

To begin this journey, it is worth reflecting upon how the availability of credit affects asset prices over time. It is widely understood that leverage and volatility tend to move in opposite directions in the later stages of the credit cycle. Leverage is high, yet equity prices are grinding up and credit spreads are stable or declining. Credit is cheap and can be readily deployed into the equity and corporate bond markets. This means that investors have the firepower to "buy the dips", which dampens downside volatility until the cycle breaks.

Historically, the US credit cycle tended to last six to eight years, measured from peak to peak. We could say with some degree of certainty where we were in the cycle. Asset booms and busts were somewhat predictable, as they corresponded to peaks and troughs in the quantity of credit available. Since 2008, however, this template has been altered by Central Banks, who now seem to equate economic stability with low asset price volatility. The expansionary phase of the current credit cycle has become extremely long in the tooth, given the ever increasing presence of the Fed.

While credit expansion usually has a stabilizing impact on asset prices, even that stability has a limit. If a large enough price shock occurs, leveraged agents will be forced to liquidate their positions as they get hit by margin calls and breach their risk limits. In recent years, banks and prime brokers have become increasingly risk averse, partly as a function of regulations enacted after the Global Financial Crisis. Brokerage houses set tighter position limits for their clients than before. This has important implications. An initial wave of selling can easily cause a cascade of forced liquidations, as other investors have to cut their positions after plunging through their loss limits. Within a Zombified market, prices can fall very rapidly, at least in the short term. Notably, the COVID-19 induced sell off in February and March 2020 started from a recent high in the S&P 500 and a very low volatility base.

## "Zombification" of Modern Markets

In the past decade, the tendency for volatility and leverage to move in opposite directions has become even more extreme—as leverage rises, volatility declines in markets awash in liquidity. (Note that this stylized fact did not rigidly apply to global equity markets in 2020, but was largely the case in the previous decade.) Before the Global Financial Crisis, the Fed's balance sheet was just under $900 billion; at the time of this writing, in early 2021, it has ballooned to over \$8 trillion. The quantity of corporate debt is now larger than ever, suggesting greater default risk—and yet the volatility of most asset classes has been persistently low.

This low level of volatility may seem puzzling since leverage ***is*** risk, in a certain sense. By definition, without the existence of leverage, there could be no defaults, with no need for margin calls. To repeat, we now find ourselves in an environment of structurally low volatility across asset classes, bloated balance sheets and negative yields. Bank deposits provide what is essentially a 0% return to savers, forcing investors to consider other riskier investments in the search for yield. Long positioning in risky strategies has become over-extended because of the lack of suitable investment alternatives. This "volatility paradox", where market fragility is high, but overall volatility is low, has become a stubborn feature of modern markets. Historically, the volatility paradox has been restricted to the later stages of a real economic cycle, where it creates a toxic blend of plentiful credit and investor complacency.

As an example, we can think about some of the forces at play in a simplified version of a housing bubble. Within the bubble, homeowners often borrow an increasing amount of money per dollar of equity, causing aggregate loan-to-value (LTV) ratios to rise. This type of borrowing is a function of market sentiment: investors and lenders are both convinced that prices will continue to go up, so they borrow and lend more. This is based on the dangerous assumption that higher housing prices in the future will push LTV ratios back down to more reasonable levels. Everyone seems to make solvency assumptions based on extrapolations from recent historical returns—and seem dangerously unaware of the risks inherent in the broader debt cycle.

We can think of this problem a bit more mechanistically. Easy credit generally increases the aggregate demand for assets. As a consequence, a fresh supply of new money enters the market and bids up asset prices, as investors fear missing out on the rally. This liquidity, partially provided by late entrants to the market, dampens downside volatility. As the rally continues, it becomes possible to borrow even more, given the rising value of the underlying collateral. It is worth observing that we live in a world where lending has become increasingly collateralized. The process becomes an archetypal, positive feedback loop.

A model describing precisely this phenomenon has been developed by Thurner (2012) and others. Minsky (2021) was one of the earliest academics to identify the problem. The volatility paradox arises as a function of the feedback between prices, risk appetite and access to credit. While "average" returns are compressed into a relatively narrow range, extreme event risk grows ever larger. With enough leverage in the system, even a moderate-sized sell off can wash a large number of over-leveraged investors out of the market. Ultimately, the sell off can cause a nasty chain of further selling—and a potential crash.

## The Challenge to Investors

No cycle lasts forever, even a distorted one, and this cycle will need to end at some point as well. But until the end of this cycle arrives, the volatility paradox can persist for a surprisingly long time. If pressures on balance sheets are high enough, the risk is that the cycle will end in a spectacular collapse. This brings us to an important point. Market Zombification presents a serious challenge to active managers. Intermittent mega-spikes in the VIX and other volatility indices increasingly occur from a low volatility base—often without much warning. This forces investors to make a difficult choice: if they stay out of the market, they collect no return; however, if they buy and hold equities or risky bonds, they may collect a small premium, but have to accept the risk of a large and sudden drawdown in return.

Taking on an over-extended market by selling futures against it is a dangerous alternative. Frothy markets have a tendency to become even frothier in the near term. Moreover, the timing of a market reversal is nearly impossible to predict in advance, which is why shorting bubbles can lead to catastrophic losses. Finally, buying insurance through the options market might seem to be a theoretically sound idea and actually is, given enough skill and over a long enough horizon. However, options strategies that decay over time require immense patience from investors in an environment when many other investors are piling on risk and Central Banks are standing guard. While it is true that active managers can blend long and short volatility strategies in their portfolios, the core problem remains an intractable one.

## An Analogy with Waiting Times

At some point, the credit cycle will turn, dragging equities and other risky assets into a bear market. Prices may drop quickly without recovering. If yields normalize somewhat, bonds may also sell off. This will be doubly toxic if we see a wave of defaults, as institutions are no longer able to finance their debt. Institutions that target a fixed return without too much regard for risk (think pensions and insurance companies) will take large losses in this scenario. It may turn out that options-based hedging is the only truly diversifying strategy left to investors if the stock and bond bubbles burst simultaneously.

The trouble is that we don't know *when* the cycle will turn. Many observers with a bearish disposition argue that every passing day makes the risk of an imminent liquidation more likely. This may well be true, but a simple analogy shows the dangers in this assumption. Imagine that you are waiting for a friend. If someone issued a guarantee that your friend would be no more than an hour late, the odds that he or she will arrive in the next 5 min would increase rapidly over time. After 55 min, the probability of arrival in the next 5 would be 100%. However, this doesn't correspond with experience. The longer you are kept waiting, the *less* likely that your friend will be coming anytime soon. Something material may have happened, which has qualitatively changed the distribution of arrival times.

## Qualitative Features of Zombification

In this new era of increased systemic risk, it appears that the economic cycle has been damaged—perhaps permanently. As we have suggested above, the price action we see across markets reflects this new reality. Equity sell offs, such as the events we observed in February 2010 and December of 2018, now occur spontaneously and often materialize out of nowhere during periods of low volatility. While these sell offs are quick to arise, they also seem to be quickly forgotten by the financial media and even market participants.

Historically, this was not always the case. The VIX and other implied volatility indicators tended to decay quite slowly after a spike. The market at large had a longer memory. Slow decay was reflected in the various econometric models that were developed by practitioners and academics alike. In the current market, however, "melt ups" are almost as violent as the meltdowns and V-shaped recoveries are increasingly common. Volatility tends to collapse quickly as investors jump back into "risk-on" mode, in an attempt to recover profits and make up for lost time in the markets.

Viewed through a wider lens, equities and fixed income have both been trending upward for an unusually long time. As of this writing, the S&P 500 has increased by a factor of 5*X* since 2009, while US bond prices have enjoyed nearly 30 years of steady positive performance. Credit markets have been underpinned by several rounds of Central Bank monetary easing in each of the major economies. Since corporate credit and equity are linked, Central

Banks have effectively acted as a backstop on the S&P 500 and other large-cap equity indices. In the meantime, US government bonds have received a nearly continuous bid from institutions. In the post-2008 regime, where loans are increasingly collateralized, the demand for sovereign debt has been remarkably high (Fig. 1.1).

Moreover, the zero interest rate policies implemented by Central Banks have incentivized excessive risk-taking in other areas. Rather than maintaining their strategic asset allocation weightings and simply accepting the lower forward returns that the current environment offers, investors have piled in *en masse* into riskier corporate bonds, illiquid assets and various short volatility strategies. Consequently, excess demand has reduced the amount of compensation they now receive for bearing risk. For example, many pensions with an annual return target of 6% to 7% have simply ramped up the credit and liquidity risk exposure in their portfolios, with something of a cavalier attitude toward extreme event risk.

Many observers, including the authors of this book, do not believe that these dynamics are sustainable indefinitely. In general, Central Banks can control either their domestic yield curves or their currency valuations, but not both at the same time. Lowering benchmark interest rates can encourage banks to increase their balance sheets, assuming that sentiment is not too bad. However, that increased velocity tends to come at a cost. Easy money policies have historically tended to weaken currency values, sometimes to disastrous effect.

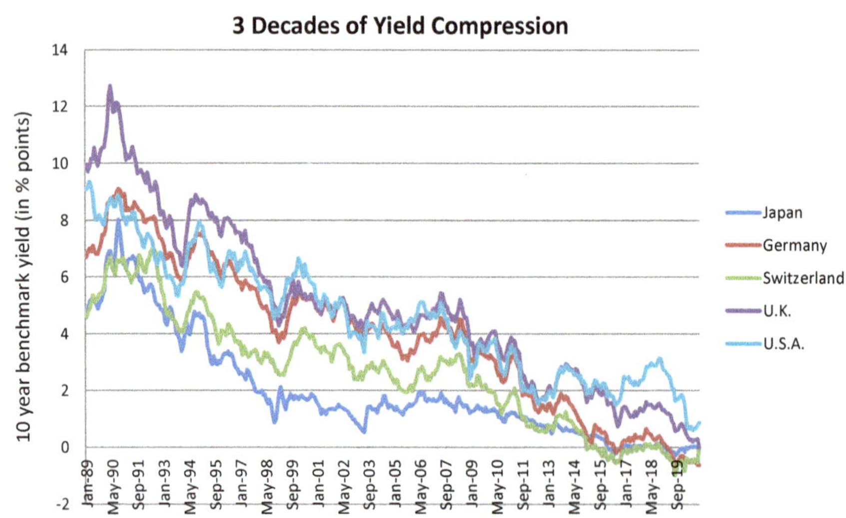


**Fig. 1.1** 30 year secular bear market for government yields (*Source* Bloomberg)

Under the current regime, it has taken a great deal of Central Bank coordination to maintain a reasonable level of stability across the major currency pairs. In the meantime, alternative forms of exchange with a fixed supply, such as gold and Bitcoin, have rallied. The Central Banks have collectively walked a tightrope in their activities. We would argue that synchronized easing is an inherently unstable process, as the financial system is highly non-linear and sentiment driven. The fault lines for a major dislocation in currency or bond markets are now in place.

## The Dilemma for Institutional Investors

Artificially low yield curves have forced many investors into areas that may not provide adequate compensation for risk. We might, for example, consider the case of a hypothetical European pension fund that is currently underfunded. In this example, using historical yields as our reference point, the situation has become dire. For the sake of simplicity, assume that the pension fund needs an average forward return of 4% on an annualized basis to meet its expected future liabilities. Current government bond yields fall well short of that threshold, as Fig. 1.1 clearly indicates.

One potential investing strategy would be to substitute Euroland debt with US Treasury bonds. After all, US bonds offer a modestly positive return over time. A 1.5% return might be a drag on a 4% return target—but something is better than nothing, right? Unfortunately, the added yield from US Treasuries introduces currency risk for European investors. Any attempt to hedge dollars back to Euros will cancel out the yield in US Treasuries. It follows that the pension fund in question needs to be an implicit currency speculator in order to get some yield from this strategy.

The other, far riskier alternative is to buy lower-quality credits, moving further down the capital structure in the process. This requires an invocation of the so-called Fed put, which is now the stuff of legend. The theory goes that Central Banks will bail out anything and everything that might be large enough to cause collateral damage to the economy. Following this line of thought, Central Banks have become an across-the-board backstop for virtually all risky assets.

If this theory were correct, it would be perfectly logical to buy the highest yielding loans possible. In the authors' view, however, this smacks of overconfidence. It is impossible to say with certainty what the Fed and other Central Banks might do if push comes to shove in the credit markets. The magnitude of QE required to calm things down may be met with political resistance among a host of other factors. What we do know is that many large buy side investors have been forced to take on enormous levels of risk in an effort to generate high single digits returns, when comparable returns could have been easily achieved with government bonds 20 years ago.

Given that investors crave yield, corporations have been happy to supply it. Figure 1.2 tracks the quantity of US corporate debt issuance over the past 25 years.

If we drill down a bit, we can see that companies that barely qualify as investment grade have been particularly active in their debt issuance (Fig. 1.3).

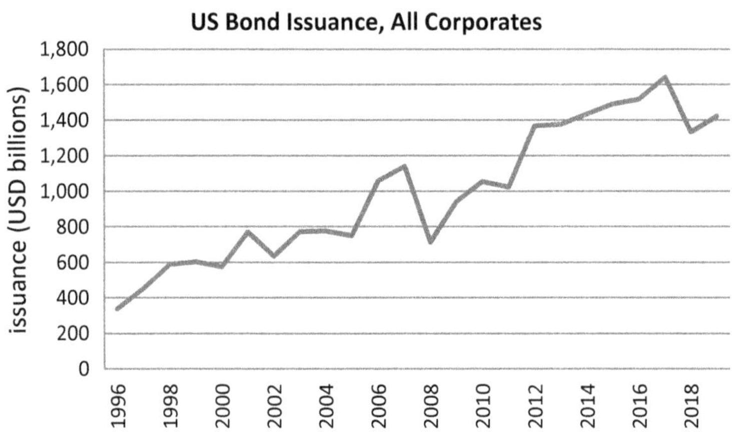


**Fig. 1.2** Historical time series of US corporate bond issuance (*Source* SIFMA)

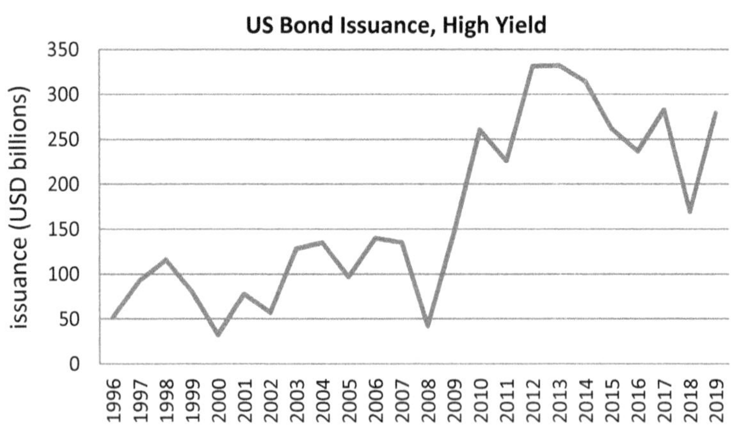


**Fig. 1.3** Historical time series of US high yield debt issuance

The indiscriminate search for yield has offered enormous benefits to companies that are large enough to securitize their debt. Corporate treasury departments have been able to issue new bonds with low coupons, reducing the burden of servicing their debt. Persistently low yields have led to narrowing credit spreads, as investors are willing to accept a large amount of risk per unit of incremental return. This, in turn, has allowed corporate treasuries to issue new bonds with low coupons. The large overhang of debt and leverage in capital markets has had destabilizing effects on the financial network.

## External and Network Risks

We now need to define a few key terms that will be helpful in our characterization of modern markets. Concisely, moderate ***exogenous*** shocks can drive increasingly large ***endogenous*** liquidations and squeezes. At the risk of stating the obvious, endogenous risks come from within the financial system, emerging from the complex interaction of agents who form the network. By contrast, exogenous risks affect prices from the outside and can arise from a wide variety of sources, such as geopolitical events and changes in technology.

There are gray areas in this coarse decomposition. Corporate earnings, for example, have both an exogenous and endogenous component. On the one hand, corporate earnings constitute news flow that affects prices once they are released (exogenous); on the other, companies are part of a global financial network, and their earnings are a function of transactions within the network (endogenous).

Endogenous network risks largely arise from a combination of factors: complex counterparty exposures, excessive leverage and overly concentrated exposure to certain asset classes or strategies. Counterparty risk played a major role in the Great Financial Crisis. It was impossible to untangle the network enough to know how much exposure to the mortgage markets a given bank faced. This caused the short-term financing markets to seize up, as the major banks doubted the solvency of each other. These markets are the lifeblood of the financial system. Leverage and over-exposure are loosely connected: when credit in the system is excessive, it eventually gets directed toward unproductive areas. This is the source of the various speculative bubbles we have seen over time. However, positioning risk can play a role even when Central Banks are not particularly dovish, e.g., when investors sell their core positions to chase returns in another asset class.

We can represent the financial system visually as a large graph. It consists of circles, or "nodes" of variable size and lines between nodes. The lines can also have variable width, based on the connection strength between two nodes. Figure 1.4 provides a stylized view of the global financial network.

Nodes are agents in the system, such as governments, banks, companies and households. When two agents transact with each other, they are joined by a line. Banks are the largest nodes, based on the size of their balance sheet and the sheer number of connections with corporations, individuals and other financial institutions. Banks are similar to major airport hubs, as a disproportionately large number of financial transactions are directed through them. Market makers, including those in the algorithmic trading space, are also large nodes, based on the percentage of order flow they service.

Conceptually, a financial network can become dangerous if the web of connections becomes too complex and convoluted or certain nodes increase beyond a reasonable size. For example, if the global banking system has become too interconnected, a shock to any part of the system may propagate throughout it and cause damage to large swathes of the network. This offers a more precise description of the source of defaults and large-scale price

**Fig. 1.4** Slightly cartoonish representation of the global financial network (*Courtesy* https://www.interaction-design.org)

moves observed during the Global Financial Crisis than the tangled web one above. Naturally, Central Banks are going to be larger than the typical household, so the real question is whether a node or related collection of nodes is acting out of proportion to its usual size. Bloated nodes can destabilize the financial network, increasing the odds of an extreme price move, as we will see in the sections below.

## Vulnerability Not Predictability

This book is decidedly not a treatise on market timing: instead, we are largely concerned with *market vulnerability*. Over time horizons longer than just a few seconds, it is nearly impossible to know for certain when a sharp sell off is going to occur. Even when looking across the very short time scales of high frequency trading, price action has a large component of randomness. To frame the argument more generally, a limit order book provides an incomplete and imperfect overview of where prices are likely to go from one moment to the next. The implication is that timing is always going to be elusive. As time horizons increase, the problem rapidly becomes more intractable. On longer time scales, randomness plays an ever-larger role, and the range of potential outcomes increases.

What we can do, however, is identify market configurations that are dangerous from a structural standpoint. These are the "market tremors" that give this book its title. Markets are constantly exposed to random shocks of varying sizes that are inherently unpredictable and essentially beyond categorization. Even if we were able to create a comprehensive list of externalities that influence corporate earnings or economic growth, for example, other market participants might already have done the same analysis. Many of the external factors that drive price action are already baked into the market at any given point in time.

Given this understanding of the uncertainty in markets, what options remain for investors to pursue? To pose the question more specifically, if attempting to build a comprehensive and predictive economic model is a fool's errand, where might we more profitably focus our attention?

A wiser course of action, in the authors' view, is to accept that random shocks occur as a matter of course in markets—and to focus instead on *regime identification*. In the simplest terms, what we are looking for are the repeatable pre-conditions for a major liquidation or a spike in volatility. Specifically, we want to know in advance when a shock of moderate size is likely to have an unusually large market impact. Under these circumstances, realized volatility might be low, but disequilibrium lurks beneath the surface. To a certain extent, these vulnerable market setups can be identified since they tend to follow predictable patterns. This is a major theme which we will expand upon at length in this book.

When the interbank lending market breaks down, as it did during the Global Financial Crisis in 2008, two things generally happen. First, highly liquid assets that can be easily posted as collateral, such as Treasuries, rally hard; currencies required for global settlement—especially the US dollar—also rally, because dollars are needed to close positions. Second, strategies that expose market participants to equity or credit risk are liquidated. The notion of diversifying across multiple risk premia capture strategies becomes secondary.

To put the general thesis into more practical terms, the two high-risk setups we will examine in this book are the following:

*First*, when the amount of leverage in the system is unsustainably high. When leverage rises, the price of risk assets inflates. This can lead to an Everything Bubble, such as the one we have largely experienced for the past decade, where the prices of stocks and bonds have both risen dramatically. When leverage is high enough, even a moderate change in market conditions will force certain agents to either liquidate their positions or to hedge them aggressively. This offers a rough explanation for the extremely sharp, short-lived sell offs we have seen in the past several years.

*Second*, when certain market participants are overly exposed to a specific asset or class of assets. When this occurs, too much of the available supply of cash and credit has been deployed into a segment of a market, which causes an asset bubble to form there. These asset bubbles can easily burst after the last marginal buyers come in during the late stages of an exhausted market.

One manifestation of over-concentration is the "pain trade". This phrase has gained a great deal of currency over the years. The pain trade is the one that will force the largest number of speculators out of the market in one go. In rising markets, there are actually two possible pain trades. If there is a large amount of tactical short interest, the pain trade can be a "melt up" where equity indices power through recent highs. Shorts have to cover their positions to avoid outsized losses. Otherwise, it tends to be a reversal, as momentum traders who have increased positions during the rally get flushed out. In bear markets, the pain trade oscillates quite rapidly between a rebound and a collapse. Shorts pile into down trends, but have tight risk controls. This can increase the degree of short-term mean reversion. Prices move sharply down; however, given a mild positive shock, momentum traders have to buy or cover their positions. Mean reversion is high as the market whips up and down. The next item on our agenda is to provide some intuition about how positioning risk arises.

## The Two Asset Base Case

The following example provides a basic framework for understanding how we will be discussing positioning risk in this book. It is important to note that positioning risk is not observable in the historical price series for a given asset. In our discussions of this topic, we have used Bookstaber (2017) as a guide.

Imagine highly simplified example where we own two assets, "Asset A" and "Asset B". Both assets are trading at $100 and have a realized volatility of 15%, measured over some past time interval. In the absence of any other information, assets A and B would appear to be equally risky, as volatility is the only input we are using to measure uncertainty.

Now, suppose that we add an extra piece of information that clearly impacts our risk model, but does not fit into a traditional risk management framework. Imagine there is a highly leveraged investor who holds a large position in Asset A. This investor has tight risk limits and will be forced out of the market for Asset A if the price drops below $97.50. In other words, after an initial $2.50 drop in the price of Asset A, our highly leveraged investor will have no choice but to hit the SELL button—and will need to liquidate the position in large blocks. By contrast, Asset B does not face the specter of liquidation risk, because it has a genuinely diversified pool of investors who are effectively unlevered.

So, which asset is riskier in our stylized example? Clearly Asset A is riskier, even though no price movements have occurred yet. Given a moderate, −2.5% down move, an investor who holds a long position in Asset A may be in some serious trouble.

Assuming that Asset A is normally distributed with 15% volatility, a down week of −2.5% or more would be expected to occur roughly 11.5% of the time. (Note that, for an asset with 15% annualized volatility, a −2.5% down move in 1 week is about 1.2 standard deviations below 0.) Something with an 11.5% probability of occurring would certainly not be classified as a rare event. However, once the large investor is forced to sell in size at that key price level, prices may drop even further because of the price impact of the selling.

What started as a modest shock now has the potential to morph into something much larger. The quantity of Asset A on sale has increased dramatically, with no change to demand.

Other agents in the system will only be willing to absorb the excess inventory of Asset A at a large discount, if at all. We are now faced with a situation where a moderate random drop has pushed Asset A's price into the danger zone. Suppose that the impact of the large investor's sell order is −5%, which corresponds to a total move of −7.4% for Asset A. For an asset with 15% volatility, the stated odds of a −7.4% or larger 1 week decline are 0.02%. Positioning has transformed a garden variety sell off into something that can easily qualify as an extreme event, if not a Black Swan.

Now suppose we like both Assets A and B equally, for example in terms of their future cash flows. We might then expect both assets to have comparable returns over a given time horizon. Without taking positioning into account, it would be reasonable to allocate the same amount of capital to assets A and B. This would reflect their historical volatility, along with our return expectations for each asset. However, given our deeper understanding of the problem, we need to allocate less to Asset A, as it has significantly higher structural draw down risk. In the language of classical portfolio theory, the "true" volatility of A is much higher than 5%—and added caution is required. The significant point here is that our leveraged investor has impacted the distribution of forward returns for A. The historical distribution needs to be modified in some way before we can use it to allocate capital responsibly.

## Textbook Description of Risk

The stylized example above is instructive—but it only accounts for two assets held by a single agent in a highly simplified sample problem. In the real-world financial system, there are billions of financial agents transacting in the network with complex overlapping exposures between them. In order to adjust the standard risk measures in a meaningful way, we need a realistic model of positioning risk that can accommodate the complexity of the real-world network.

Can we generalize our example to these more pragmatic, real-world cases? Happily, we can apply some very helpful ideas from statistical physics and game theory to reduce the network's complexity while retaining its most important features. We will describe the underlying methodology thoroughly in Chapter 2. In this section, we will simply attempt to define the scope of the problem.

It is helpful to divide risk models into two categories: first, models of price dynamics that **do not** make reference to specific agents within the financial network, and second models of price dynamics that **do** account for agents in the network. The models from each category form two poles of theoretical difficulty and computational feasibility.

First, if we ignore the network of agents entirely, we get a simplified representation of market reality. These simplified models are the type that appears in introductory finance textbooks. Markowitz (1952) is usually given credit for developing Modern Portfolio Theory, which was further developed by Sharpe (1964) and a legion of other financial economists. The original Markowitz model equates risk with the variance of a static distribution of asset returns, while more sophisticated models allow for return distributions that are not normal and vary over time. Second, at the other extreme, models that account for the full specification of the financial network can be incredibly complex.

We can begin by examining models that do not account for the full specification of the network in determining price. In the simplest version of this model, asset returns are assumed to evolve according to a random walk with a 0% average return. Prices go up and down from one time step to the next without reference to the recent trend. The direction of future movements is entirely unpredictable. The only thing we can infer is the range of future outcomes, based on the volatility of a given asset in the past. In this category of model, we do not need to understand anything at the granular agent-to-agent interaction level. Following the theory, the most important properties of a system are best observed after averaging over the very many trades that go through the market. This simplifies things from a practical calculation standpoint, as it is far easier to collect a bunch of historical prices than develop a mechanistic model of price action from first principles.

The random walk approach makes several stringent assumptions. Significantly, today's returns do not depend on the pattern of historical prices or any information that was known to investors in the past. In other words, asset returns have no memory. Over time, paths are effectively created by a series of independent random draws, which are analogous to repeated coin flips or spins of the wheel in a game of roulette. In addition, the distribution of returns does not change over time. We can phrase this in another more revealing way: while future outcomes are uncertain, the rules of the game do not change over time. The only source of uncertainty is *which* return will be drawn from the range of possibilities at a given point in time. The likelihood of any given return within the range is constant.

These assumptions underpin the various incarnations of portfolio theory that appear in finance textbooks. Using some ideas from probability, it can be shown that the random walk hypothesis implies that returns are normally distributed over time. This has an important implication. Normal distributions have very narrow tails. In more technical terms, 99.7% of all returns fall within 3 standard deviations of the mean, as we can see in Fig. 1.5.

Moves that are larger than four standard deviations essentially *never* occur. When outliers are as rare as this, we can conclude that the "tails" of a normal distribution are extremely thin. The possibility of high synchronization within the financial network, to the point where extreme events occur, is virtually negligible. It would virtually take a Martian landing to move prices far into the left or right tail of the distribution. In the textbook description, it also holds that no single player has the power to disrupt the distribution that the collective has created: only the activity of the collective is observable. All of this makes our stylized two-asset example above rather perplexing. Textbook theory is clearly violated when network effects dominate the system, since the simplified models cannot easily account for multiple standard deviation moves that occur without warning.

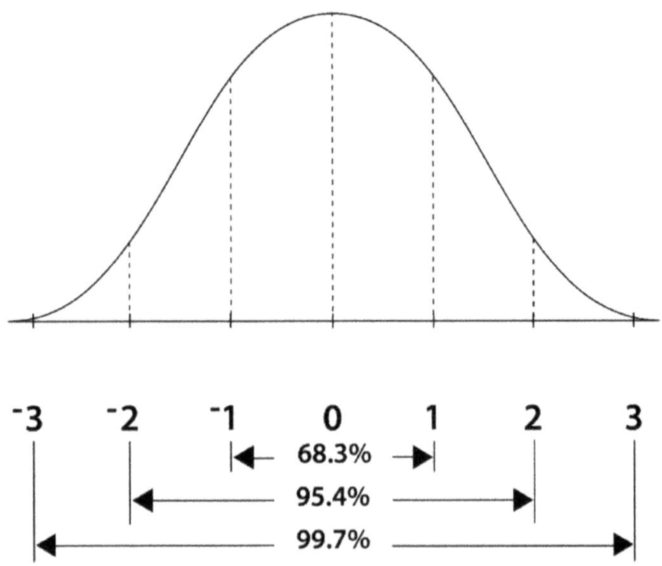


**Fig. 1.5** Normal distributions assign virtually 0 probability to moves much larger than 3 standard deviations up or down (*Courtesy* https://www.geyerinstructional.com)

This does not by any means imply that Modern Portfolio Theory is useless. In most regimes, asset returns can be approximated by something that resembles a normal distribution. Textbook theory offers a reasonable approximation of reality when nothing unusual is happening within the financial network. Framed in slightly more technical language, portfolio theory provides a good framework for understanding price dynamics when ***endogenous risks***—or risks that arise from within financial networks, rather than from external news flow—are not warping the distribution of returns.

As we mentioned previously, a long line of improvements have been made to the original random walk model over the years. These changes to the theory attempt to account for what is actually observed in financial time series data. In later-generation econometric models, for example, volatility is allowed to change over time. Even more complex models allow the correlation across assets to vary, both as a function of time and as a function of how far the market has moved. However, none of these approaches deals with the risks that emerge from ***within*** the financial network directly, such as complex feedback loops and the propagation of credit through the system. Framed slightly differently, even the most complex second-generation econometric models ignore financial flows, the amount of leverage in the system, and where that leverage is allocated in the market.

Credit and positioning are the twin heralds of risk—and yet they rarely appear in portfolio theory textbooks at all.

## A Parallel Universe

It is possible to imagine a financial universe with relatively low network risk. In the low network risk universe, prices would reflect information flows and investor sentiment without distortions or amplifications. In other words, bubbles and liquidations would be far less severe, and classical portfolio theory would offer a reasonably accurate reflection of markets there. Large price gyrations would generally only occur after a dramatic and unexpected shock to the broader economy.

In the alternate reality we have envisioned, money and credit would flow more slowly through the system, and counterparty exposure would not propagate far from the source. Major currencies might be "hard", meaning backed by gold or another asset with limited supply, which would put a brake on the ability of governments to issue large quantities of debt while using their Central Banks to suppress financing costs. Nation states could no longer debase their currency to increase exports or artificially stimulate demand.

Moreover, banks would revert to their original mandate, focusing on making well-researched loans to local businesses and individuals. The loans themselves would be conservative, generally requiring significant collateral. The derivatives markets, which allow the transfer of undiversifiable risk to the global capital markets, might still exist—but the derivatives would be exchange-traded and restricted to futures and options with simple payout structures. Finally, there would be less commoditization of investment strategies, and copycat investing would play a smaller role. Pensions and insurance companies would feel less pressure to manufacture "carry" by selling options, taking excessive credit risk, or over-allocating to global equity markets. (In this context, "carry" refers to any investment strategy that generates a steady return only as long as the market remains stable.) The land grab for yield in our alternate universe would be contained. Financial markets, along with the global economy, would be largely de-centralized.

This alternate universe would also dramatically slow the capital formation process by restricting credit flow through the financial system. From the perspective of investors who use leverage to exploit small price inefficiencies, it would also be an exceedingly dreary place to trade. A hedge fund manager transported from our world to the low network risk universe would be tempted to take a nap or reschedule Happy Hour to the early afternoon.

Still, in this monochrome alternate reality, the risk of global financial contagion would be extremely low. We could ignore the possibility of significant endogenous risk almost entirely. Individual banks might go out of business, but they would rarely blow up. If a bank defaulted, it would be very unlikely to drag down other financial institutions into insolvency with it. Similarly, government budgets would be constrained by the need to hold physical gold, which would keep currencies relatively stable.

As we will discover in subsequent chapters, this alternate reality bears little resemblance to our own. Not only do exogenous events affect prices in real-world markets, but complex feedback loops within the financial system can also cause them to spread and intensify—like a forest fire through bone-dry grass and timber. In fact, network effects may play a larger role in financial crises than pandemics, wars and natural disasters in determining the distribution of asset price returns.

## The Full Network Model

At the opposite end of the spectrum from the low network effect universe, a full-blown network model of financial markets can be extremely complex. The full network effect model relies on the idea that, within the network, every transaction and every agent matters. To repeat, any individual or entity that completes a financial transaction must be added as a node to the network model. Additionally, any transaction with a new counterparty creates a new network connection.

This broad analytic framework is capable of explaining or at least describing many phenomena observed in the markets that traditional models cannot. Leverage, overlapping exposures and counterparty risks clearly have played a significant role in the bubbles and crashes that have occurred throughout history. We also know that certain agents, such as Central Banks, have the power to change price outcomes—although those modified outcomes are never entirely predictable. Using a network model, we have the flexibility to generate virtually any form of price action observable in markets.

A network-based description of markets is obviously valid at a very granular level, on a transaction-by-transaction basis. Therefore, equating price movements to some aggregation of all transactions must be correct, by definition. Asset prices could never move if no transactions ever took place. However, this does not mean that a big data approach to the financial markets is the best way to understand systemic risk.

The market consists of a large number of agents, such as banks and institutional investors. These agents obviously play an important role in determining market price levels. For example, if we somehow removed banks from the network, most asset prices would be lower than they are today. There would be less credit available to create demand for financial assets. Network connections clearly also play a role. Agents with a high degree of connectivity to other agents within the financial network play a critical role in market stability. Banks and very active players in the derivatives markets (think Long Term Capital in 1998) fall into this category. These agents need to be monitored at some level, as they can cause considerable damage to the network if forced to unwind their positions. Network counterparty risks can be exposed when credit dries up. The Global Financial Crisis in 2007 and 2008 is effectively a demonstration of risks that can emerge from high levels of connectivity across a global financial network. Network counterparty risks can be exposed when credit dries up.

While conceptually correct, network models force us to consider a vital question: Do they have any practical use in the real world? When we try to draw practical conclusions from a network model, several cracks begin to appear. A well-specified model might generate the right sort of complex phenomena—but it is generally not suitable for making predictions. (We are not referring to price prediction here, which can be a Herculean task; rather, the network models we know of do not generate concrete numerical risk estimates either.) Using a network model, there are no associated volatility or drawdown forecasts. These models speak a different language from most risk managers. There is no direct way to convert network risk to a number that allows for position sizing. For example, we cannot make assertions such as: "the amount of credit available to a certain subset of agents in the network has recently increased by 50%; therefore, the volatility of the assets they are exposed to should be decreased by 10%". Nothing is stated in cold numerical terms—implying that quantitative investment decisions cannot be made on the basis of a network model.

Referring to Haldane (2019) and Bookstaber (2017), complex network models are currently useful as simulation tools. We accept that this is an important function. Economists can explore the range of outcomes that a policy change might produce in a qualitative way. Rough testing can be performed to see how a change might propagate through the financial markets. For example, Central Bank policy levers can first be pulled in a simulated network, without immediately performing a Frankenstein-like experiment on the real economy. A well-specified model allows policymakers to build some intuition about possible outcomes of a given action—before turning on the real-world liquidity spigot.

## Steering a Middle Course

These ideas all lead us to a critical point in our discussion, where we have to deal with the two crucial issues associated with building a network model. Specifically:

1. Can we build models that are *complete* enough to capture endogenous risk within the financial network?
2. Will these models be *simple* enough to generate stable quantitative risk estimates that can be compared with real-world outcomes? Any model that relies upon full specification of the network is likely to be unstable, given the highly non-linear nature of financial networks.

Our goal is to put financial network models on a firm practical footing.

As we begin to explore these issues, it is important to summarize the main challenges we face in our endeavor. First, within a complex network, we do not know how every agent is currently positioned, let alone their typical behavior patterns. This means that we cannot easily predict future positioning. The rules of the game are not known at a granular level. If we, the authors, do not know our own utility functions, it would seem unreasonable to specify anyone else's.

As we will discover in Chapter 2, even a near-complete knowledge of these factors would not be enough. Building a complete model of the economy from first principles is computationally infeasible. There are simply too many agents, financial products and counterparty exposures to contend with. As we have mentioned above, a full-blown model is also likely to be unstable. With all the moving parts and the introduction of leverage through the banking system, small changes in model assumptions are likely to generate vastly different results. It is widely accepted that leverage has an asymmetric impact on the financial network. While a moderate increase in the amount of credit available does not tend to have too much impact on prices, an equivalent decline can be highly destabilizing.

However, there is a path through the noise—at least under certain conditions. Our solution is to use a concept from statistical physics called Mean Field Theory ("MFT") to create a hybrid between classical portfolio theory and complete specification of the financial network. If we had to summarize the core idea behind this book on the back of a postcard, this would be it. We will develop this idea in great detail as we go along.

It is important to understand that we are not trying to make a small incremental change to textbook theory here, for example, by allowing volatility to vary over time within a standard model. Those improvements can be significant—but we are seeking a much larger conceptual reinterpretation of risk here. The Mean Field approach is developed in Chapter 2 and constitutes the main theoretical idea in this book. Note that our underlying idea is not original, but the practical applications of MFT will be.

As we explore this material in detail, our book takes the following narrative path.

Chapter 2 presents a basic framework for the more detailed chapters that follow. Here, we give an informal overview of Mean Field Theory and specify where it offers a reasonable description of market reality. When the conditions for a Mean Field description are satisfied, textbook portfolio theory may be acceptable. However, when certain agents in the network become very large or active, they have the power to distort the forward distribution of returns. They can amplify bubbles and crashes over a wide range of time horizons.

Chapter 3 targets Exchange-Traded Products ("ETPs"). These include listed funds and notes. As we will see, certain ETPs can dominate the markets they are supposed to track. Their impact is measurable and given the right conditions, induces extreme event risk.

Chapter 4 focuses on ETPs that track various VIX futures strategies. We will show how inverse VIX products caused an explosion in volatility during February 2018 that could not be predicted by backward looking risk models. Our revised estimate, taking ETP positioning into account, demonstrates that the "Volmageddon" was *not* a Black Swan-type event. Indeed, a volatility spike of this magnitude was likely to occur in 2018 or 2019, based on the forced reaction of ETPs to an initial volatility shock. Using our simplified, agent-based model, the Volmageddon could have been foreseen and predicted.

Chapter 5 turns our attention toward listed products that track corporate bond indices. Here, the problem is not leverage, but a mismatch in liquidity between ETPs and the cash bonds underpinning the benchmark indices. We study the consequences of the sort of technical sell off in high yield bond ETPs that occurs frequently in equity markets. Our risk estimates point to an unusually large drop in the junk bond market and the potential failure of the ETPs that track them. Our initial 2019 analysis turned out to be prescient in March and April 2020. Namely, the Fed had to buy various bond ETPs directly to prevent the underlying markets from crashing.

Chapters 4 and 5 place agent-based risk models on a solid and practical footing. More broadly, we will find that investors who rely on exchange-traded products to express their views may be in for some nasty surprises. Many passive investments, such as ETFs, can add to extreme event risk in the indices they supposedly track. We will also challenge the widely held belief that ETPs give highly reliable exposure to a benchmark of choice.

Chapter 6 moves to options market makers, who can have a disproportionately large impact on prices over multi-day horizons. While market makers may not have large balance sheets, they take at least one side of a high percentage of orders that go through the market. Given the right conditions, market makers can cause large dislocations in the underlying equity and futures markets without much warning. Using statistical tests, we analyze the impact of market maker positioning on S&P 500 volatility and extreme event risk.

Chapter 7 focuses on banks and Central Banks ("CBs") as mega agents in the market. These agents are of obvious interest in the post-Lehman market environment. As the scope and influence of commercial banks have decreased, CBs have become increasingly dominant. We will find that, when

CB balance sheet expansion is strongly above trend, credit spreads tend to decline. In addition, an increase in domestic debt can support high equity valuations for a surprisingly long time. For investors and borrowers, CBs tend to improve median outcomes. However, there is no guarantee that rounds of quantitative easing will reduce extreme event risk in the future.

Finally, Chapter 8 reviews the main ideas in this book in an informal and concise way, while providing some practical takeaways.

# 2

# Financial Networks in the Presence of a Dominant Agent

By and by, a loosened mass of the hanging shelf we sat on tumbled into the lake, jarring the surroundings like an earthquake and delivering a suggestion that may have been intended for a hint, and may not. We did not wait to see.

"Roughing It", Mark Twain

## Reviewing the Core Ideas

In Chapter 1, we described some of the principal challenges in modeling the behavior of financial markets, explored several key concepts that are essential to grasp how market risk is evaluated and introduced the foundation of our new Mean Field Theory ("MFT") model.

We are now ready to explain how our MFT approach works at a conceptual level. While we will explore a more quantitative treatment of the subject later in the book, we can outline how to develop a hybrid of standard portfolio theory and a complex network model. Our goal will be to capture the most important features of the financial network in specific cases, without adding any unnecessary complexity.

We will restrict ourselves to liquid instruments, such as Exchange-Traded Funds, listed futures and options in what follows. These allow us to create historical return distributions that are not corrupted by stale prices or model-based estimates of fair value. In most markets, most of the time, the historical distribution of returns is a decent proxy for the range of plausible outcomes in the future. Here, textbook portfolio theory is appropriate when describing


H. P. Krishnan and A. Bennington, *Market Tremors*,
https://doi.org/10.1007/978-3-030-79253-4_2

future outcomes that are not too far from the mean. The historical distribution effectively characterizes the average behavior of all agents in the financial network in the past, as well as likely behavior in the future.

In this paradigm, no single investor has the power or at least the incentive to change the distribution materially. Prices do not have to move too far to find a nearly equal balance of many buyers and sellers. We wind up with a distribution that does not give much information about the likelihood of extreme outliers, but is useful for assigning probabilities to more moderate outcomes.

We observe that there are many ways to estimate a historical return distribution and no universal agreement as to the best way. In addition, we have not specified a time horizon for the distribution. Are we characterizing returns over 1 minute, 1 day or 1 year forward horizons? We have glossed over these details to make our narrative as clear as possible.

The **historical distribution** can be thought of as an estimate of the so-called **Mean Field** that every investor faces. These two terms can be used interchangeably, without much loss of precision. The only difference is that, while Mean Fields make direct reference to particle or agent interactions, distributions do not. In our context, a Mean Field represents the average behavior of a large number of agents within the financial network, as it relates to the price movement of a given asset. Significantly, a Mean Field can be more easily modified to account for the presence of very large players in the network. We know from experience that some agents are many orders of magnitude larger than others. Banks, for example, have vastly larger balance sheets than a typical household. However, assuming that these large agents do not act differently from the way they have in the past, the **Mean Field = historical distribution** approximation is likely to suffice. We do not need to have a detailed understanding of the players or their motivations to make practical investment decisions. A macroscopic picture of risk is sufficient.

To put things in context, suppose we know the Mean Field for a given asset. As we have said, it reduces to a distribution of returns, estimated from past data. Then, we simply need to decide, based on our risk tolerance and other constraints, how much exposure to the distribution we want to have. Different assets naturally have different distributions. A risk-averse investor would allocate more to assets with a narrow spread of returns, such as Treasury Bills, rather than something whose distribution is much wider, such as Natural Gas futures. Treasury Bills have more certain future outcomes than Natural Gas futures, something that is accurately reflected in the historical distribution.

This brings us to our main point of departure from standard risk models. **The standard models fail when agent interactions do not average out.** These situations cannot be discounted, as they often lead to outsized market moves. When certain agents grow to an abnormal size or act unusually aggressively at the margins, historical distributions are no longer indicative of future risk. A qualitative change has occurred, that has the potential to affect future outcomes, even if it is not observable in recent price action.

All agents might initially face the historical distribution. In addition, assuming that prices remain in a narrow range, the presence of abnormally large agents may not be felt for a long time. Then, the historical distribution may still seem to be valid. However, it is on very shaky ground. Market tremors are lurking below the surface, effectively changing the tails of the distribution. Given a large enough price disturbance generated by the original (historical) Mean Field, things will change dramatically. As the majority players or Dominant Agents are forced into the market, they have the capacity to push prices much further in the same direction. They can amplify random fluctuations beyond recognition. 2 standard deviation moves according to the original distribution can easily turn into 4+ standard deviation ones. These would be considered highly improbable in the absence of network effects.

Extreme price changes are a direct consequence of **price impact**, over a range of time horizons. When Dominant Agents are forced to hedge or liquidate positions without regard to value, prices can accelerate at an alarming rate. Large unidirectional trades are the drivers of outsized moves. Quantifying the impact of fire sales and short covering requires a certain amount of mathematical technique. As we attempt to measure network risk, rather than simply describe it, we will need to develop techniques for estimating impact in Chapters 4 and 5. The end game is a hybrid system that is computationally closer to textbook portfolio theory than a full network model, but incorporates important feedback effects within the network.

Econometricians might refer to the set up as a Mean Field Game with majority players. We prefer to call these players Dominant Agents in what follows, given that they can disrupt the normal functioning of markets when forced to act in size. However, we will not concern ourselves with the strict accuracy of the Mean Field Game analogy for now. What we are concerned about is the feedback loop between the historical distribution and a few large players. If the original Mean Field creates a path that forces the large players to rebalance in size, their actions will change the Mean Field. It is as simple as that. Leverage and positioning risk were always there, but have now risen to the fore. Once the Mean Field changes to account for unexpectedly large price moves, another feedback loop is possible. Things can become even more extreme, as the same or other agents are forced to sell or cover their shorts again.

## Contrast with Reactive Approaches

The Oscar Wilde quote at the beginning of Chapter 1 now seems particularly relevant. Waiting for a volatility spike before reducing exposure can be dangerous. Some practitioners argue that modern risk systems are responsive enough to get you out of trouble reactively. Assuming this is correct, you can wait until the market is giving signals of distress before exiting. Prices are sampled at reasonably high frequency, numbers are crunched rapidly and the models flash RED when there is a potential break in the market. We accept that there is some merit to this approach. It is perfectly reasonable to use as much price data as possible and scale in and out of positions using automated execution strategies.

However, if relied upon too much, the faster systems can also lead to overly aggressive positioning. This is, especially true in a Zombified market. Suppose that the market has been in "risk on" mode for a while, with rising equity and corporate bond prices and low volatility. Intraday ranges are low and cross-asset correlations stable. The faster systems would actually encourage larger positions than usual, based on low levels of short-term realized risk. They are ill-equipped to deal with sell offs that emerge very rapidly, such as the US equity flash crash in May 2010. Algorithmic trading has increased the speed of crashes in various markets beyond the capability of most dynamic allocation schemes. It has also increased the number of false crash signals, where a given contract recovers almost as quickly as it fell.

## An Emphasis on Practicality

We have to admit that this book does deal with several theoretical concepts. In particular, we borrow some ideas from statistical physics as a way to reduce the complexity of the financial network in this chapter. In Chapter 7, we veer in the direction of Modern Monetary Theory when we describe how liabilities mechanistically transform into bonds and cash. However, we will try to restrict ourselves to ideas that can be transformed into actionable risk numbers. Certain ideas can deepen our understanding of market function, but are insufficient when it comes to protecting capital. In our opinion, every good theory needs some concrete examples to provide meaning and motivation. At some point, you may actually want to calculate things. Theories without meaningful special cases tend to wither on the vine.

Our overriding goal is to identify dangerous market set ups or traps. We can think of these as situations that have a larger than normal probability of leading to serious losses. As discussed above, the **twin heralds of credit and positioning** are usually in play. These situations have certain common elements. Investors are confident, possibly even complacent. Volatility is low, signaling to the marketplace that no significant risks are looming on the horizon. Nevertheless, based on our framework, the market is structurally weak. Things look extremely dodgy from a credit and positioning perspective.

In the pages that follow, we will quantify the notions of contracting credit and over-extended markets. We will put some substance behind the "things look dodgy" phrase. It should then be possible to reduce exposure in advance of a crisis or alternatively, to hedge cheaply before the horse bolts from the stable. We give some guidelines for using the core ideas in this book in Chapter 8. Along the way, we will develop various strategies to infer who the large players are, how large they might be and how much leverage they might be applying. These are case studies that demonstrate the relevance and effectiveness of our approach.

## Buying Options in Fragile Markets

While this is not a book on trading strategies, it addresses the following practical question. How can we play the long in the tooth equity bull market or overcrowded strategy, from a trading standpoint? What do we do if yield hungry investors have loaded into credit to the point where spreads no longer reflect default risk? One reasonable strategy is to stockpile insurance in markets that have low realized volatility, yet are structurally fragile. Options are the ultimate "bubble fighters", as they allow investors to profit from severe corrections with bounded risk. Taking on the market directly with futures, trades against the direction of the trend can be treacherous. Assuming that no important releases (such as a rate decision) are looming on the horizon, assets with low realized volatility generally also have low implied volatility. Ordinarily, we would not expect the spread between implied and realized volatility to be very large. If implied volatility were much higher than realized, it would be easy to sell options, hedge gamma risk with the underlying asset and extract a likely profit. It follows that options on assets with low realized volatility will generally be cheap, once our structural risk indicators start to flash RED. As a consequence, options that offer protection against a sharp reversal are likely to be relatively cheap.

We emphasize that buying options on a stock before an earnings report or on a currency before a Brexit-type vote is markedly different from what we will discuss here. In that case, market makers ratchet up their options quotes, reflecting very high implied volatility, before an event that is known to have a binary outcome. This offsets the theoretical advantage of a long options trade in advance of a major event on a known date.

Of course, there is no guarantee that we will make money on a long options position that is theoretically underpriced. Our edge, so to speak, is statistical. We are putting our money into something that has a very attractive asymmetric payout. We can get more leverage (as a function of dollars invested) from a put or call when volatility is low. This brings us to an important point that motivates the ideas developed in this book. When an asset class has low volatility but high positioning risk, the odds skew even further in our favor. The "true" probability of making a large gain from a fixed cost options position is significantly higher than the market thinks. Some of the great macro-hedge fund managers have historically taken this approach, burying long options positions in their portfolio, both as a hedge and a source of episodic or "crisis" alpha. Once we buy an option, we have a convex trade in place. While the probability of winning before maturity may be somewhat uncertain, the payout, if we do win, will be vastly higher than the premium we have paid for the option. This can qualify as a trading edge. In the late stages of an extended bull market, options structures that would usually be considered hedges transform into potential alpha generators.

Admittedly, it might take a while for structural risk to transform itself into realized volatility. That is the downside to measuring subterranean risk, the **risk of being early**. We may have correctly characterized the current regime as "calm but unsafe", which is superior to buying options whenever volatility is cheap, without regard to market internals. Although we have a theoretical edge, our options structures might lose money for a while. However, when they *do* payout, our trading gains are likely to more than offset previous losses. Why? We bought options when risk was underpriced by the market.

## The Standard Approach to Modeling Risk

Now that we have supplied a conceptual basis for our MFT approach, we can explore how standard risk management practices rely on the problematic assumption that future price patterns will look like price patterns observed in the past—at least in a probabilistic sense.

If we want to characterize the risk in an asset or portfolio, we need to understand the range of outcomes that it can produce. This requires estimating the distribution of forward returns. Assuming that the future will produce the same range of patterns as the past, we can use the historical distribution as a proxy for the forward distribution.

For example, assume we are interested in the distribution of returns over some time period, which we can call $\Delta t$, or "delta t". If we want to characterize the range of 1-day outcomes for our portfolio, we would set delta $t$ equal to one day. We could then take our historical price series, slice it into intervals of size $\Delta t = 1$ day, and then calculate the percentage change in price over each interval, and finally tabulate the data.

We can then build a histogram of realized returns, as in the following diagram. The histogram places returns into various bins, based on their size. In the chart below, our source data consists of daily returns for the Indian Rupee rate (relative to the US Dollar) from 2003 to the present. Here, we have divided the data into 100 equally sized bins. Along the y-axis, we can see how often the daily return fell into a given bin (Fig. 2.1).

Here, the vast majority of returns fall into the $-2$ to $+2\%$ range, represented by the interval $[-0.02, 0.02]$ in the graph. There are a few returns in the $+2$ to $+4\%$ range, where the Rupee weakened sharply after some combination of external information flow and technical selling. The distribution appears to be positively skewed: large price moves are more likely to occur when the Rupee weakens than strengthens relative to the US Dollar.

According to textbook theory, supply and demand change as new information becomes available from outside the system. Network effects are relatively unimportant. This new information affects agent perceptions of risk and opportunity. We can say that news flow is a source of "exogenous" risk, arising from anywhere outside the financial network.

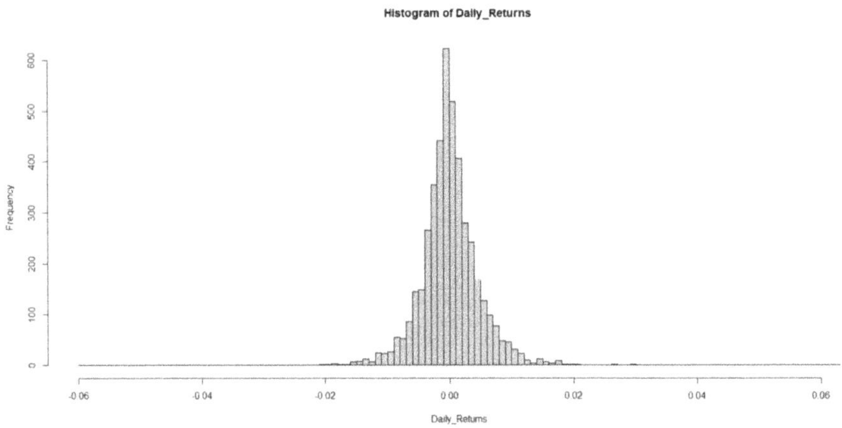


**Fig. 2.1** Histogram of daily returns for the INR/USD exchange rate (*Source* Yahoo! Finance)

Significantly, this histogram only gives a good representation of future outcomes if certain conditions are satisfied. First, the underlying process needs to be **stationary**, or invariant over time. In other words, in order for the histogram to be valid, we have to hope that the invisible "machine" that randomly generates prices has not changed its rules in the past and will not change them in the future. If we are going to slice time into small increments, we also need to convince ourselves that prices are **path independent**. Path independence requires that the return *at* time step delta t does not depend on whether prices were trending up or down *before* we reached $\Delta t$. Under these assumptions, we can reasonably view each return as the result of an independent experiment. Given enough data, our histogram should eventually converge to the "true" distribution of returns.

Once we have estimated the forward distribution of portfolio returns, we can directly calculate a wide range of traditional risk statistics such as downside deviation, Value at Risk, expected shortfall and so on. (Note: we are not making a value judgment about the usefulness of any particular risk metric in this discussion.)

These risk metrics provide some information about how much an investor is likely to lose in a typical, quantifiable downside scenario. They act as a data compression tool—mapping a wide distribution of returns onto a discrete risk number. However, as we discussed earlier, a correctly estimated distribution gives far more detailed information than any single summary statistic can.

## The Mean Field Interpretation

Applying some concepts from statistical physics in new ways, we can reinterpret the distribution. At first, it may seem as though we are simply assigning new names to standard concepts in portfolio theory—but, as we continue to build on the theory, the advantages of our alternative framework will become clear.

As we have mentioned above, the distribution of returns for a given asset can be thought of as a "Mean Field" generated by a subset of agents in the financial network. These are the agents who trade the asset directly or supply funds to other agents who trade it. Mean Fields are used in areas of statistical physics where a very large number of particles are interacting. The benefit of Mean Fields is that they characterize the state of a system without requiring a detailed understanding of the nearly infinite number of potential particle interactions within the system.

Mean Fields add some precision to a very rough but intuitive idea: given enough particles moving randomly according to roughly the same distribution, most particle interactions "average out". No single particle contributes too much to the whole. For example, suppose that we want to measure the temperature in a closed room. Without recourse to the concept of Mean Fields, we might think of estimating the temperature at any given location by calculating and summing the kinetic energy of every particle passing near that location shortly before and after a specific point in time. This is a technically correct description of the problem.

However, such a calculation would be impossible in practice, given the number of particles in the room and all of the possible particle collisions that could occur along the way. A more sensible and practical approach involves modeling the evolution of temperature directly, using something called a diffusion equation.

In a diffusion equation, particle motions do not appear explicitly. Rather, temperature is thought to be a **distribution** that evolves over time. It is a macro-level quantity, not explicitly dependent on the dynamics of energized particles. It tells us everything we need to know about how hot any small region is at some point in time. If we wanted to measure a quantity other than temperature, we might have to use a different approach or model particle interactions directly. However, for the problem at hand, we repeat that the time-dependent temperature distribution provides all the information we need.

In the same way, we can think of the distribution of returns for a given asset at any point in time as a Mean Field. Using a bit of notation, the Mean Field $H(r, \Delta t)$ gives the likelihood of a return of fixed size $r$ over some time interval $\Delta t$. For standard distributions, such as the Gaussian distribution, $H$ decays as we move further away from the mean. While space is 3-dimensional when we model the temperature in a room, $r$ is only 1 dimensional for a single asset. This would appear to simplify the problem considerably. However, when dealing with agents rather than inanimate particles, we face other sources of complexity. Agents in the network play the role of particles in our most basic Mean Field setup. They create supply and demand for a given asset, with transactions very roughly playing the role of particle collisions. In reality, however, agents have the capacity to change their behavior over time. By contrast, particles obey a fixed set of rules as they move through space.

To repeat, the quantity we are searching for is the distribution of future returns for a given asset. We might not be able to build a microeconomic model of price formation, based on a characterization of individual agent behavior across the entire network. However, if we believe that the historical distribution $H$ above gives a reasonable and stable description of the collective behavior of all agents, then $H$ *is* our Mean Field. We do not need to know anything about local network interactions to construct a Mean Field. So long as network effects largely average out, we can model everything from a high-level perspective.

## Indistinguishability: A Hidden but Crucial Assumption

There are various ways to improve upon the Mean Field model to make it more realistic. For example, we might look at the time series data and decide that risk levels vary over time. Sometimes, the range of outcomes is quite narrow, while other periods are characterized by high levels of uncertainty.

We can express this idea by making the Mean Field dynamic. In the simplest case, we might allow volatility to fluctuate over time. Various econometric models try to account for the time-varying nature of risk.

GARCH models, originally developed by Engle (1982), update volatility (or more accurately, variance) as a function of the most recent squared return and an estimate of long-term volatility. In this context, estimated volatility varies over time. GARCH and its various incarnations are based on two observations that are qualitatively correct: volatility tends to increase after a large price move in one direction or another and eventually reverts to some long-term average over time.

Other techniques use options prices to incorporate market expectations into the Mean Field distribution. This is a direction that Derman (2003) and others have taken. It allows for the distribution of a given asset to be highly non-normal when investor demand for extreme event insurance is high. Note that we are not concerned with models that describe the correlation or more generally, co-movement of different assets for now. We are solely focused on estimating the return distribution of a single asset for now.

The models above make various refinements to the original random walk model. If used correctly, they can lead to improved risk estimates and more accurate sizing of positions in a portfolio. However, each of these models makes a hidden assumption that is only revealed when we think of things in a Mean Field context. In particular, the network of agents needs to satisfy an indistinguishability condition. To repeat, the Mean Field can only be defined without direct reference to the underlying financial network given this condition.

Indistinguishability means that every agent faces the same Mean Field. No agent dominates the system, in the same way that no single particle has a material impact on the temperature of a room. Equivalently, if you removed any one agent from the network, the distribution of returns would not change. If this condition holds, risk models that rely upon historical price data can perform fairly well on an out-of-sample basis. However, if indistinguishability fails, network effects *have* to be included if we want to properly measure risk.

We can consider a non-technical example where indistinguishability is violated. Imagine a quaint town with many beautiful, old, low-rise brownstone buildings. Unfortunately, the town is also home to a twenty-story monstrosity of an office tower built during the 1970s. The ugly office tower is located near the middle of town, and we can distinguish it from the rest of the buildings in two ways: first, a view from the twentieth story of the office tower looks out across many of the other, smaller buildings in the town; second, the ugly office tower is likely to be included in the panoramas of any of the low-rise buildings. Under these circumstances, there is no "average" view in the town: a viewer from the top of the 20-story tower faces a qualitatively different collection of buildings than a viewer from the roof deck of any of the low-rise buildings.

Now let us revert to the base case. Assuming that the indistinguishability condition is satisfied, and we can reasonably specify the Mean Field, either for an asset, index or portfolio, we have a complete description of risk in the system. The actions of a single agent can never be enough to change the Mean Field materially. In the following diagram, we can see how the process works. We have mapped a highly complex network of agents onto a single distribution of returns (Fig. 2.2).

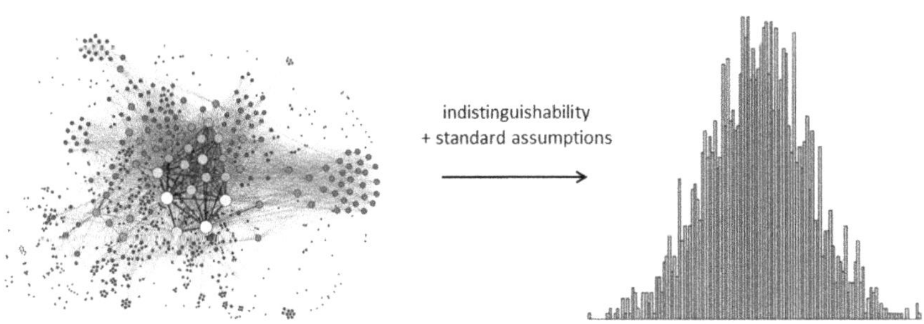


**Fig. 2.2** Conditions where the Mean Field approximation makes sense (*Source* https://www.interaction-design.org/)

Given the right conditions, a Mean Field approximation is certainly tidy. However, it loses its validity on those occasions certain nodes have a disproportionate impact on the network. Here, ordinary price discovery can be overwhelmed by a number of internal factors, such as forced liquidation of margin accounts and bank defaults. We will explore this idea further in the next section, but need to make a technical comment beforehand.

Aside from the indistinguishability condition, we emphasize that Mean Fields only exist for **large** ensembles of particles or agents. The Mean Field derived from a network will only be well-specified if it is an average of the behavior of very many indistinguishable agents. This may be one reason why private and thinly traded markets do not have distributions that are easy to characterize. There are not enough agents or transactions to justify averaging over them.

## From Mean Fields to the Entire Financial Network

The following diagram, borrowed from https://www.finexus.uzh.ch/en/events/past-events/bigdatafinance-school.html, is a somewhat more detailed representation of a financial network than the one above. Importantly, it also has a stronger core, implying that a relatively small fraction of agents account for the vast majority of activity in the system (Fig. 2.3).

The nodes in the center are typically intermediaries who lend money or provide liquidity in various asset classes. These include global banks and market makers. Central nodes are characterized by a very large number of counterparty exposures. The density of connecting lines is very high at the core. At the periphery, we might find households, who hold checking accounts at their local credit union or the local loan shark in town, who charges extortionate rates to individuals who sadly cannot access other forms of credit.

We can easily see from the diagram that indistinguishability is violated. The only question is whether it is violated badly enough that no Mean Field exists and the standard models do not apply. For now, let us explain why the indistinguishability condition is violated, by way of example. A small regional bank faces a different set of agents than a primary dealer that transacts with the Fed. Citigroup has over 200 million clients in roughly 160 countries, stretching its tentacles into any market where it can find enough profit per unit of perceived risk. By contrast, small US credit unions, which act as cooperatives, may only hold a few million US dollars in deposits.

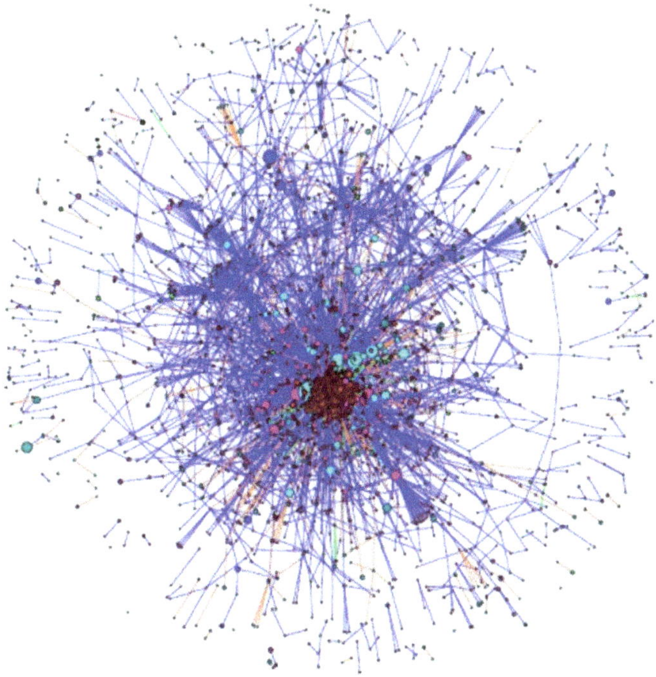

**Fig. 2.3** Representation of the financial network: dense core with massive number of interconnections (*Source* https://www.finexus.uzh.ch/en/events/past-events/bigdatafinance-school.html)

The next question is whether we can remove any the large nodes in the center, without material effect. As we have mentioned above, this is a test for indistinguishability. Before 2008, it was widely thought that network stabilization could be achieved through risk spreading. Loans could be securitized, sliced into small pieces and offered to a relatively large number of end investors. At least in theory, derivatives allowed for the transfer of risk to agents who had the balance sheets to absorb it. As it famously turned out in 2008, risk could not be easily spread without dramatically increasing the complexity of the global financial network. A reasonable analogy was one of a telecommunications network that distributes resources until it reaches the point of overload and collapses.

In the aftermath of the Lehman default and the Global Financial Crisis, we now know that the system is very vulnerable to changes at the center. Network effects are vital in the general case. Without a technical shortcut, we are now faced with the massive challenge of modeling the propagation of shocks through the network. Even for a lattice, where each node is only connected to its neighbors, chaotic dynamics can be observed. By comparison, the structure of the financial network is hideously complex, suggesting phenomena that are even harder to model. We have our work cut out for us in the general case.

Without delving into the details of the Global Financial Crisis, we can give a rough description of how risk propagates through the system. Suppose that a company that has borrowed money from a bank defaults. This can trigger a pernicious chain of events. The bank has to absorb losses when it writes off the loan, making it less solvent. If the loss is large enough, it may have to divest assets or restrict lending activities elsewhere. Every dollar lost in loans is a dollar lost in deposits (once the money is spent), which reduces consumption and potential investment in other areas of the market. To a large extent, fractional reserve banking is a confidence game. If depositors worry about a given bank's solvency, they are likely to pull money out, compounding the problem. Once a bank fails, things can get much worse. It may take quite a while before positions can be liquidated and liabilities paid. This can put pressure on other financial institutions that need short-term funds, leading to more perceived solvency issues and ultimately a widespread breakdown in the banking system. Endogenous risk operates on a "house of cards" principle: if one agent defaults or is forced into a "fire sale" of assets, other agents are likely to take a hit. If the liquidating agent is deeply entrenched in the network, losses will generally be large and widespread.

Now that we have been thrown headlong into a network description of markets, we face not only modeling issues but also raw computational ones. This is the topic of the next section.

## Computational Issues in the Full Network Model

At a basic level, endogenous risks are easy to categorize. These risks are generally reducible to two primary categories: access to credit and positioning risk. Liquidations occur when large quantities of speculative capital are forced out of the market, for example, in the presence of margin calls. However, this observation alone is insufficient when we try to estimate risk within a large network.

Even if we knew every agent's name, along with a precise specification of each utility function, our problem would rapidly grow computationally intractable as the number of agents scaled up to the size of the financial system. A complete financial network would have many billions of nodes, one for each individual, corporation or financial intermediaries, such as banks, pension funds, or asset managers. To fully document all network interactions, a line would need to be drawn connecting every relevant buyer and seller in the network whenever a transaction was made.

As the system's complexity increases, we become ensconced in the domain of combinatorics as we attempt to specify the total number of connections in the financial network. Assuming that only one transaction took place between every pair of $n$nodes, which is a significant understatement, the number of connections would be on the order of $n^2$. This quantity increases at an astounding rate. For example, suppose that our network has 10,000,000,000 agents. Then, there are $\frac{(10{,}000{,}000{,}000)(9{,}999{,}999{,}999)}{2}$, or an $5 \times 10^{19}$ possible pairs of agents that can transact. This number corresponds to 50 quintillion pair—or, perhaps more plainly, 50 million sets of 1 trillion pairs! Aside from a few exceptions, the fastest computers can only handle $10^{15}$ low-level instructions per second. This suggests that even counting the number of connections, without performing any useful calculations or storing any information them, would take approximately a minute—and a realistic network model would require far more detail than that. The implication is clear: the only way we can build a network model of risk is by reducing the complexity or dimensionality of the system while preserving its essential features. We will begin that journey in the next section.

## Mean Field–Majority Agent Interactions

Imagine that a large number of agents are active in a given market, such as S&P 500 futures, VIX futures, or the cash bond markets. Initially, no agent is dominating the market. Some agents, such as ETF providers, might be large in terms of ownership and balance sheet power. Other agents, such as broker/dealers, might be active in providing liquidity to the market.

While these players violate network indistinguishability in the strictest sense, their activities are not distorting prices. The historical distribution of returns has already accounted for these agents, so long as they act in a way that's consistent with the recent past. This is a weak version of the indistinguishability assumption we made earlier in the chapter—but a practical one.

In addition, each agent acts fairly independently from the others. Note that we are not using the word "independent" in a rigorous way here, meaning there is likely to be some overlap in the ways various agents behave; we simply want to ensure that no one is too worried about what any other specific agent might be doing. In this instance, there are no equivalents to the Hunt brothers, who tried to corner the silver markets in 1980. Hedge funds are not in liquidation mode, and Central Banks are not making radical changes to their balance sheets. Each agent bases its investment strategy solely on its estimate of returns generated by the Mean Field, rather than a game-theoretical decision about what the largest market players are likely to do.

Now, we can make a significant alteration to the structure of our network model, one that will make us wonder whether our Mean Field assumptions are still valid. Suppose that, over time, one of the following scenarios plays out.

- An agent (or small number of agents) with strict risk controls or a systematic rebalancing strategy grows to the point where it owns a disproportionate amount of a given asset class. This category might include levered hedge funds, or certain structured products.
- An agent that is always large, such as a Central Bank or always active, such as an options market maker, changes its behavior dramatically.

We now have a modified setup, where a one or a small number of majority agents interact with the Mean Field. Indistinguishability is critically violated now: a majority agent's response to random draws from the Mean Field has the potential to modify the field.

There are now two categories of players: Dominant Agents and everyone else in the market. The original distribution, or Mean Field, is now involved in a feedback loop. As we will see, this loop can sometimes have a stabilizing effect on market prices. However, the feedback loop also has the potential to become toxic. As we will discover in the case studies that follow in Chapters 4–7, the Mean Field—Dominant Agent grouping does not need to be too precise to create meaningful estimates of credit and positioning risk.

It is reasonable to assume that most agents initially do not change their behavior as a majority agent emerges. Algorithms, as well as discretionary traders, tend to be attached to recent price patters, rather than structural changes to the system that may not have manifested themselves yet. Collectively, their activities are still producing something that resembles the Mean Field estimated from historical data. At the same time, we know that the Dominant Agents will have a large impact on the distribution of returns if they decide to—or are forced to—act in size. Depending on their function, strategy and the path that prices take, these agents may distort ordinary price formation as they react to random draws from the Mean Field. The danger is that, given a large enough random draw, it will trade in a way that exaggerates the move. This can serve to increase the probability of a tail event.

## Quantifying Feedback from the Dominant Agent

From a pragmatic standpoint, we must now ask a critical question: is feedback from a Dominant Agent measurable?

As we explore this question, it soon becomes clear that three conditions must be satisfied before we can measure Dominant Agent feedback. Specifically:

- First, we must be able to track the Dominant Agent's size over time. (Here, "size" has an ambiguous meaning, as it can refer to assets under management, notional exposure, or the percentage of total volume traded in a given market.)
- Second, we must identify the levels where the Dominant Agent will be drawn into the market as a large-scale buyer or seller. (This is based on the assumption that our Dominant Agent will respond in a reasonably predictable way to large movements in price; naturally, we will have to justify this assumption in each of the case studies that follow.)
- Third, we need to estimate the quantity—measured in shares, contracts, dollars, or proportion of the underlying market—that the Dominant Agent will trade in response to an initial price shock.

Based on the assumption that we can measure the price impact of a Dominant Agent rebalancing, we can adjust the historical Mean Field accordingly.

As we will see in Chapters 5 and 6, certain Exchange-Traded Products satisfy these conditions directly and are useful subjects for our agent-based risk calculations. These ETPs engage in transparent strategies that are legally binding, according to a prospectus. In the language of futures trading, the goal is to identify specific levels, or "stops", where Dominant Agents will be forced to transact in the market.

We are now ready to introduce a simple algorithm that modifies the Mean Field in the presence of a Dominant Agent. This is a crucial section in our narrative, as it conceptually underpins our case studies in later chapters.

## The Basic Mean Field—Majority Agent Algorithm

We can now present a series of steps for updating the Mean Field distribution in the presence of a Dominant Agent. So long as prices are restricted within some range, it will appear as though this Agent has no impact on the Mean Field distribution. Positioning risk is invisible to the market. However, given a sufficiently large return drawn from the Mean Field distribution, the Dominant Agent's actions have the potential to transform a return that was previously considered large into something *much* larger, further along the tail of the distribution. (Note that, under certain conditions, Dominant Agents can also serve to stabilize prices. For now, we are more concerned with their potential to disrupt the Mean Field distribution.)

For simplicity, we will restrict ourselves to a **single feedback loop** and one Dominant Agent in the description that follows. As the Dominant Agent responds to a sufficiently random draw from the Mean Field, the Mean Field then changes through the price impact of the large BUY or SELL order. For our purposes, that constitutes the end of the loop.

Of course, we cannot exclude the possibility that our updated Mean Field will generate even larger values that will force the dominant agent back into the market, in a second round of feedback. However, this adds an unwieldy layer of complexity to our problem, given the rudimentary tools we have at our disposal.

The following algorithm is fairly straightforward. The algorithm samples from the original Mean Field distribution, keeping small values, while modifying those outside some pre-defined range. With a certain range, the algorithm behaves as expected; the real action occurs when a large enough return is drawn from the distribution. We emphasize that this return does not need to be extremely large, just large enough for a Dominant Agent to rebalance in size. Depending on the situation, the actions of the Dominant Agent can be stabilizing or de-stabilizing.

If the Dominant Agent needs to buy dips and sell rallies, large random draws will be pushed back to 0. This serves to increase the frequency of small to moderate outcomes, while dampening the tails of the distribution. By contrast, if the Dominant Agent trades momentum or has to liquidate a losing position, its actions can dramatically increase the tails. De-stabilization is largely what we are concerned about in this book.

Specifically, here are the steps involved in our algorithm.

**Algorithm 2.1**

- We first draw a random return $\xi$ from our Mean Field $H$. The Dominant Agent has done nothing so far.
- Next, we decide whether the Dominant Agent will be forced to trade, based on the sign and magnitude of $\xi$.
- If YES, we estimate how much $\xi$ is expected to change, based on the estimated size of the Dominant Agent's trade and the likely price impact of such a trade.

- We continue with the YES scenario. Suppose that price impact pushes $\xi$ to a new value $\hat{\xi}$ under the action of the Dominant Agent. Then, we discard $\xi$ and treat $\hat{\xi}$ as a random sample from the new distribution.
- If NO, we treat $\xi$ as a sample from our new distribution, without alteration. $\hat{\xi} = \xi$ in this case.
- Once we draw enough $\xi$'s and follow the recipe above, we can construct a revised forward distribution of returns in the presence of a Dominant Agent. Our new histogram tabulates the adjusted $\hat{\xi}$'s that we have sampled.
- We can call our new, approximated field $H^*$ ($H$ Star). In practical terms, $H^*$ can be represented as a histogram of modified returns $\hat{\xi}$ generated by our simulation.

After a few samples, suppose that no return is large enough to force the Dominant Agent into the market. As Taleb (1997) might say, we are currently in "Mediocristan". All returns are moderate and the original Mean Field $H$ offers a good representation of future outcomes so far. Structural risk caused by a disruptive Dominant Agent is latent for now. However, the added risk has not really disappeared. Once a large enough $\xi$ is drawn, our Dominant Agent will be forced into action. This is why our algorithm requires a reasonably large number of samples to adequately estimate the modified Mean Field $H^*$.

## Estimating Price Impact: Practical Considerations

In practical applications, mapping a random draw $\xi$ to $\hat{\xi}$ is probably the most challenging part of our problem. Algorithm 2.1 requires some sort of price impact model. Price impact, especially during liquidations and other large-scale events, can be noisy. Impact can also be asset class specific and conditional on the prevailing risk regime. For example, illiquid corporate bonds during high volatility regimes have a vastly different impact function than liquid futures contracts. Here, impact tends to increase in tandem with market volatility. This means that we are going to have to apply some domain knowledge when we measure impact in a specific segment of the market.

Even for small trades in the most liquid equity and futures markets, a fairly wide and disparate range of impact models exists. We refer to Bouchaud (2009) for more details about the range of options available. In some sense, our problem is even more intractable. We have to estimate the impact of forced trades occurring in larger size and over longer horizons than the market microstructure literature can easily handle. However, it turns out that *very* large trades can have more quantifiable impact than small ones. As in Mean Field Theory, the macro picture is easier to understand than an assembly of trades logged in the order book. Fire sales (e.g., where a prime broker liquidates a client's portfolio without regard to value) and hostile takeovers (where an activist investor assumes control of a company by purchasing over 50% of its shares) resemble large block trades that go through the market. These trades are not easily disguised by an automated execution algorithm.

In particular, considerable research has been devoted to the hostile takeover premium. In Chapters 5 and 6, we will draw from the relevant corporate finance literature when measuring the impact of very large-scale trades.

## Properties of the Modified Distribution

We can reflect upon the properties of Algorithm 2.1 a bit more. While our algorithm produces the modified Mean Field $H^*$ in a way that corresponds to experience, a technical issue arises: the new distribution might not fall into a class found in standard probability textbooks.

For concreteness, suppose that the Dominant Agent liquidates according to a hard threshold. A random draw from the original distribution is only modified if it is less than some fixed negative value $C$. In the following graph, we have sampled from a normal distribution and mapped it to a modified one. Any sample more than 2.5 standard deviations below the mean is pushed by a random amount to the left, according to a uniform distribution. The 2.5 standard deviation threshold is marked by a thick red bar. We can see that fairly extreme negative outcomes are far more likely than equally sized positive ones (Fig. 2.4).

Here, the modified distribution $H^*$ has some properties that would be considered undesirable, from a strictly mathematical standpoint. The graph threatens to be bimodal (i.e., with two distinct peaks) or at least very flat in the vicinity of the red bar. In the language of dynamical systems, the red bar can be thought of as a "saddle point", with prices shooting through as the Dominant Agent sells into a falling market.

However, is this really an issue? After all, we are focused on characterizing real-world phenomena, rather than finding elegant analytic solutions to idealized problems. In the presence of a Dominant Agent, an irregular tail may be more realistic than a steadily decaying one. A simple intraday trading example may serve to clarify things. Suppose that a futures contract is trading at 100, and an institutional manager has placed a very large STOP SELL order at 95. We want to model the distribution of returns over a 10-second interval. The

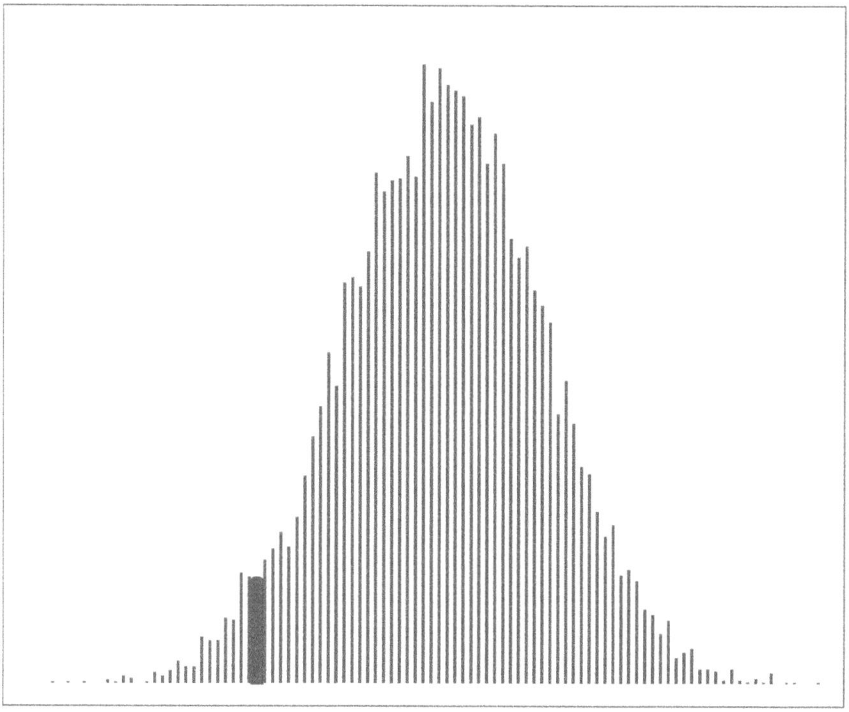

Fig. 2.4 Simulated distribution based on feedback from a Dominant Agent

contract is roughly moving according to a random walk, with one exception: if a trade is printed at 95 or below, the stop will turn into a market SELL order. Once the boundary is hit, the market impact of the STOP SELL is almost certain to be large. The futures will smash through 95, causing a sharp qualitative change to the distribution of returns. We will explore this point further as this chapter progresses.

## Reflections on Parameter Stability

Our hard threshold example raises the question of parameter stability in Algorithm 2.1. In general, we can only estimate the price threshold that will force a Dominant Agent into the market. Unless explicit stops are placed in the order book or open interest is unusually high at a known options strike, we cannot know exactly where the pressure points in the market are. This poses a fundamental problem for Algorithm 2.1: if our threshold is slightly misspecified, will we wind up with a modified distribution that is very different from the correct one? The following example should help assure the reader that our results are not too sensitive to the choice of threshold.

Suppose that a certain Commodity Trading Advisor, or "CTA", has grown dramatically. Note that a CTA is a regulated entity authorized to trade futures and futures options in external client accounts. It now accounts for 25% of the open interest in a certain futures contract. The CTA uses a fully automated trend following system for trade entry and exit. In other words, it mechanically scales into rallies and sell offs, according to rules that have been hardwired into a trading system. Once a trade is entered, an internal stop level is set. In all but the most extreme market regimes, this allows the system to exit losing trades with bounded downside risk. (Naturally, stop levels are adjusted for trades that are well in the money, as a profit-taking mechanism when a trend reverses.)

The futures are currently trading at 100, and the CTA has placed a large stop SELL order at 97. (Placing large stop orders in the order book is not the wisest idea, but useful for the purposes of illustration.) According to our original Mean Field, the odds of a −3% or greater drop in this contract over some time interval are 1 in 100. In standard risk management terms, −3% is our non-agent based estimate of Value-at-Risk, or VAR, at a 99% confidence level. Recall that VAR estimates the least an investor is likely to lose over a given horizon, in a measurable worst-case scenario. It gives an optimistic appraisal of a bad downside scenario. We have chosen to express VAR in percentage, rather than dollar terms for now. Our futures contract would then be expected to lose −3% or more every 1 out of 100 days.

Note that we are neither recommending VAR as a risk management tool, nor condemning it. We have simply chosen VAR because we had to choose *something*, preferably an industry standard. Our immediate goal is to demonstrate how a widely used risk estimate can be improved with an agent-based adjustment.

We can now continue with our example. The initial −3% VAR estimate might be reasonable, given the original Mean Field $H$. However, $H$ is no longer accurate, given the current unbalanced state of the network. Too much risk has become concentrated in a single Dominant Agent. Our CTA is going to amplify a sufficiently large initial move to the downside. Once the market hits our original VAR threshold, the CTA will be forced into action, dragging the market lower. In particular, a fixed size mega SELL order will go through the market, with large price impact. For example, suppose that this Dominant Agent's order is likely to push prices down by a further −2%. Then, a legitimate Value at Risk estimate for the futures contract should be closer to $-5\% = -3\% - 2\%$ than our original −3% calculation. Why? A large proportion of −3% initial drops are going to turn into −5% total drops in the presence of the whale.

After a long prologue, we are now ready to discuss the issue of parameter and model stability, in the context of this example. Suppose that our original VAR estimate is slightly too severe. In the absence of the Dominant Agent CTA, VAR is really −2.9%, rather than −3%. Will the whale still be forced to execute its stop SELL order? If we assume the −2.9% number is exact and assume no other forces come into play, the answer has to be no. The CTA's hard stop will be hit fewer than 1 out of 100 times and the original VAR estimate stands. Naturally, this ignores the fact that losses beyond the −2.9% threshold will be larger than before. However, any increase in expected shortfall (i.e., the expected loss beyond the VAR threshold) does not impact VAR at a 99% confidence level. According to these stringent assumptions, a −5% feedback-generated calculation overstates risk, as stated in VAR terms.

However, our −2.9% VAR estimate is flawed, as it ignores the market ecosystem completely. **Smaller technical traders come to the rescue** in defense of a −5% VAR estimate. These agents typically operate over intraday horizons, although they need not fall into the high frequency camp, relying on very low latency connections to exchanges. Once prices approach a large stop level, agents who try to profit from short-term breakouts are incentivized to push them through by placing a sequence of small SELL orders in the market. An alpha opportunity will appear as soon as the price hits the stop. After the forced Dominant Agent SELL order is triggered, prices are likely to drop sharply lower, at least in the short term. The smaller agents can then cover their shorts at a likely profit. We can get a feel for the underlying dynamics in the diagram below. Given the gap move down, it is clear that the distribution of intraday returns is far from normal (Fig. 2.5).

**Fig. 2.5** An intraday jump caused by concentrated STOP SELL orders at a specific price

Now that we have dealt with the issue of parameter stability, we are ready to incorporate network effects into a tractable risk model, without letting non-essential technical details derail us for now.

## Contrast with Impact-Adjusted VAR

There is an important distinction between our Mean Field—Dominant Agent approach and liquidity-adjusted VAR, as in Angelidis and others. In the liquidity-adjusted case you are the actor. By contrast, in our case, you are (initially at least) the observer who has to mark your portfolio to market as others liquidate. Liquidity-adjusted VAR estimates how much you stand to lose if your VAR limit is hit and *you* are forced to liquidate. In actively traded markets, this typically results in a modest adjustment to ordinary VAR. The behavior of agents other than yourself is not considered. To repeat, the liquidity adjustment is simply a function of trading costs as you reduce risk.

In our case, the situation is markedly different. We are deeply concerned about what *others* in the network are up to. In particular, we want to identify Dominant Agents who have the power to distort the historical Mean Field in a significant way. More poetically, we are just one of the minnows, assessing the potential impact of the CTA whale.

## Algorithm Requirements

Our next challenge is to apply Algorithm 2.1 in a practical real-world context. At this stage of the game, the main requirement is **domain knowledge**, rather than technical expertise. In particular, we need to identify segments of the market where certain players are playing a dominant role and track what the consequences of their actions may be. This may require detailed knowledge of specific regions within the global financial network. If we had to write a rough prescription for adjusting risk estimates in the presence of a Dominant Agent, it would be guided by the following questions.

- Who are the main players in a given market or asset class?
- How big are they, in terms of balance sheet size, ownership or percentage of volume traded?
- What is their typical behavior? Do they trade in the direction of a price move, trade against it or do they display chameleon-like behavior based on prevailing market conditions?

- How much will they be forced to trade, given a sufficiently large price shock in a specific direction?
- What is the likely price impact of forced rebalancing of fixed size?

A more sophisticated algorithm than ours would also address the following issue. We might refer to it as higher-order feedback.

- Will Dominant Agent rebalancing trigger price moves that are large enough to require **more rebalancing** from other agents (second order feedback)? Will this in turn draw the Dominant Agents back into the market (even higher-order feedback)?

Various enlightened practitioners, such as Serafini (personal communication), have built frameworks for trading around the dealers, structured products and systematic strategies that are dominating a given market. The interactions between these agents can be highly complex, involving multiple rounds of feedback within the network. In our opinion, these frameworks are both conceptually correct and (in the right hands) practically useful. However, from a modeling standpoint, complex feedback models involving multiple agents acting with different lags introduce radical uncertainty to a problem that is already challenging. Accordingly, in the analysis that follows, we will restrict ourselves to a **single round of feedback from a single Dominant Agent**. In our search for concrete risk adjustments rather than more complete but rougher characterizations of markets as complex systems, we need to constrain the problem as much as possible.

## Searching for Dominant Agents

Let us start with the first question from the list above. How can we identify potential Dominant Agents in a given market? One idea is to look for strategies and asset classes that have been performing well for a while. As investors chase returns, these will tend to become progressively more crowded. In certain cases, they may even be in bubble territory: late entrants buy, spurred by Fear of Missing Out, narratives justifying the extended move emerge, and prices become over-extended. Sometimes (as we have seen in 2021), speculators buy call options to gain leveraged exposure to a single stock. Market makers absorb the other side of the position, forcing them to hit the BUY button as prices rise, to hedge their exposure. (The reader need not worry about the mechanism behind this, as we will explain how market maker hedging can exaggerate directional moves in Chapter 6.) Forced hedging can cause parabolic rises that bear no relation to fundamentals, yet are nearly impossible to fade.

The intersection of crowded markets and areas where Exchange-Traded Products ("ETPs") dominate is a particularly interesting one. One obvious area to look for market distortions caused by overcrowding is in the Exchange-Traded Funds, or "ETF", space. While actively managed funds have been experiencing sluggish growth or net outflows over the past decade, ETF growth has been remarkable. (Note that there are other types of Exchange-Traded Products, such as structured notes. We will focus on VIX Exchange-Traded Notes in Chapter 4, but for now restrict ourselves to funds.) (Fig. 2.6).

The "passive revolution" has been characterized by large inflows into vehicles that track specific indices with low explicit costs. Armed with the tools to screen for the "best performing" ETFs across multiple categories, many investors have turned into pure performance chasers, without much regard for valuation, structural or credit issues. This has led to bloated allocations to specific stocks and various segments of the market. Here we come to an important point.

Most ETFs track an index according to a rigid rebalancing schedule that can often be anticipated by other agents. Once they get to a certain size, these funds can turn into Dominant Agents, trading mechanically in large

**Fig. 2.6** Parabolic growth of ETF assets, leading to flow-driven market dynamics (*Source* FRED [St. Louis Federal Reserve Database])

size according to investor flows, along with supply and demand considerations. These considerations drive the spread between the price of an ETF and the value of its reference index, calculated on a share-adjusted basis. When there is excess demand for an ETF, it will trade at a premium to the benchmark. Conversely, when investors are scrambling to reduce exposure by selling the most liquid instrument possible, an index ETF may trade at a severe discount.

In Chapters 4 and 5, we will use certain ETPs as fodder for Algorithm 2.1. While unlisted structured products can also create large-scale market distortions, their market impact is relatively hard to model. Structured products can have bespoke terms, and it is not very easy to track their notional size over time. By contrast, the market capitalization of an ETP *has* to be published on a regular basis. We know exactly how large an entity we are dealing with as we apply our algorithm. This data is in the public domain. At a more granular level, large positions, country and sector allocations are given on a periodic basis. Finally, all ETPs are required to issue a legally binding prospectus. This significantly reduces the amount of discretion they can apply when tracking an index. For example, a leveraged long Exchange-Traded Fund does not have the flexibility to "ride out" losses when the market is oversold. It *has* to liquidate some of its portfolio at the close of trading, given its hard leverage constraint. We will explain how the rebalancing mechanism works for levered ETPs in Chapter 3.

## Other Likely Culprits: Banks, Dealers and Market Makers

Another viable strategy is to focus on agents that are always large or are nearly always involved in a significant percentage of trades that go through the market. Banks, especially Central Banks, fall into the first category. By contrast, market makers and certain high frequency trading systems might not have large balance sheets, but take at least one side of a large percentage of trades that go through the market. Sometimes, these potential Dominant Agents do not exert much influence on prices and act as hidden giants. At other times, they can dominate the market with their trades.

In the high frequency space, where the players typically do not like to hold positions overnight, liquidations are quite common. At the extreme, cascading liquidations can lead to "flash crashes", such as the one observed in the S&P 500 on May 6, 2010. The underlying mechanism is a behavioral switch from liquidity provision to liquidity taking, during times of extreme stress. High frequency traders (or "HFTs") often act as liquidity providers, posting quotes at or inside the current bid/ask spread, based on the structure of the order book. However, if markets move too far in one direction or another, they either pull their quotes or more perniciously, turn into liquidity takers, dumping their accumulated inventory. This can lead to contagion, where short-term traders sell into the move and other agents short index futures to hedge their core portfolio. While market makers typically are small, i.e., in terms of risk limits, they dominate activity at the margins, taking at least one side of the majority of trades that go through the markets. Options market makers can also contribute to extreme price moves when they are short, a large quantity of puts or calls, and have to hedge in the underlying market. This "tail wagging the dog" phenomenon (e.g., where options activity on the S&P 500 can cause outsized moves in the index) has gained importance over time and is a central feature of modern market structure.

Here, though, we come to a sticking point. HFT and market-making activity are harder to track than ETF rebalancing. Market maker "size" is almost irrelevant. The main objective of a liquidity provider (this category includes designated market makers and unofficial ones, in the high frequency space) is to trade as many contracts as possible, without accumulating a net position. Liquidity providers make money by repeatedly buying at the bid and selling at the ask price. The goal is to be flat at the end of the day, as this eliminates overnight risk. We observe that, in the modern marketplace, a market maker is anyone who provides enough liquidity (in volume terms) to the market. Market makers no longer wear bright jackets and stand on the floor of an exchange. This is an outdated conception. Currently, market making is largely algorithmic, with a large percentage of trades in single stocks occurring in "dark pools" outside of the main exchanges. To repeat, the market maker function can take many forms.

However, there are meaningful things we can still do. In particular, *options* market makers engage in somewhat predictable behavior once they have accumulated enough inventory. These agents "delta hedge", mechanically buying and selling the underlying asset. This serves to neutralize the net directional exposure in their portfolios. In quiet markets, market makers do not have to rebalance their hedges very much. A larger move, though, can force them into the market, buying or selling the underlying aggressively to avoid large losses on their options books. This can lead to large one-sided flow that increases the probability of a tail event that can last from a few hours to several days.

The implication is clear. If we can infer what market makers collectively hold and levels where they have to hedge, we have nearly all the ingredients for a Mean Field—Majority Agent model. For example, suppose that speculators have significant ownership in a call options on a stock such as GameStop. Then, we know that market makers are likely to be net short those options. If the stock goes up enough, they have to hedge by purchasing the stock, smashing prices further to the upside. Whenever a stock or futures contract has an unusual amount of options open interest (and this is publicly available data), market makers have the potential to act as Dominant Agents. Structural positioning is largely a function of end investor preferences, while hedging levels depend on the amount of open interest at each options strike. This is an idea that we will develop in Chapter 6. We will use something called the "Gamma Index", or GEX to infer how much market makers will have to hedge for a given short-term move in S&P 500 futures. The danger scenario is where these agents are short "gamma", meaning that they have to trade aggressively in the direction of an initial random move. This can cause volatility to spike beyond bounds that were previously considered reasonable.

While market makers can act as majority players through their activity, banks dominate based on a combination of activity, interconnectedness and sheer size. The following diagram highlights the number and intensity of large counterparty exposures in the Australian banking system alone. Note that arrows point from borrowers to lenders, implying that small banks typically require funding from larger ones to sustain their business (Fig. 2.7).

Moving up the hierarchy, to large banks and beyond, we wind up with Central Banks. These giants increasingly exert control over other banks and the markets at large. It has even been argued that, in the end game, Central Banks will subsume many of the responsibilities of the major commercial banks. Central Banks influence their domestic yield curves across multiple durations, act as a lender of first resort when conditions deteriorate and soak up longer-dated bonds when the government needs to borrow. They are *the* Dominant Agents in the markets, whenever they choose to be. A Central Bank does not have any fractional reserve requirements. The following graph tracks Central Bank asset growth from 2002 to 2020. It suggests that there are no hard limits on Central Bank balance sheet expansion (Fig. 2.8).

## More Reflections on the Central Banks

Given the increasing importance of Central Banks in the global financial network, we will devote Chapter 7 to them. Since Central Banks are *always* large, we will construct an indicator based on balance sheet trend strength, rather than raw size. Our hypothesis is that Central Banks have the power

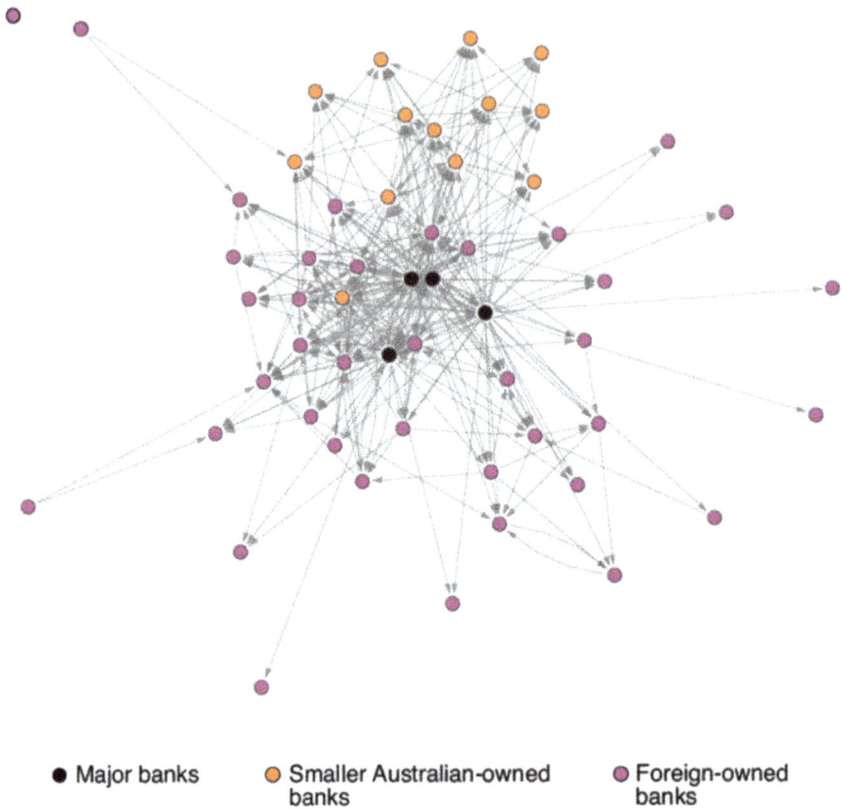


Fig. 2.7 Counterparty exposures within the Australian Banking System (*Source* Mapping the Australian Banking System Network | RBA, https://www.rba.gov.au/publications/bulletin/2013/jun/6.html)

to alter the distribution of asset price returns when they act out of line with their usual behavior.

We will find that, in the median case, trend strength is stabilizing for the credit markets over horizons lasting several months. However, we emphasize that our statistical conclusions do *not* constitute an ironclad guarantee. There are not enough blocks of unorthodox policy data to conclude anything about extreme outcomes. The challenges we face when dealing with the banking system are somewhat different from the case studies we pursue in Chapters 3–6. A wide range of data is available from the Center for Financial Stability, US Treasury and various branches of the Fed. This is helpful. We can track detailed changes to the Fed's balance sheet (both on the asset and liability side of the ledger), at weekly frequency, from 1914 to the present. The trouble with this data is the transmission mechanism from Central Banks to capital

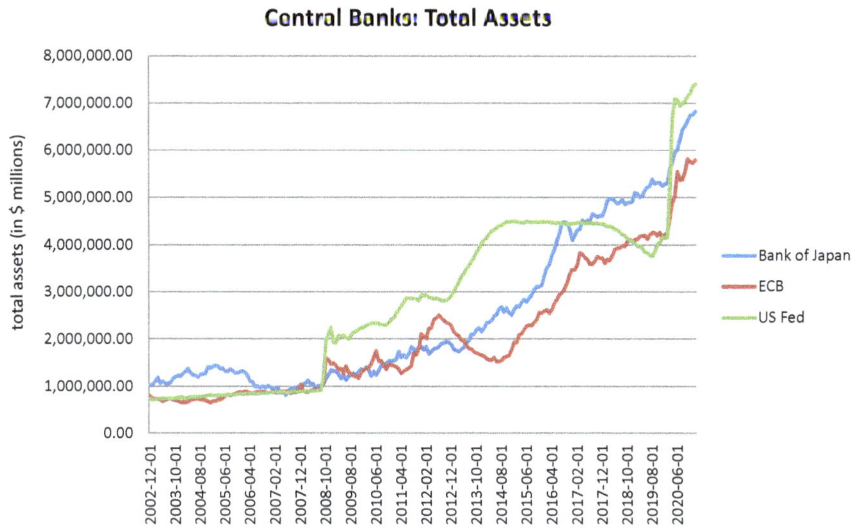


**Fig. 2.8** Extraordinary balance sheet expansion among the leading Central Banks (*Source* FRED [St. Louis Federal Reserve Database])

markets can be muddy. The Fed can swap cash for bonds with Primary Dealer banks, improving their reserve status. However, this does not mean that these banks will immediately decide to lend more, nor that investor sentiment will immediately improve. Short of buying risk assets directly (which historically was out of the Fed's remit), Central Banks can only exert so much control over the credit and equity markets.

We can describe the transmission mechanism in more detail. Why should the domestic equity market go up when a Central Bank expands its balance sheet? In the absence of a raw Pavlovian response to the news, we need the following sequence of events to occur.

1. Viewed in isolation, and increase in reserves should encourage member banks to lend. However, they actually have to decide to do so. Negative sentiment, regulatory changes and other factors can counteract any impulse to lend.
2. Deposits naturally increase if and when new loans are extended. While these deposits increase aggregate demand (i.e., more credit is available to chase a given supply of assets), investors need to be confident enough to put them to work in the capital markets.
3. Suppose that Central Bank easing operates with a lag on the domestic corporate bond market. This has historically been the case. For example, it might ordinarily take 6 months before credit increases, and deposits are

invested on a large enough scale. If a shock hits the economy or capital markets within this interval, lagged policy may not be enough to overcome the shock.

In Chapter 7, we will conduct two sets of statistical tests to gauge the impact of Central Bank balance sheet expansion on asset prices. First, we will analyze the relationship between trend strength in Fed assets and forward credit spreads. We will also summarize an intricate argument from The Philosophical Economist (2013), which relates flows to long-term equity returns, testing the model over various horizons.

## Conclusions

We have developed a simple but general technique for altering the distribution of historical returns in the presence of a Dominant Agent. Algorithm 2.1 exploits vital positioning risk, which is beyond the reach of traditional models. We can now use our modified Mean Field, along with our knowledge of the major players, to create more realistic loss estimates during a liquidation event. This is the primary subject of the chapters that follow.

## Addendum: Complimentary Models to Ours

### The JLS Model

The "JLS" model, developed by Johansen et al. (1999, 2000), shares some similarities with ours. While it is relatively technical, the JLS model also converts a network description of markets into a practical tool for identifying unsustainable bubbles that are likely to pop in the near future.

A key parameter in the model measures the degree to which various agents in the network are synchronized. When random noise dominates the system, the model generates the sort of dynamics observed in finance textbooks. However, when a disproportionate number of agents want to buy or sell, prices accelerate according to a somewhat predictable pattern. At critical levels of synchronization, crashes are more likely to occur. According to Sornette, Johansen and Bouchaud (1996), once prices start to rise rapidly enough, while oscillating at a certain rate, a "singularity" or air pocket move to the downside is much more likely than usual. Feigenbaum and Freund (1998) independently developed a similar model.

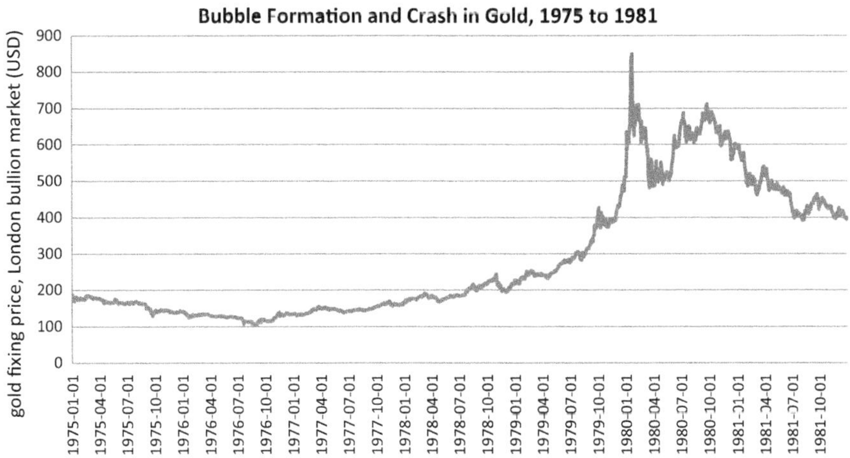


**Fig. 2.9** Gold: an archetypal LJS bubble and crash in 1979 and 1980 (*Source* Bloomberg)

In practical terms, we can check for danger by fitting specific curves through the price series for any asset or index. The following diagram tracks the development of an LPPL-type bubble that turns into a crash (Fig. 2.9).

The "LPPL" or Log Periodic Power Law method is considerably more general than our Mean Field—Dominant Agent approach, as it does not rely upon any knowledge of the specific players in a given market.

At least on a retrospective basis, the LJS model has identified many bubbles that have eventually burst. However, at other times, serious excesses have built up in the system without prices having gone exponential. Here, our Mean Field—Dominant Agent paradigm adds significant value. In the next section, we will explore some of the limitations of a crash model that largely focuses on exaggerated price action.

## Limitations of the LPPL Model

While we find the LPPL model to be conceptually appealing, it has certain limitations. This is understandable, as any model by its very nature is a simplification of reality. A curve fitting approach that equates bubbles to accelerating price action is guaranteed to miss many crashes. To complicate matters further, risk indicators such as the VIX have a higher tendency to spike from a low initial level than ever before. Realized volatility sometimes seems to emerge from nowhere. According to Scoblic and Tetlock (2020), forecasting should be blended with regime identification and scenario analysis in situations where moderate shocks can have very large impact. For example, when a currency peg breaks, prices jump from a base of nearly 0% volatility. Instantaneous volatility is almost infinite at this point. In the Mexican Peso graph below, we see discrete jumps in 1994, 2008 and 2020, without much price warning beforehand (Fig. 2.10).

Governments, who intermittently act as Dominant Agents within the financial network, either decide that they cannot or do not want to defend the peg.

As in Chapter 5, we observe that a bubble can emerge *without* prices ever accelerating to the upside. When insurance selling strategies become overcrowded, volatility can actually become compressed: the amount of return that can be collected per unit of leverage is lower than previously. The following chart is a regurgitation of the "Volmageddon" in February 2018 (Fig. 2.11).

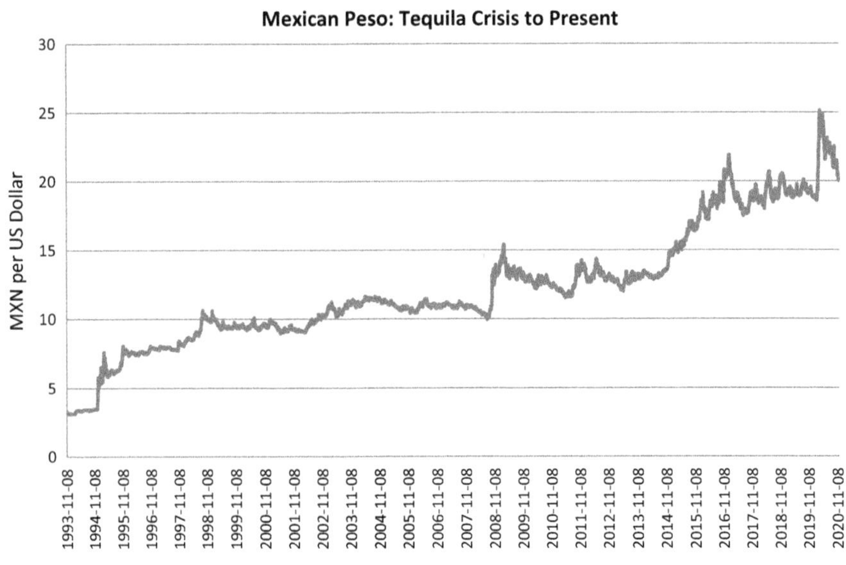


**Fig. 2.10** Mexican Peso rate: violent jumps do not require parabolic moves beforehand (*Source* Bloomberg)

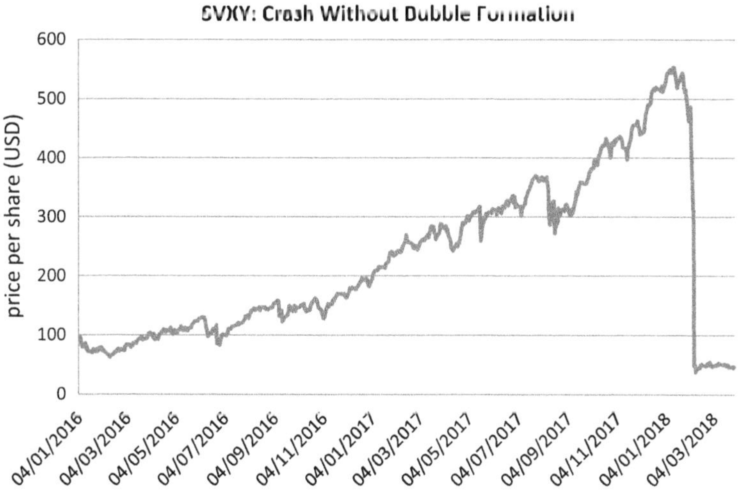


**Fig. 2.11** Short volatility strategies tend to grind up before collapsing (*Source* Bloomberg)

## Mean Field Games with a Majority Player

Lasry and Lions (2007), along with Carmona and Delarue (2013), have developed far more general and sophisticated models than ours, to account for the interaction of a small number of Dominant Agents with a Mean Field distribution.

In their formulation, there are very many agents, but only a few large ones. Each agent is trying to maximize their own utility function. The small agents can all be replaced by a Mean Field distribution, as their individual actions wash out. However, the actions of the Dominant Agents need to be taken into account individually. From a technical perspective, we wind up with a large number of stochastic differential equations with a variable drift term that depends on the actions of the collective Mean Field and the individual Dominant Agents. A given asset's forward returns are directly affected by Dominant Agent rebalancing.

The main goal in these papers is to identify Nash equilibria, given the system of equations and each agent's utility function. Specifically, a Nash equilibrium is a state of the system where no agent can increase their utility with a small change in their behavior.

While the identification of equilibria generates some very deep and interesting mathematics, it is not the focus of this book. We do not try to prove the existence of stable states of the financial network. Following Janeway (2018), given the complexity of the interaction between governments, corporations and speculators, the financial markets are probably a system where no stable equilibria exist.

# 3

# Exchange-Traded Products as a Source of Network Risk

A caricature is putting the face of a joke on the body of a truth.

—Joseph Conrad, Victory

Exchange-traded funds, or "ETFs", have grown rapidly in recent years, taking market share from mutual funds. This is evident from the following chart. As of early 2020, the US ETF industry accounted for roughly $4.5 trillion in assets (Fig. 3.1).

As we will see in the following sections, the ETF industry has enjoyed parabolic growth as a function of cost, tradability and control. Many products, such as the SPDR S&P 500 ETF ("SPY"), have straightforward design features. The SPY has historically tracked the S&P 500 index very closely (including cash dividends), with an expense ratio of roughly 0.1% per year. It offers targeted exposure at low cost.

A unit of SPY represents fractional ownership in a basket of shares that very closely resembles the S&P 500 index. The SPY, along with the basket that underpins it, is usually very liquid. This reduces the basis risk that State Street (the ETF provider) has to manage and the risk that end investors face. An agent who buys the SPY can essentially think of it as a share, without worrying too much about the underlying construction.

However, certain other ETFs can be dangerous. Exchange-traded notes ("ETNs"), the close cousins of ETFs, generally carry even greater risk than a garden variety ETF. For both ETFs and ETNs, the core problem is one of incentives. Generally, providers are in the business of gathering assets, without


H. P. Krishnan and A. Bennington, *Market Tremors*,
https://doi.org/10.1007/978-3-030-79253-4_3

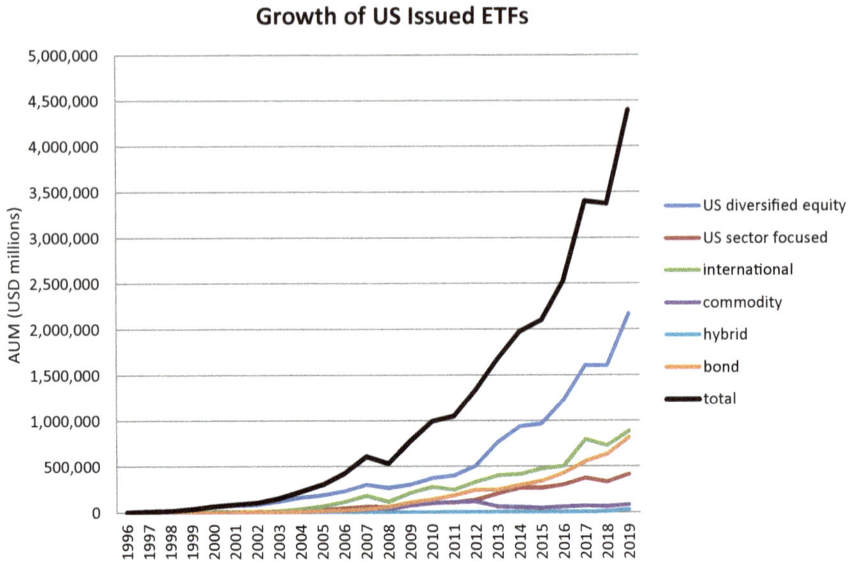


**Fig. 3.1** Rapid growth of ETFs, with equities leading the way (*Source* Investment Company Institute)

too much consideration about the quality of product delivered. They generate revenue based on scale, letting end users decide where they want exposure. Performance chasing is fine and even desirable from the provider's standpoint, as it leads to the creation of new shares and more revenues in the short term.

To repeat, stable design features are a secondary consideration to size. This has important implications. Once a product grows too large, latent design flaws can rise to the surface. Then, exchange-traded products and the dealers that support them can turn into destabilizing Dominant Agents. A decent-sized random shock is simply required to set things in motion.

In order of severity, a bloated ETF or ETN can

- drift from its reference index
- engage in forced rebalancing that destroys the link between the share price and the reference index and
- through the price impact of rebalancing, cause damage to the underlying market.

Using the formulation from Chapter 2, ETFs can distort the Mean Field distribution of the markets they trade in. This may increase the probability of a tail event.

Here, the naïve interpretation of an exchange-traded product as an ordinary share is deeply flawed. Hidden design complexities simply must be taken into consideration. In reality, these ETFs and ETNs represent investments in leveraged strategies ore ones that rely on normal market liquidity to function.

Exchange-traded products generally track a reference index or benchmark, by mandate. This increases transparency and the predictability of performance in median scenarios. However, it comes at a cost. Index replication requires rebalancing according to a strict schedule. Meanwhile, large mechanical rebalancing can exaggerate price moves in a product and ultimately in the index that supports it. Other agents in the network can make matters worse, from a price stability standpoint. They are incentivized to front run exchange-traded product dealers after a large enough intraday move, based on predictable rebalancing. This is perfectly legal, as it does not rely on private information. ETP prospectuses are generally available on the internet.

Once shorter-term traders understand how a given index is constructed, they can set parameters for how and when the relevant ETP will rebalance. This can lead to cascading BUY or SELL orders, where informed agents act first, ETPs trade in size and other players subsequently have to cut their risk. Moreover, if underlying market conditions are weak, large price moves in one market can propagate to other segments of the financial network.

Note that we are not claiming that all exchange-traded products are dangerous. Large cap index products in developed markets are generally quite safe, so long as they are not geared. Since, the stocks underpinning these ETFs are at least nearly as liquid as the ETFs themselves, a large premium or discount to net asset value ("NAV") is unlikely to develop. Rather, our focus is on ETPs that EITHER (1) use excessive leverage relative to the volatility of the underlying OR (2) trade illiquid assets AND (3) have grown too large for the underlying market to support. In the next section, we will describe exchange-traded products in more detail, while explaining why they have become so popular over the past decade.

## Easy Access for the Retail Investor

ETFs are a good place to start, as they hold vastly more assets than ETNs and easier to comprehend. ETFs represent an actual stake in a pool of assets. They bear a stronger resemblance to a run-of-the-mill stock or bond portfolio than ETNs do.

As the name suggests, ETFs are funds that have the functional characteristics of individual securities and trade on an exchange. Mapping a portfolio onto a security offers several advantages, such as real-time pricing and reliable settlement. By comparison, mutual funds trade at end of day prices. A sharp intraday drop followed by a reversal cannot be exploited in mutual fund format.

ETFs have greatly benefited from the flow of capital from actively managed funds into inexpensive passive vehicles. The 2015–2020 environment, with very sharp equity sell offs followed by nearly equally sudden recoveries, has made alpha generation more difficult for many stock selection strategies. Many investors have become frustrated with active managers who have struggled to generate alpha net of fees. Another factor behind the rise of ETFs is a change in mindset. Millennials and Generation Z typically want to take more control of their investments, using modern technology. They can easily use their smart phones and a piece of application software to vary their asset allocation or screen for inexpensive ways to gain exposure to a given asset class or strategy.

A given ETF might be poorly designed, but it is likely to be cheaper than an actively managed alternative. While it is true that some vendors, such as Vanguard, offer index-tracking mutual funds with very low fees, comparable ETFs generally have an even lower cost basis once they reach scale. The following chart, based on data compiled by the Investment Company Institute in a 2019 report, compares the cost of mutual funds and index ETFs, based on asset class (Fig. 3.2).

ETFs appear to be uniformly cheaper, with the largest differential in the fixed income space. Recall that the expense ratio for a given fund equals the

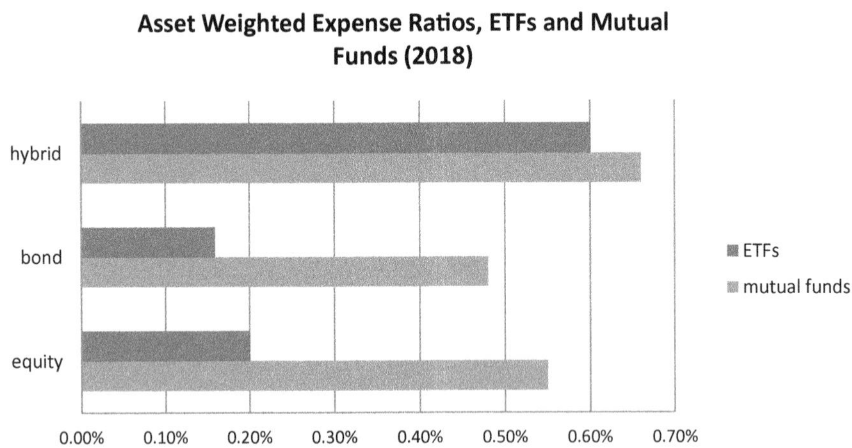


**Fig. 3.2** Ignoring the price impact of investor flows, ETFs offer a cost advantage (*Source* Investment Company Institute)

annual cost to run the fund divided by its assets under management. The investment management team usually takes the lion's share of fees, with a smaller fraction taken by custodial services, accounting, audit and legal fees.

Significantly, the price impact of trading, along with execution fees, is not included as an explicit cost. This is understandable, as it is impossible to predict how much a fund will wind up trading in the future. However, this can paint a misleading picture to end investors. ETFs, even "passive" ones, often trade more actively and in far higher volumes than actively managed mutual funds. Whenever money flows into an ETF, securities need to be bought on the day, without regard to valuation. When money flows out, securities need to be sold. Given their constraints, ETFs generally act as liquidity takers. In highly volatile markets, a trading desk supporting an ETF can turn into a forced seller in a market where the bid has disappeared. Impact acts as a variable implicit fee passed on to investors. By contrast, a mutual fund manager has more latitude when facing net subscriptions or redemptions. Trades do not have to be done on the day and some tracking error is acceptable until conditions stabilize. Flexibility generally leads to better fills over the long term.

However, the main point remains. Investors who are trying to decide how to gain exposure to a given asset class see lower headline costs for ETFs. This acts as an enticement.

For the more ambitious investor, the ability to trade in and out of an ETF can be attractive. Silber (1991) and others have argued that this liquidity option does not have much economic value, as market timing is considered to be extremely difficult. However, the "weight" of academic literature has not deterred the legion of active investors who believe that they too can beat the market, especially over short horizons. An agent can dip in and out of an exchange-traded product on an intraday basis. In addition, for the most liquid products, market impact is generally low. These factors are a source of their growth. According to Statista (https://www.statista.com/topics/2365/exchange-traded-funds/), global ETFs accounted for over $5 trillion as of November 2018. This was equivalent to roughly 3% of stock and bond market capitalization worldwide.

Before ETFs started to gain traction, retail investors had to resort to mutual funds to express their tactical views. Index futures were and generally still are too large and complex (from an operational standpoint) to consider. Actively managed mutual funds do not offer an ideal solution for investors seeking precise targeted exposure. While these funds generally do try to control tracking error relative to a stated benchmark, they muddy the waters in an attempt to outperform it. The search for alpha can lead to sector and country tilts that the end investor has no control over.

## Premium/Discount to NAV

Many exchange-traded products do appear to provide reliable exposure to a given benchmark. For example, the iShares Core S&P 500 ETF ("IVV") has nearly always traded within 0.20% of NAV. Even in March 2020, when the VIX spiked to 85, the IVV and S&P 500 benchmark never drifted much more than 0.40% apart.

ETFs generally have an "arbitrage mechanism" that encourages nominated dealers to minimize any premium or discount to NAV. This is true in theory, at least. Suppose, for instance, that the IWW drops well below NAV. In other words, the cash equities comprising the S&P 500 (weighted according to the index) are trading at a higher price than the SPY. The index is worth more than the ETF, on a share-adjusted basis. Designated market makers then have an incentive to buy SPY shares and swap them with the index provider for a representative if not identical basket of equities underpinning the index. Assuming that the impact of buying IWW shares and selling the basket is not too large, dealers can then sell shares into the market at a higher price than they paid for the SPY. In general, large cap US equities are liquid enough to support the arbitrage mechanism for an actively traded ETF.

In a volatile market, dealers can also use S&P futures to hedge any residual exposure. Futures act as a stopgap: when conditions stabilize, they can cover their futures and sell S&P 500 component shares directly into the market. In relative terms at least, S&P E-mini futures are extremely liquid. They have surpassed US 10 Year Note futures as the most actively traded contracts in the world and rarely depart much from fair value. In other words, their "basis" (the difference between the futures price and the value of the index) tends to be extremely stable.

The implication for the SPY, IWW, QQQ (which tracks the NASDAQ 100) and other large cap equity ETFs is straightforward is that a large premium or discount should almost never develop between a large cap equity ETF and its reference index. Other agents within the network also help to keep tracking error low. For example, high frequency agents actively trade the spread between the SPY and its components, with the realization that dealers will step in if prices move too far out of line.

In the following sections, we will explore the arbitrage mechanism further and see where it has the potential to break down.

## Major Players in the ETF Space

Asset managers, such as Blackrock, State Street and Vanguard, act as ETF providers. They design new products, launch them and subsequently manage them. After launch, providers are responsible for the custody of assets, new share issuance and the appointment of dealers to manage inflows and outflows. An appointed dealer is known as an authorized person, or "AP". APs are incentivized to act as a backstop if the spread between an ETF and NAV widens too much. They tend to include major banks and specialty dealers in the securities that underpin a given ETF.

As we mentioned above, the mere presence of APs can encourage fair pricing throughout the trading day. Other agents can buy discounted ETFs and sell ones that are trading at a premium, on the assumption that dealers will protect them if the spread becomes too large. However, we emphasize that the creation/redemption process introduces another layer of complexity, which can break down in extreme market conditions. When liquidity in the underlying market breaks down, APs can simply drop out of the market. APs differ from traditional market makers in a crucial way: they are under no obligation to trade.

To repeat, the arbitrage mechanism tends to break down in illiquid asset classes during risk off regimes. Various agents leave potential trading opportunities on the table as they scramble to cut risk. This important detail, which can cause an ETF to break down when other markets are falling, tends to be glossed over by ETF marketing departments. Since providers do not take much reputational risk when they launch a new product, the attrition rate for ETPs has historically been quite high. For asset gatherers, the reward for a successful launch outweighs the risk of failure.

## How the Creation/Redemption Process Works

We can now provide a more detailed example to deepen our understanding. Suppose that an ETF has 10,000,000 shares outstanding at some point in time. By mandate, the ETF has to track a specific equity index. Next, suppose that the ETF provider currently has $1 billion of assets. No excess cash is held, implying that $1 billion is invested into a basket of stocks that replicate the index.

Then, the ETF's share price should be close to $\frac{\$1{,}000{,}000{,}000}{10{,}000{,}000}$, or $100. This simple relation ensures that the dollar value of what all investors hold matches the dollar value of what the provider holds. On a mark to market basis, investors hold $1,000,000,000 in ETF shares and equivalently, the provider holds $1,000,000,000 in underlying securities that make up the index. The ETF is trading in line with NAV. The provider has a strong incentive to hold a portfolio that matches the index as closely as possible. This should serve to minimize tracking error over long-term.

However, even if a provider holds all index components in exactly the right proportions, ETF supply and demand imbalances can cause the ETF to drift away from fair value. For simplicity, assume that the ETF share price sharply drops to $99, based on a large supply and demand imbalance. The move is purely technical and restricted to the ETF. The individual shares in the index have not moved much. In a frictionless market without network effects, an AP would be highly incentivized to arbitrage the $1 difference in value. Technically, arbitraging the difference would involve a share redemption, which we describe below. The following steps rely upon the fact that ETFs are "open-ended" investment trusts: new shares can be created or destroyed upon demand.

1. The AP would first buy $\frac{0.01}{10{,}000{,}000} = 100,000$ETF shares at $99 in the market. The cost to the AP would be 100,000 * 99 or $9.9 million in this case. To repeat, we are assuming no price impact in our "frictionless" market.
2. The AP would then deliver these to the ETF provider.
3. In exchange, the AP would receive 100,000/10,000,000 or 1% of the portfolio held by the provider, namely a basket of individual stocks that very closely resembles the index.
4. Next, the provider would remove the 100,000 ETF shares from circulation, reducing supply.
5. The dollar value of investor and provider holdings would again be equal, now at $990 million.
6. Finally, the dealer would sell its stock portfolio back into the market. Again assuming no price impact, it would receive $10 million in cash proceeds. The net gain to the AP would be, $10,000,000–$9,900,000, which amounts to "risk free" a $100,000 profit in this highly idealized example.

Once an AP decides to redeem some shares, the size of an ETF shrinks. This holds whether we measure size in dollars or number of shares. An equivalent dollar amount of underlying securities is released to the market.

In the example above, we have made the very stringent assumption that prices do not move when the dealer enters the market. In practice, an AP might buy somewhat fewer than 100,000 lots to account for the dual cost of buying ETF shares and selling individual securities in the market. Still, price impact is assumed to be very low when trading either exchange-traded products or individual securities.

The assumption of a nearly frictionless market will be violated in Chapter 5 and completely obliterated when we analyze corporate bond ETFs in Chapter 6. Ultimately, prices are based on real transactions rather than theoretical assessments of value. If a large enough BUY or SELL order goes through the market, prices will rise or drop in the short term, whatever the reason might be. When the assets underpinning an index are illiquid, the very notion of arbitrage comes into question. It can be impossible to decide how many shares to redeem or whether a spread trade is even possible.

We accept that the arbitrage process is helped along by a few factors, even though these are not ironclad. Providers have a bit of wiggle room in terms of what they can deliver to APs during a share redemption. For example, illiquid single names do not need to be included in the deliverable basket. There are also various contingencies where cash can be substituted for ETF shares or shares in the underlying basket, as a liquidity buffer. This, of course, assumes that both parties agree to the exchange. These technical exceptions are specified in an ETF's prospectus.

However, the basic point remains. In all but the most extreme conditions, "in kind" delivery requires that a highly representative basket of stocks is exchanged for any ETF that tracks an index.

## Where It Can All Go Wrong

The arbitrage mechanism faces serious difficulties when we replace the phrase "highly liquid stock" with a less liquid asset, such as "corporate bond". In the second case, a large ETF dislocation may actually signal a breakdown in the market rather than an easy arbitrage opportunity.

During an ETF share redemption, selling bonds (especially in the high yield sector) into the market can have serious price impact. Suppose that a segment of the bond market freezes up, which has a tendency to happen at the end of the credit cycle. Then, it might not be possible to sell any inventory back to the market in a reasonable amount of time. When one leg of a relative value trade needs to be held for a while before a profit can be realized, we cannot classify the trade as anything resembling "arbitrage". At best, a dealer is trying to capture a premium for taking on significant liquidity risk.

No amount of financial engineering can transform an illiquid basket of securities into a liquid derivative that is resilient to market shocks. The false alchemy of liquidity comes at a cost, namely extreme event risk. If a derivative suddenly jumps away from the underlying basket, there may be no way to arbitrage the difference. Any attempt to compress the spread is only going to worsen the problem.

This brings us to a related point. Certain "passive" vehicles can be more dangerous than active ones. Passive funds are purely benchmark driven and the more rigidly a product needs to track a specific benchmark, the more toxic it can become. We emphasize that passive vehicles require active trading in the underlying securities to manage inflows and outflows of capital. Large-scale rebalancing generally needs to occur within the trading day, in the correct proportions. For example, if there are net redemptions on a given day, securities need to be sold according to their index weights.

Since other market agents know how an index ETF has to behave, they can anticipate orders, withdrawing liquidity from one side of the market. Investors in an ETF have to bear to cost of large telegraphed trades that go through the market during the rebalancing stage. At the extreme, risk can migrate from what seemed to be an innocent-looking passive product to the market at large. If the price impact of rebalancing is large enough, other agents may have to liquidate, in a vicious feedback loop.

Our next objective is to explain the mechanics of Exchange-Traded Notes ("ETNs"). In some ways, ETNs are close cousins of ETFs. However, as we will see, they carry different risks.

## ETNs: Debt Trading on Equity Exchanges

Externally, ETFs and ETNs might seem indistinguishable to many investors. Indeed, they share many common features. Both are listed on stock exchanges: they functionally trade like shares. In addition, ETFs and ETNs generally offer targeted asset class or strategy exposure, with a significantly lower cost of entry than most futures contracts. Retail investors can take a view on volatility, physical commodities and a variety of other asset classes using a combination of the two.

However, internally, ETFs and ETNs are materially different. While ETNs may trade on stock exchanges, they are notes issued by a bank. To repeat, they are debt instruments in the issuing bank's capital structure. The debt is generally senior but unsecured. The issuer promises to pay the total return of a stated benchmark at redemption or maturity, net of fees. This means that

ETNs have a fixed expiration date. Close to maturity, a new ETN will be issued (given sufficient demand) with identical features, other than a revised maturity date.

Significantly, an ETN investor does not hold any assets in the benchmark. Rather, the issuing bank promises to deliver a series of returns matching the reference index. What we are really looking at is a structured product that trades freely on an exchange. Issuers do not have a contractual obligation to hold securities in a given index, according to the index weights. In fact, they have no obligation to hold anything. However, it is generally in their best interests to do so, to avoid making an out of pocket payment at maturity. By contrast, ETF owners do have an indirect stake in a physical portfolio. Recall, however, that ETFs have an added layer of complexity, as they require arbitrageurs to maintain a reliable connection with the benchmark.

Bank trading desks generally support ETNs. We can refer to them as flow desks. Their stated role is to manage risk that accumulates through a bank's various lines of business. These agents hedge against any shortfall that will have to be paid at maturity, while trying to skim some outperformance relative to the benchmark. After all, trading desk profits usually translate into a larger bonus at the end of the year. However, index replication is the main objective. If a desk does not hedge enough exposure in an ETN that rises sharply, the issuing bank will have to take a loss at maturity.

The blowup risk of an ETN has to be higher than the blowup risk of a senior unsecured bond with the same duration on the issuing bank. It is not hard to reason why. Barring some special covenants, if the issuer defaults, the ETN will also default. There are insufficient funds to pay investors. However, an ETN can get wiped out even if the underwriting bank is solvent, given large enough moves in the underlying market. As we will discover in Chapter 5, this is exactly what happened to certain VIX ETNs during the February 2018 "Volmageddon".

## Safety Considerations

Ignoring bank default risk for a moment, an ETN is likely to be relatively safe if it satisfies the following conditions.

- It tracks a benchmark index that can be replicated using highly liquid securities or futures contracts.
- The ETN is small enough that the relevant flow desk can reproduce the benchmark without impacting the market too severely.
- It does not apply significant leverage either on the long or short side. Gearing can be particularly dangerous if the reference index is volatile.

By contrast, a large geared product can be highly disruptive to the market it is trying to track. As we have already mentioned, trading desks that support an ETN do not need to hold the index exactly. However, they are highly motivated to hedge against any shortfall that investors will be paid at maturity. This requires at least some replication of the benchmark.

Suppose that at least one of the three conditions above is not satisfied. After a significant intraday price move, hedging may require large liquidity-taking trades. When trading desks have to rebalance in size, they can quickly turn into Dominant Agents in the markets where they are active. However, the problem is larger than that. Once they realize that the trading desk "whales" are coming, other agents are incentivized to push prices in a direction where the whales will have to trade in even larger size. This allows the smaller agents to make a likely in and out profit.

Desks that have to hedge a large amount of ETN exposure can cause short-term bubbles and crashes, without having taken any directional view on the market in the first place. This is part of a larger "tail wagging the dog" issue that has become increasingly prominent in recent years. Clearly, derivatives (such as futures, options and exchange-traded products) settle based on the price of the underlying. It would seem logical, then, that derivatives prices should be a function of underlying prices over time. Indeed, options prices are the dependent variable in Black-Scholes and virtually any other pricing model.

Increasingly, however, the largest derivatives markets actually drive the cash markets that determine their settlement prices. They can be the real-time arbiters of fair value. This is, especially true during crisis periods, as agents transact in the most liquid contracts available, with the underlying markets catching up over time.

From a research perspective, we are obviously interested in products that have dangerous design features. These feature in Chapters 5 and 6, in our investigation of ETNs based on the VIX and corporate bond ETFs, respectively. The structured products industry at large has had a large influence on market volatility for several decades. However, exchange-traded products are considerably easier to track. We can download the size of a given ETF or ETN at the end of each trading day. We also have access to detailed information about the composition of any given benchmark. Finally, we can tell when a dislocation develops between an ETF and its NAV. An unusually large discount or premium to NAV indicates a problem: for whatever reason, liquidity has dried up in the ETF or the securities in the benchmark. These key inputs for a network risk calculation are in the public domain and allow us to estimate what and how much a given product has to trade in order to deliver the benchmark.

Finally, if we can gauge the price impact of a large trade, we can apply Algorithm 2.1, which models the impact from a given shock in the presence of a Dominant Agent. To repeat, various structures offered by banks to large institutions can also dominate the market. However, it is hard to pin down their size and precise characteristics. Algorithm 2.1 cannot be applied without reasonably well-specified inputs. For example, we might find in a research report that $250 billion of assets have been invested in a specific risk targeting strategy at some point in time. At best, this is a rough estimate and one that can change over time without our realizing it. However, different versions of the strategy might target different levels of volatility, measure volatility in different ways and rebalance according to a different schedule.

We are by no means making the blanket statement that all exchange-traded products are inherently dangerous. Minor design flaws might lead to persistent but controlled underperformance or tracking error relative to the stated benchmark. There can also be issues with benchmark construction, leading to outcomes that are not catastrophic, but simply different from what investors expected.

Things become more serious when we move to products that track an illiquid asset pool or have an embedded short volatility profile of some sort. The short volatility products typically generate attractive returns during extended quiet market regimes, drawing investors in. These are similar to some of the structures offered by banks to Japanese investors in the 1990s and 2000s, collecting a steady premium in exchange for large positive returns in either direction. Recall that Japan was the first major economy to enter an extended low interest rate regime. 10-year rates have been bounded below 2% since 1999, luring investors into strategies that offer alternative forms of carry. However, there is a price to pay for the added carry. Once these strategies become bloated, they can influence the benchmarks they supposedly track in uncontrollable ways. A large enough spike in volatility will force dealers to rebalance in size, causing severe technical damage to the reference index.

Levered products are particularly dangerous, as they have significant path dependence and require more aggressive rebalancing. The problem is compounded when leverage is applied to an asset that is already volatile, such as natural gas or VIX futures. These contracts can move by 20% or more in a single day, forcing dealing desks that support an ETN to trade in significant size. Very large orders near the close can cause fractures in the underlying market. We will focus on leveraged products in the sections that follow.

## Levered Exchange-Traded Products

Some advisors refer to levered ETFs and ETNs as “enhanced” products. The sales pitch goes as follows. Investors have the potential to realize outsized gains, but can never lose more than their initial investment. Exchange-traded products offer limited liability to investors, while leverage provides the juice. However, there is a catch: limited liability requires a rebalancing strategy that dynamically adds to gains and cuts losses on a daily basis. In other words, a 1-day momentum strategy is embedded in levered products, including those that have dedicated short exposure to an index.

We will describe the precise rebalancing mechanism for a leveraged product in the next section. While the reference index for a leveraged ETF or ETN mechanically reduces exposure after losses, serious problems can still arise to an end investor. We can proceed by analogy with a slightly contrived example, for a less regulated vehicle. Imagine a $1,000,000 investment in a very highly leveraged Limited Partnership (“L.P.”). The ratio of notional exposure to equity is a mighty 10 : 1. The investment is exposed to $10,000,000 of market risk. As a Limited Partner, it is strictly true that an investor can never lose more than the initial $1,000,000. However, this does not negate the fact that the strategy carries high risk. The probability of a very large drawdown is much higher than for a fund with more reasonable gearing. Moreover, the price impact of forced liquidation can be damaging to the broader market. “Passive” leveraged funds are in fact very active, as they have to respond to changes in the underlying index as well as investor flows.

## Where is the Bid?

While leveraged and short products account for a relatively small percentage of ETF assets under management (“AUM”), it is not difficult to construct scenarios where they destabilize the benchmarks they supposedly track.

If we search for the largest US-levered products according to AUM, we wind up with the following chart. For reference, the chart dates from March 2021. It forms a useful starting point for a rough agent-based study. Note that we will take a considerably more precise and comprehensive approach in Chapters 5 and 6. Many of the assumptions below are debatable. In addition, a significant amount of risk can be offloaded to the NASDAQ futures market. However, in our opinion, the general line of reasoning is qualitatively correct (Fig. 3.3).

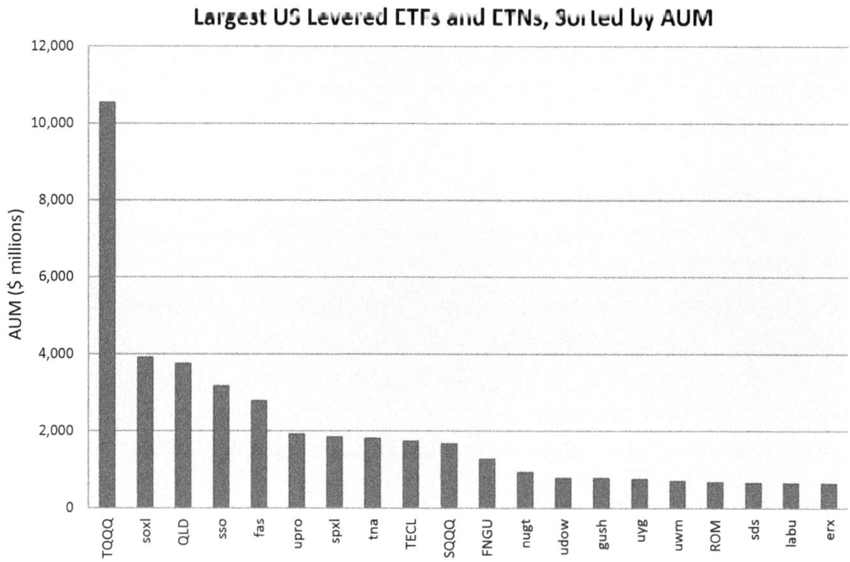


**Fig. 3.3** Largest levered Exchange-Traded Products, as of March 2021. Tech dominated products in CAPS (*Source* ETF Database [etfdb.com])

Vehicles with unusually large exposure to the Amazon, Apple, Facebook, Google and Microsoft appear in capital letters along the *x*-axis. We will refer to these as "mega cap tech" for the time being. For example, mega cap tech securities account for roughly 40% of market capitalization in the NASDAQ 100. Representation is even higher for products such as the FGNU, a 3*X* levered ETN on the FAANG stocks. FGNU is one of those "in for a penny, in for a pound" type retail products.

We can now make a few back of the envelope calculations, as follows.

- Assume that the FAANGs (excluding Netflix) account for 50% of the ETFs and ETNs in capital letters, and 10% of the other 20 largest leveraged products.
- As of March 2021, mega cap tech-dominated products in the chart above accounted for roughly $20 billion of assets under management.
- Adjusting for leverage, this number jumps to roughly $55 billion.
- Leverage-adjusted exposure for the remaining names on the list is also around $55 billion.
- We wind up with $0.5 * 55 + 0.1 * 55$ billion USD, or around $33 billion of exposure to mega cap tech in the largest levered US exchange-traded products.

$33 billion may seem to be a small number relative to the market cap of Apple, which was in excess of $2 trillion as of March 2021. However, if we think in terms of trading volumes, rather than sheer size, things get much more interesting.

- Suppose that daily dollar trading volumes for the mega cap tech names are around $35 billion. This is consistent with the 3-month trailing average as of early 2021.
- Next, suppose that 50% of assets in US equities are in the hands of external managers, while the remainder is managed internally.
- The external money is split equally between active and passive managers.
- Even if the active managers are generally value buyers, any bid they might provide to the market after a sell off is offset by momentum-driven passive strategies.

We wind up with a situation where internally managed portfolios are the only entities that can provide a *net* bid to equities during a sharp sell off. Now assume that 25% of these entities trade actively and have a value tilt. Then, latent demand is only around $0.5 * 0.25 * 35$ billion USD, or $4 billion, for mega cap tech stocks over a 1 day horizon.

After a −5% intraday drop in the NASDAQ 100, short and levered ETFs will have to sell $-0.05 * 33$ billion USD, or roughly $1.7 billion in Amazon, Apple, Facebook, Google and Microsoft. This alone accounts for over 40% of volume that the market can conceivably support, executed at or near the close!

## Underperformance of Leveraged ETFs and ETNs

According to a recent Bloomberg article (https://www.bloomberg.com/professional/blog/passive-likely-overtakes-active-by-2026-earlier-if-bear-market/), passive vehicles now control a larger percentage of the US equity market than actively managed funds. It is likely that the rise of passive vehicles has increased the degree of price momentum in equity markets. When an index such as the S&P 500 rises, investor flows into passive products that track the index tend to be positive. Nominated dealers then have to buy individual securities in the index, proportional to their weights, without regard to fundamentals.

In the extended period where active managers dominated, index and individual security prices tended to be more tethered to future cash flows.

(The .com bubble was a notable exception to this rule.) Traditional stock pickers were less likely to chase stocks that were rising rapidly, with a greater tendency to buy companies that were trading at very low multiples to earnings, sales or book value.

Leveraged products amplify the momentum phenomenon, at least in the equity markets, where passive vehicles have really taken root. By construction, both levered and short ETFs and ETNs are momentum strategies in disguise. Each day, they mechanically cut losses or add to winning positions. Leveraged products typically perform beyond expectations during strongly trending markets. A significant directional move with relatively low volatility is ideal. We will analyze the dynamics of levered products in more detail in the next section.

By contrast, these ETNs can perform surprisingly poorly in choppy markets characterized by short-term reversals. Leveraged products also tend to have high trading costs, as they require active daily rebalancing even in the absence of investor flows. In the following graph, we can see the gulf in performance between a 1X and 2X levered gold miners ETF from 2016 to early 2021. Specifically, the GDX refers to the VanEck Vectors Gold Miners ETF, while the NUGT is the Direxion Daily Gold Miners Bull 2X levered ETF. (It is important to realize that, since GDX and NUGT have a strong loading to the price of gold, they behave differently from the large tech companies that currently dominate the S&P 500.) (Fig. 3.4)

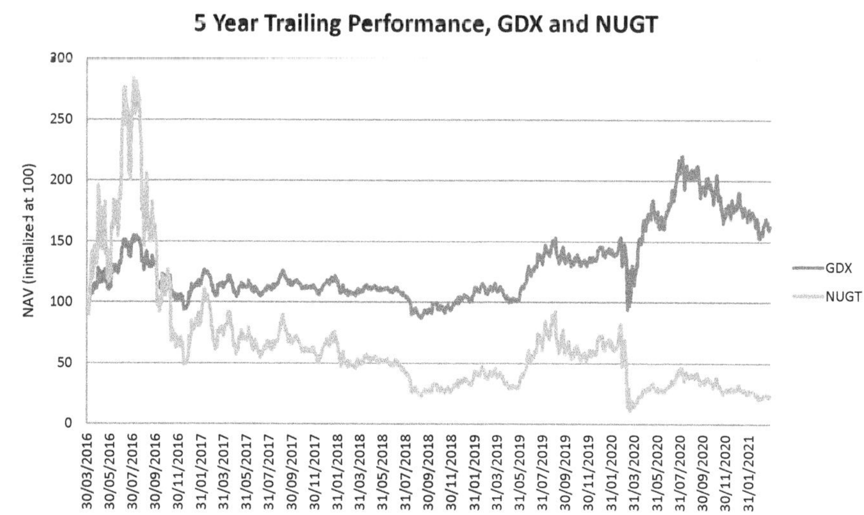


**Fig. 3.4** Surprising divergence in performance between levered and unlevered gold ETFs over longer horizons (*Source* Yahoo! Finance)

While the unlevered GDX gained 62% over the period, the 2X geared NUGT lost nearly –77%!

We can now supply some intuition as to why this is so. A levered exchange-traded product aims to deliver a fixed multiple of the index return on any given day. This requires daily rebalancing. A simple example shows why this is the case. Suppose that a $2X$levered ETF has \$100 of equity at the close of a given day. Appropriately, the provider decides to replicate the index exactly. Dealers would need to buy \$200 worth of the index to reach $2X$ leverage. Then, \$100 of investment would create \$200 of exposure. In other words, \$100 would have to be borrowed to support the position. Note that we have used the convention that \$200 of exposure on \$100 of equity constitutes $2X$ leverage.

Next, suppose that the index goes up by +10% on the next day. This is an admittedly large but round number. At this point, the ETF has \$220 = 1.1 * \$200 of notional exposure and \$120 = \$100 + \$20 of equity. \$20 is the day's profit, pushing leverage below$2X$. In particular, notional exposure is now $\frac{220}{120}$ or 1.83 times equity. Since the ETF is mandated to deliver $2X$ of $I$'s return again on the next day, it needs to buy \$20 more shares or contracts on margin. This would bring the exposure/equity ratio back to $\frac{240}{120}$ or $2X$. To repeat, the ETF has to build its long position after every up day, while reducing exposure whenever the index drops. On any day where the index is not completely flat, the ETF is an active participant in the market.

For completeness, we can also consider a $1X$short ETF on a reference index with \$100 of equity. It targets the negative of the index return on any given day, gross of costs. We might refer to this as a "bear" ETF, as it benefits from declines in the index. Although it may not be immediately obvious, the provider has to follow the same rebalancing pattern as in the $2X$ levered case. Short products also have to trade momentum to avoid going bankrupt. We can again proceed by example. Suppose that the reference index returns + 10% on day 1. While equity has dropped from \$100 to \$90, short exposure now stands at \$110, implying that the ETP is $\frac{110}{90} = 1.22X$ geared. \$20 of the position needs to be "covered", or bought back, to deliver minus 1 times the index return on the next day.

If the reference index is even slightly mean reverting from one day to the next, a $2X$ levered ETF is likely to generate a return much lower than 2 times the index over longer horizons. Similarly, a short ETF is likely to underperform the inverse of the benchmark.

From 2016 to early 2021, the serial correlation of GDX returns from one day to the next was roughly −0.04%. This number is low but negative, offering an explanation why NUGT's return has been dramatically lower than 2 times GDX's. It is also likely that NUGT has incurred significantly higher trading costs (including fees and price impact), based on its daily risk reweighting schedule.

In the next section, we will demonstrate that even mild mean reversion in an index creates a substantial headwind for a levered ETF or ETN over longer horizons. This section is somewhat technical and can be skipped by readers who want to move directly to the case studies in Chapters 5 and 6.

## Path Dependence over Longer Horizons

We can extrapolate the rebalancing strategy of a levered product over multiple days.

We want to compare the performance of two strategies on the same benchmark. As above, both start with $100 of equity.

- **Strategy 1** is a $2X$levered ETF on the benchmark, with leverage reset on a daily basis.
- **Strategy 2** borrows $100 to create $200 of benchmark exposure on day 1 and simply holds the position over time. The only contingency is that Strategy 2 is liquidated if the equity in the position gets close enough to 0.

Observe that while Strategy 1 needs to rebalance on a daily basis, Strategy 2 incurs no intermediate trading costs. This creates a headwind for Strategy 1.

Suppose that the benchmark goes up with a strong enough trend for a while. Then, Strategy 1 should outperform Strategy 2. Strategy 1 steadily borrows more as the index moves in its favor to buy more units of the benchmark. During an extended positive trend, an early investor in the levered long ETF will make more than a late entrant, as a percentage of initial dollars invested.

Similarly, levered ETFs and ETNs mechanically decrease exposure during a strong bear trend. Rebalancing acts as a risk mitigation device, with Strategy 1 preserving capital more effectively than Strategy 2. Both lose money, but Strategy 1 loses less. The path dependency in Strategy 1 is not designed to improve performance. Rather, it is largely based on a solvency constraint. The provider does not want to accept unbounded risk when end investors have limited liability. For a $2X$ fund or note, rebalancing ensures that equity will remain positive unless the benchmark drops -50% or more in a single day. Ignoring certain commodity and volatility index futures for a moment, exchange protocols halt trading well before a −50% 1-day move can occur.

Even $3X$ geared products are generally protected by circuit breakers on the major securities exchanges.

In Chapter 5, we will direct our attention to the potentially violent interaction between leverage and large-scale rebalancing in the volatile VIX futures market. For now, however, we will content ourselves with the mildly but persistently painful case where mean reversion undermines long-term performance. If an asset oscillates too much relative to trend, Strategy 1 will dramatically underperform Strategy 2.

## Conclusions

In this chapter, we have described the basic features of ETFs and ETNs.

Both types of products are effectively derivatives, typically with more internal complexity than standard futures or options contracts. Equating ETFs to a fractional stake in a portfolio of securities understates structural risk. Products that use leverage or track a basket of illiquid securities need to be viewed with particular caution. In particular, leveraged and dedicated short products are heavily path dependent, leading to disappointing performance in choppy markets.

We are now prepared for the case studies in Chapters 5 and 6. These focus on ETNs tied to the VIX and ETFs on a basket of illiquid corporate bonds. In particular, we will create revised risk estimates for the VIX futures and high yield corporate bond markets, with VIX ETNs and bond ETFs acting as the Dominant Agents.

## Endnote: The Effect of Mean Reversion on Levered and Inverse Exchange-Traded Products

Suppose that our benchmark mildly reverts to its short-term trailing average over time. Its price moves according to the following equation.

$$P_{t+t} - P_t = \theta(\mu - P_t)\Delta t + \sigma\sqrt{\Delta t}\xi \tag{3.1}$$

Note that we are modeling prices, rather than returns, here. Equation 3.1 can be thought of as a discrete time Ornstein-Uhlenbeck equation. It was originally used in mechanics and later applied to interest rate dynamics, as in the Vasicek model (1977).

$\Delta t$ is our discrete time step, set to 1 trading day. $\sigma$ is the annualized standard deviation of daily price changes and $\xi \sim N(0, 1)$ is a normally distributed random variable with mean 0 and standard deviation 1. $\theta > 0$ is the key parameter for our purposes, as it measures the strength of mean reversion. Prices have a tendency to mean revert when $\theta > 0$, for the following reason. When $P_t < \mu$, the drift is positive. The right hand side of equation above has a positive expected value: $\theta(\mu - P_t) > 0$, $\Delta t > 0$ and $\sigma\sqrt{\Delta t}\xi$ has a mean of 0. In other words, $P_{t+\Delta t}$ will on average be larger than $P_t$. By the same token, when $P_t > \mu$, the drift will be negative. As $\theta$ increases, $P$ gets pulled more strongly back to its historical mean.

Since, we have no way of specifying $\mu$ without looking at the data, we can just calculate it using a rolling historical window. In our example, we will assume that $P_t$ is tethered to its trailing average over the past 5 trading days. In particular, $\mu = \frac{1}{5}\sum_{i=1}^{5} P_{t-1}$. Dynamically, $P$ does not like to drift too far away from its location over a trailing 5-day window. This is a restrictive assumption, but suitable for the purposes of exposition. Continuing on, we set $\theta$ equal to 0.001 and $\sigma$ equal to 15%. Naturally, $\mu = \mu_t$ varies over time and the most recent series of prices.

We observe that our choice of $\theta = 0.001$ only introduces a small amount of mean reversion. The average serial correlation of daily returns is only around $-2\%$.

Using Eq. 3.1, we simulated 1,000 paths for $P_t$, with 1,000 daily time steps for each path. For each simulation, we then calculated the amount of equity in Strategy 1 and Strategy 2 at each time step. We can think of this in terms of the Net Asset Value, or "NAV", of each strategy. Transactions costs and price impact were set to 0, biasing the scales toward Strategy 1, given its active rebalancing schedule. For any path that wiped out Strategy 2's equity, we halted trading for Strategy 2. Strategy 2's NAV for that path was then set to 0.

In each simulation, we calculated the spread $S_t$ between the final NAV for Strategy 2 and Strategy 1. Even though $\theta$ is extremely small, the static borrow Strategy 2 outperforms Strategy 1 roughly 70% of the time. With 99% confidence, the mean of $S_t$ is in the interval [0.23, 2.19]. Strategy 2 generates negative alpha over the long term, simply based on its momentum bias, even without taking costs into account.

# 4

# The VIX "Volmaggedon", with Exchange-Traded Notes Destabilizing the Market

> Says a writer whom few know, "Forty years after a battle it is easy for a non-combatant to reason about how it ought to have been fought. It is another thing personally and under fire to direct the fighting while involved in the obscuring smoke of it."
>
> Herman Melville, "Billy Budd"

The following chart sets the stage for the rest of this chapter, in the most direct possible terms. We have simply tracked the quoted VIX index and front month VIX futures contract from 2017 to early 2018 (Fig. 4.1).

We observe an epic spike on February 5, followed by a sharp reversal. February 5 is obviously the day where the Armageddon in volatility, or "Volmageddon", occurred. The inverse VIX ETN complex suffered catastrophic losses, with the XIV closing shortly thereafter. We can infer more from the intraday chart (Fig. 4.2).

Near the close, we can see a classic "squeeze". Certain large agents obviously had to cover their short positions in short order, driving the market up almost vertically. For whatever reasons, they simply could not hold out to the next trading day. Once the liquidation was over, the VIX normalized quickly, showing little memory of the Volmageddon. Even without knowing the players, we can reasonably conclude that some damage to the network, rather than changes in fundamentals, caused the move.

We are left with the following questions: *who* had to liquidate and *why*? More ambitiously, could the magnitude of the VIX futures spike


H. P. Krishnan and A. Bennington, *Market Tremors*,
https://doi.org/10.1007/978-3-030-79253-4_4

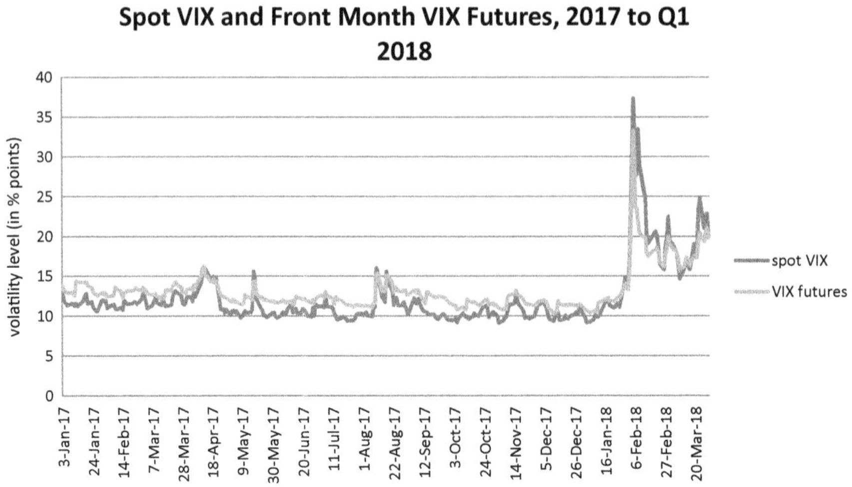


**Fig. 4.1** The Volpocalypse occurred nearly without warning in February 2018 (*Source* Bloomberg)

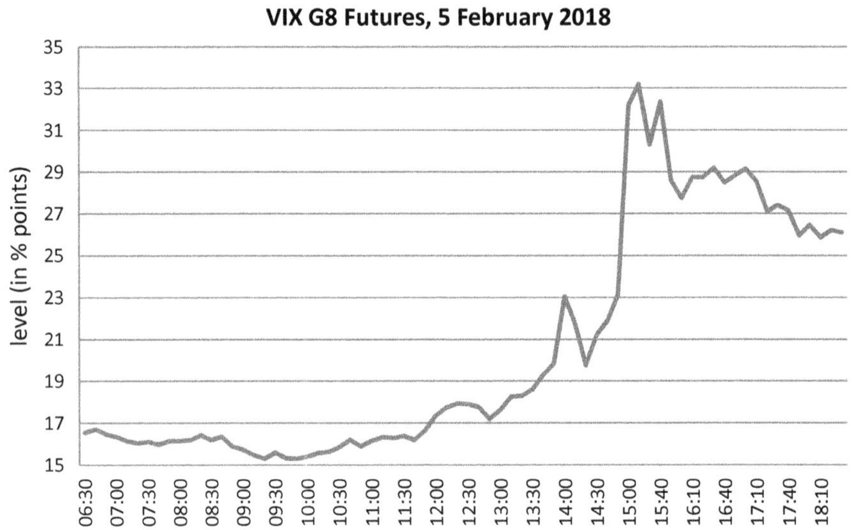


**Fig. 4.2** Intraday price moves for front month VIX futures on February 5, 2018 (*Source* Bloomberg)

have been predicted? In what follows, we will address all of these questions directly, using the Mean Field—Dominant Agent framework we developed in Chapter 2. Specifically, we will

- identify the main players in the VIX futures complex, as of early 2018

- show how they became too large for the market to support based on customer demand
- estimate the impact of their trading once they became Dominant Agents
- demonstrate that a massive spike in VIX futures was almost inevitable within a Mean Field—Dominant Agent feedback loop.

Our analysis will require a series of assumption and approximations, which are not written in stone. However, we believe that each intermediate step has a solid basis, leading to risk estimates that are not only qualitatively correct but practically useful.

## Initial Demand for Long VIX ETNs

The story of the "Volmageddon" begins in February 2009, with the launch of the VXX. The VXX is an Exchange-Traded Note, or "ETN", issued by Barclays. It tracks the performance of a rolling long position in short-term VIX futures contracts. VIX futures allow investors to take a view on forward VIX, i.e., where S&P 500 implied volatility will be at some discrete point in the future.

As we will see, VIX futures are far from a perfect substitute for the spot VIX. However, they are highly correlated with the spot over short time horizons. The following scatter plot maps daily changes in the VIX to changes in the shortest-term VIX futures contract that has at least 7 days to maturity (Fig.4.3). We might refer to this as the "front month" VIX futures contract.

By February 2009, it was not clear that the Great Financial Crisis was over. (Some financial historians consider June 2009, four months later, as the end of the GFC.) The S&P 500 was still in a severe down trend and fear gauges remained extremely high across global markets. These factors created a large amount of demand for an exchange-traded product that offered exposure to the VIX.

As a rule of thumb, the market's memory of a sell off is roughly proportional to the size of the sell off. Major declines have a psychological impact for a relatively long time. Many investors took a severe hit in 2008, leading to a nervous reaction whenever equities showed signs of dropping again. These agents wanted access to a high-octane hedging vehicle that was easy to trade. Given the large amount of equity exposure in US domestic portfolios, something based on the VIX seemed ideally suited to the task.

A modest allocation to the spot VIX improved nearly any back-test, dampening drawdowns and hence increasing compounded returns. For example,

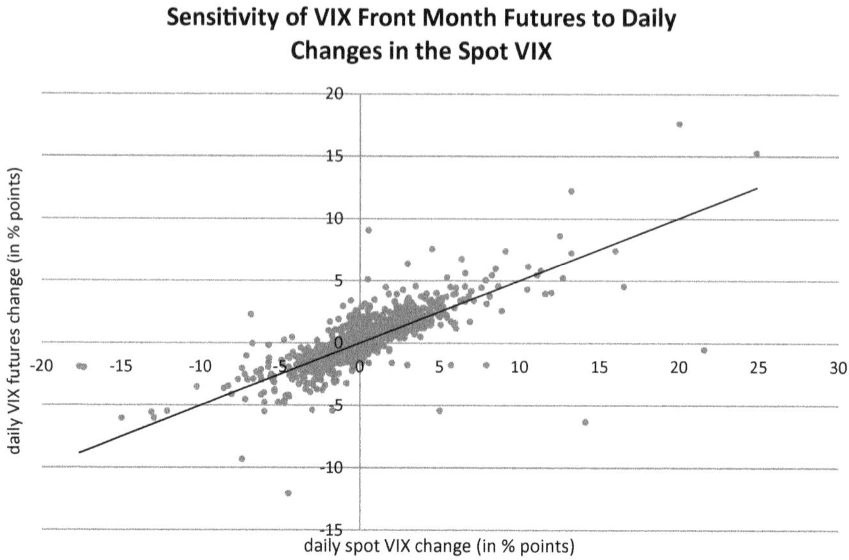


**Fig. 4.3** Over daily intervals, front month VIX futures provide reliable exposure to the spot VIX (*Source* Bloomberg)

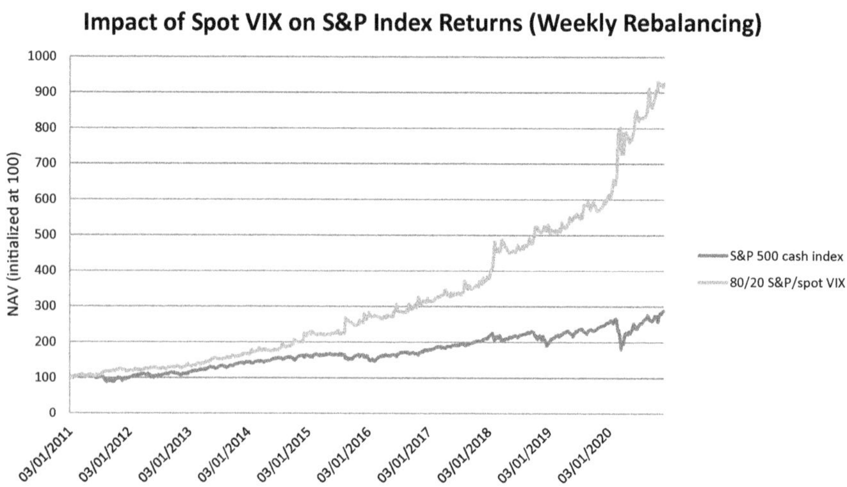


**Fig. 4.4** Remarkable impact of the spot VIX on a long equity portfolio (*Source* Yahoo! Finance)

the following graph shows the impact of a 20% allocation to the VIX on a core S&P 500 portfolio. (Note that we have not included dividends in the S&P index return. While this somewhat accentuates the difference in performance, the results are qualitatively the same in either case.) (Fig. 4.4).

This simple example demonstrates that a hedging instrument does not need to have a positive expected return to add significant value in the context of a larger portfolio. Any strongly convex payout, at reasonable cost, is enough. Historically, the VIX has accelerated into an S&P sell off, providing reliable portfolio protection.

Importantly, the VIX is **structurally** as well as statistically diversifying. It offers far more than an asset that has been negatively correlated to equities over some historical window. Investors can be at least reasonably confident that it will continue to act as an effective hedge in the future. VIX formula is entirely based on the prices of S&P options at various strikes. These options are tied to the index directly.

By contrast, other asset classes, such as US Treasuries, are not functionally connected to the S&P. While Treasuries have been reliable performers during equity crashes since the 1980s, the "protection" they offer is regime-dependent. For example, during a period of stagflation (as in the 1970s), Treasuries did not offer much, if any, protection during equity down trends. Treasuries offer one-sided protection: they only hedge against deflationary shocks.

The spot VIX is particularly attractive as a defensive play when volatility is low. (At least, this would be true if the spot were investable.) For example, suppose you could buy the VIX at a handle of 12. Using its historical range as a guide, you would only have about 3 points of downside risk, with the potential to make roughly 70 points in October 2008 and March 2020. Long volatility hedge fund managers fantasize about leveraged asymmetrical payouts such as this one, with win: loss ratios in the 20:1 range.

In reality, replication of the spot VIX is infeasible: it requires a nearly continuous rebalancing strategy involving hundreds of individual S&P options. There is no VIX to buy. In addition, far out of the money puts have a disproportionate weight in the VIX formula. The price impact of buying every S&P put with non-0 open interest would be prohibitive, as a percentage of premium paid. Many options are not easily tradable, yet factor into the VIX calculation directly; a return stream based on the spot VIX is not deliverable to investors directly. The costs of replication are simply too high.

However, it is possible to buy and roll VIX futures, which move in tandem with the spot VIX over short horizons. This theoretically appealing idea underpins the VXX ETN, which we describe in more detail in the next section. Unfortunately, as we will soon find out, theory does not always agree with market reality.

## VXX Implementation Details

In the aftermath of the Great Financial Crisis, many investors were reluctant to invest in the various long S&P volatility structures offered by banks. These carried counterparty risk: a given structure might not be priced correctly or (in the event of a default) pay out at all. Demand for an exchange-traded volatility product was high. VIX futures offered a relatively transparent, **listed** alternative to various over the counter structures, including S&P variance swaps. Even if variance swaps have superior design features (namely, higher convexity in the event of a crash), counterparty risk was to be strictly avoided. Accordingly, the VXX ETN used a rolling VIX futures strategy as a benchmark.

Before we can describe exactly how the VXX works, we need to give a qualitative description of VIX futures contracts. These underpin the VXX as well as other VIX-related products. While weekly futures are available in the front two months, the most liquid VIX contracts are listed at monthly intervals. Maturities typically range from less than a month to 9 months. Collectively, these futures form the VIX term structure. Standard monthly contracts mature on the Wednesday after the 3rd Friday of a given month. The term structure serves as the market's expression of forward volatility expectations. The following graph depicts the VIX term structure on December 9, 2020. We can see that the curve is in contango: futures with a longer time to maturity are trading at a premium to nearby futures. During quiet market regimes, this is the default state (Fig. 4.5). Longer term insurance, which requires

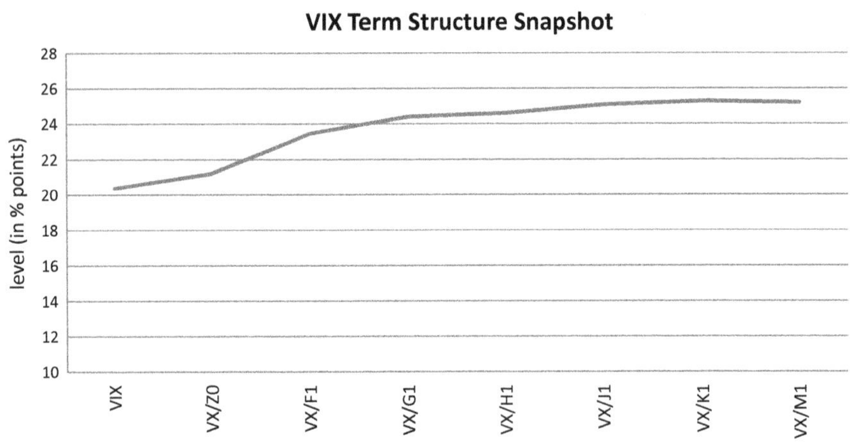


**Fig. 4.5** In quiet markets, the VIX futures curve tends to be in severe contango (*Source* Bloomberg)

relatively little rebalancing, has a higher absolute cost.

When the spot VIX moves, the various futures contracts typically go in the same direction. The futures are closely interlinked. For example, when the VIX spikes, the entire term structure also rises. However, different points along the curve move at different rates. Front month futures are particularly responsive to changes in the spot, as we can see in the graph below. Here, we have calculated the historical beta of each monthly contract along the term structure to the spot VIX, using data from 2010 to June 2020. In this context, "beta" measures the expected change in a given contract when the spot VIX increases by 1 point (Fig. 4.6).

We can see that beta decreases for longer maturities. Longer-dated futures are not very elastic to changes in the spot. The market is essentially saying that bouts of high volatility in the S&P are transitory. Things will calm down eventually. At the other end of the spectrum, when the spot VIX is low, the futures market is assuming that very low volatility is unlikely to persist indefinitely. As the market reprices the VIX futures curve, it assumes that volatility is mean reverting over time.

To repeat, the short end of the VIX futures term structure is particularly sensitive to changes in the spot VIX. This is of interest: the VXX is based on the front two contracts only, which give the biggest bang for the buck when the VIX spikes. In Bloomberg, these contracts have generic tickers $UX1$ and$UX2$. Here, the word "generic" means that the front two contracts do not have fixed expiration dates. They move as the front month contract matures and new contracts are added. (Recall that most investors roll several days before expiration. We are simply following the rolling convention of

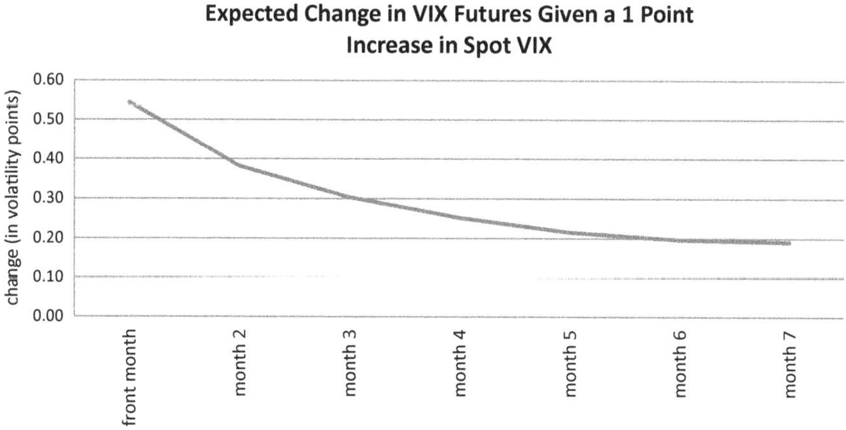


**Fig. 4.6** The front end of the VIX term structure is relatively responsive to changes in the spot VIX (*Source* Bloomberg)

the VXX for now.) For example, June 24, 2020 was the expiration date for the June 2020 VIX futures contract. Before 24 June, $UX1$ and $UX2$ were the June and July 2020 contracts, respectively. After this date, the front two months switched to July and August 2020.

Once $UX1$ expires, it is replaced by the old $UX2$ and we have to go to the next calendar month to find a new $UX2$. In practice, we do not have to roll on the last day before maturity. From a liquidity standpoint, better options are available. For example, we might want to roll roughly a week before expiration, as open interest drains out of the front month contract. While this rule is preferable for investors who want to trade VIX futures directly, it is not necessary for the discussion that follows.

Given these preliminaries, we can now describe how the VXX works. First of all, it is an exchange-traded *note*, rather than a fund. ETNs are favored for benchmarks that are calculated using futures contracts, rather than the prices of securities that can be held indefinitely. Historically, the largest ETNs have offered exposure to commodities or the VIX. Recalling this chapter, the VXX is internally a bond with fixed maturity, but trades more like a stock. It tracks a benchmark known as the S&P VIX Short-Term Futures Index Total Return, or "*SPVXSTR*". At maturity, the issuer (Barclays) promises to deliver the return of the *SPVXSTR*, net of fees. The benchmark index itself derives from the performance of a pre-defined rolling VIX futures strategy. Only the front two months in the term structure are involved in its construction.

The reference index has a constant 30 day maturity, which requires a variable blend of $UX1$ and $UX2$. $UX2$'s weight increases each day, until $UX1$ drops off the screen. For example, suppose that $UX1$ and $UX2$ have $n_1$ and $n_2$ days to expiration and $0 < n_1 \leq 30 \leq n_2$. We want to know what the percentage weight $w$ of dollars allocated to $UX1$ has to be. $UX1$ has less than 30 days to expiration and $UX2$ has more. Given that the *SPVXSTR* benchmark is fully invested, $w' = (1 - w)$ has to be the allocation to $UX2$. The weights of $UX1$ and $UX2$ add up to 100%. Then, a bit of algebra allows us to solve for $w = 1 - \frac{30 - n_1}{(n_2 - n_1)}$. For example, if $n_1 = 10$ and $n_2 = 40$ days, then $w = 0.33$. One day later, with $n_1 = 9$ and $n_2 = 39$, $w = 0.30$. The front month contract gradually peels off until it matures, at which point the second month becomes the front and the process is repeated again.

## Sound Reasons for Launching the VXX

Intuitively, a financial product will only be successful if there is sufficient supply *and* demand for it. Two-sided interest is a requirement for healthy order flow. Hedgers, in particular, play a vital role because they provide reliable depth on the buy side. In addition, imbalances caused by hedging activity can create price distortions that will eventually attract momentum traders and other types of speculators. Designated market makers can support a product for a while, but cannot really replace real money, institutional demand over the long term. These rough comments set the stage for the following assertion: VXX liquidity initially benefitted from a lively two-sided market of hedgers and speculative volatility sellers, as we can see in the normalized chart, Fig. 4.7.

As exchange-traded products go, launching the VXX was a reasonable idea. It responded directly to investor demand. The following graph tracks the performance of hypothetical *SPVXSTR* from early 2018 to the launch of the VXX in February 2009.

Judging from this graph alone, the *SPVXSTR* appeared to be an excellent crisis fighting instrument. It nearly doubled leading up to the Lehman default and continued to perform well even after the spot VIX declined from its highest levels in October 2008.

For the sake of completeness, it is worth mentioning that, while the *SPVXSTR* index does not have a fixed maturity, the various ETNs that deliver it do. For example, the VXX "A" series was issued as a 10 year note, expiring in early 2019. A "B" series note, with an identical mandate, was released in 2018. In our discussion, however, it will not be necessary to distinguish

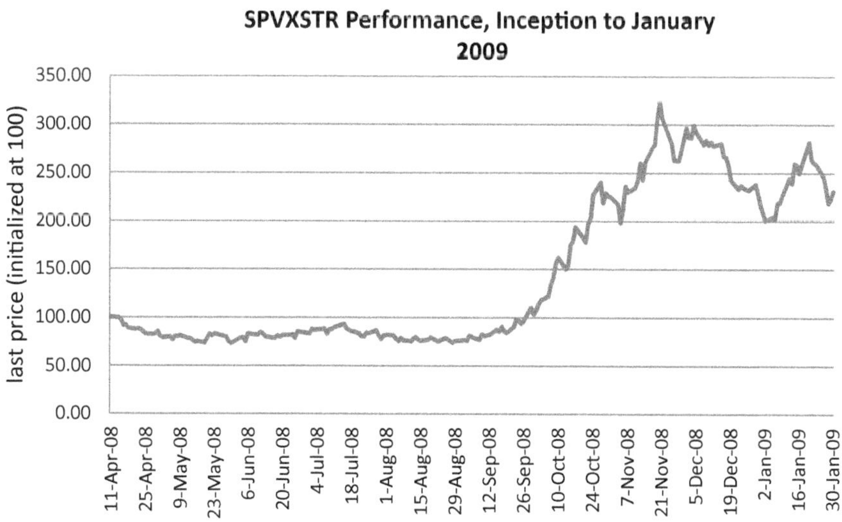


**Fig. 4.7** Performance of rolling VIX futures benchmark in 2008 and early 2009 (*Source* Bloomberg)

between the “A” and “B” series. The Volmageddon occurred entirely within the lifetime of VXX “A”.

## Impact of the VIX Futures Term Structure on Carry

While the VXX could easily be justified from a marketing standpoint, its design features turned out to be problematic if not disastrous for buy and hold investors. The product only had the capability to deliver positive returns given near perfect entry and exit timing, with a maximum holding period of a month or two. Otherwise, carry costs would be overwhelming. To understand the problem, we need to recap the rolling strategy that underpins the VXX. Each day, a small dollar amount of the front month VIX futures contract needs to be sold and an equal amount of the second month bought. The constant 30 day maturity target for the *SPVXSTR* is maintained by a series of self-financing daily rolls. In other words, if \$100 of front month futures are sold, only \$100 is available to buy the second month.

This process has two important implications. If the term structure is upward sloping (namely, the second month is trading at a relatively high price), rolling comes at a cost. The *SPVXSTR* has to sell the front month low and buy the back month high to satisfy its 30 day constant maturity mandate. This loss is monetized. The rebalanced position is also less potent, in the sense that fewer contracts are bought than sold. For every \$100 of investment, the portfolio holds progressively fewer VIX futures over time, so long as the term structure is upward sloping.

By contrast, there is no cost associated with holding the mythical spot VIX. The only hard constraint on the futures is that the front month has to converge to the index price at settlement. This implies, for example, that the price of a 3 month futures contract reflects the market’s current estimate of the VIX’s settlement value in 3 months.

The spread between VIX futures and the spot VIX is typically referred to as the VIX “basis”. Significantly, it is considerably more fluid than the basis for a physical commodity, currency or a basket of individual securities. The VIX curve reflects forward volatility expectations, along with a term premium. It is not simply a function of storage and other fixed costs. The typical VIX premium expresses the idea that, during relatively quiet market regimes, speculators require more compensation for selling volatility over longer horizons. Given a long enough time, something is likely to disrupt the markets. By the same token, many institutional agents are reluctant to rebalance their hedges too frequently. Since calm regimes tend to last longer than highly volatile ones, the VIX term structure tends to be upward sloping.

Notably, the VIX term structure does not depend on quantifiable inputs, such as dividend income, financing, storage costs and so on. There is nothing to store or deliver. If investors expect the VIX to rise in the next several months, long-dated futures will trade above shorter-dated ones. The curve will then be in "contango". If the reverse is true, the futures curve will be downward sloping, a state known as "backwardation". The shape of the curve typically depends upon the amount of mean reversion expected, supply and demand imbalances for S&P options and a binary event (such as an election) looming on the horizon.

The following diagram shows two historical VIX term structures, on November 30, 2006 and the other on October 10, 2008. On the first date, volatility was extremely low and the term structure upward sloping (i.e., in contango). The second date was at the very teeth of the Lehman default. The VIX reached multi-decade highs, with near term risk priced at a premium. The curve was severely downward sloping (i.e., in backwardation) at that point (Fig. 4.8).

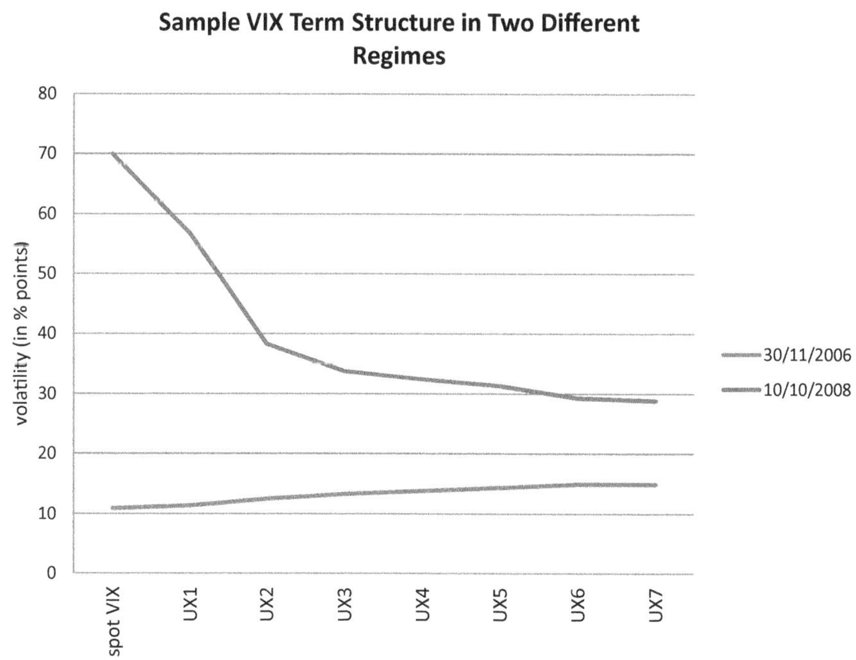


**Fig. 4.8** Contango in quiet markets, backwardation after a risk event (*Source* Bloomberg)

## Costs of Rolling a Long VIX Futures Position

Contango is the default state, especially in an upward trending equity market. Markets tend to be "risk seeking" most of the time. In the years following 2009, US equities moved into a strong bull market. Realized volatility declined, pulling implied volatility down along with it. In other words, relative value traders could no longer offset the high premium paid for an option by delta hedging in the underlying. Short-dated implied volatility took a disproportionately large hit.

Taking a broader perspective, investors were relatively sanguine about nearby outcomes, while remaining cautious about the end game of Central Bank experimentation. This pushed the VIX term structure into a state of persistent contango. Front month VIX futures traded at a discount to other VIX futures contracts an unusually high percentage of the time.

In a quiet market, front month VIX futures are almost by definition low, though higher than the spot VIX. Investors are sanguine about short term outcomes, but wary of the dangers that the future may present. The next chart tracks the percentage spread between the front two monthly contracts along the VIX term structure over time. It takes the difference between the second month futures price and the front month price, then divides by the front month price. We have smoothed the series with a trailing 3 month average of the percentage spread over time (Fig. 4.9).

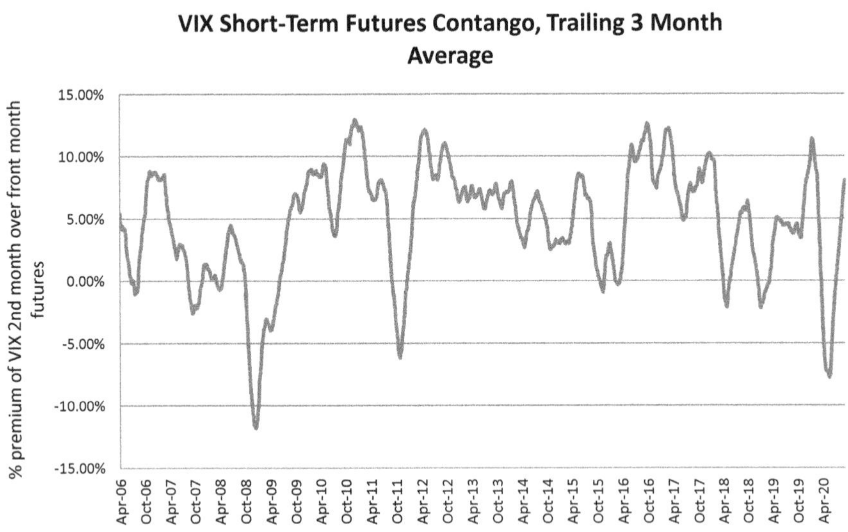


**Fig. 4.9** Historical steepness at the short end of the VIX futures curve (*Source* Bloomberg)

The average level of contango from January 2006 to January 2018 was + 5.09%. In other words, **every month**, an investor in front month VIX futures would have to pay an average of + 5.09% for the "privilege" of maintaining a long position. Five percentage is an extremely high rent to pay.

From 2009 to early 2018, term structure effects caused the VXX (which replicates a rolling futures strategy) and spot VIX to diverge extremely widely. The VXX swooned, while the spot held relatively firm. However, in 2009, many agents considered the VXX to be a close enough approximation, especially if deployed tactically. The VIX term structure had experienced long stretches of backwardation in 2008, as we can see in the chart above. Contango was not considered the default state at the time.

We have already shown that VIX futures, which underpin the VXX, have a high daily correlation to the spot VIX. An investor who had a sizable position in the VXX shortly in advance of a "flash crash" would make a giant dollar profit on the day. These factors contributed to the VXX's early growth.

The trouble is that the violent price dynamics observed in late 2008 are relatively rare in frequency, if not impact. Given the term premium for volatility, the natural state for the VIX term structure is contango. Once the VIX futures curve normalized, a long position in the VXX entered a few months too early had lost potency when the sell off came: a −30% 6 month drawdown in the VXX would require a +43% 1 month spike just to break even. We can conclude that, on a buy and hold basis, the *SPVXSTR* is a poor substitute for the spot VIX. It "bleeds" far too much during calm market regimes. The following cumulative return chart for tells the story. (Note that the VXX adds fees to the *SPVXSTR* return stream, creating an even larger drag on returns.) (Fig. 4.10).

The decay in the chart is so severe that we have had to use log units to make any sense of recent performance. A hypothetical investor in the *SPVXSTR* from inception to February 2, 2018 would have lost −99.92% of equity! This is astounding. Several reverse splits were required to keep the share price at a tradable level. Note that the cumulative return from inception to December 31, 2020 was even worse, at −99.96%. Remarkably, this extended period includes both the Volpocalypse and the Covid-19 crisis in early 2020.

Replacing the VIX with the *SPVXSTR* in the blended 80%/20% portfolio above, we get a vastly different result (Fig. 4.11). The blended portfolio is now a losing strategy.

If the window from 2008 to 2018 is any guide, we have all the evidence we need. The VXX is too expensive to hold, relative to the protection it offers. In a typical month, front month futures would have to rise by several points

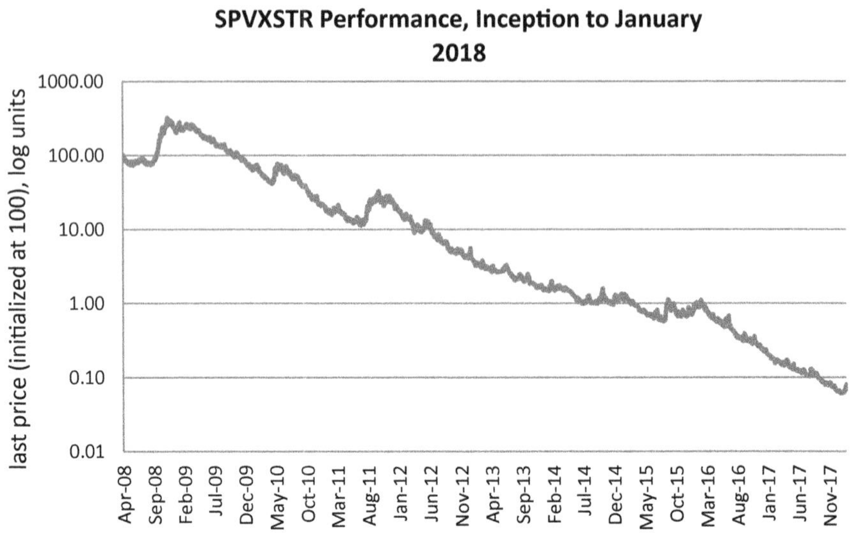


**Fig. 4.10** Long VIX futures: roll costs overwhelm protection offered, when viewed over the long term (*Source* Bloomberg)

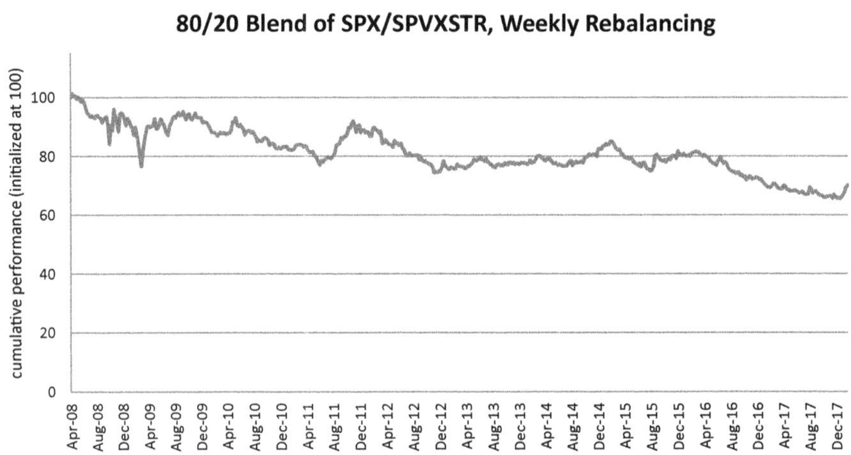


**Fig. 4.11** VIX futures erode any risk premium that the S&P 500 may offer (*Source* Bloomberg)

for a rolling long front month futures strategy to break even. Roll costs are a massive drag on performance when compounded over time.

## Speculators Complete the Market

As 2009 went along, credit and equity markets stabilized. Speculators came back to the market in force, looking for ways to profit from a return to normalcy. An obvious idea was to short the VIX in one form or another. While a VIX at 40, say, might be justified given the recent market crash, it implied an average daily move of at least $\frac{0.40}{\sqrt{250}}$ or 2.5% in one direction or another. Note that 250 is a rough scaling factor that allows us to convert annualized volatility to 1 day volatility, given that there are about 250 trading days in a calendar year. This rescaling assumes that the variance of S&P returns varies linearly with time, which is not strictly accurate. However, our back of the envelope calculation paints a reasonable picture. If the S&P continued to stabilize, 40% implied volatility would be expensive relative to realized variations in the index. The index would simply not be able to bounce around by 2% or 3% every day.

Certain agents were also able to exploit the large demand for the VXX and other long VIX strategies. As dealers supporting ETNs and other structured products rolled a long position from one month to the next, the term structure would naturally steepen. Demand for protection increased carry costs for long volatility investors, to the benefit of investors who wanted to short VIX futures.

## Short VIX ETNs Enter the Fray

Given the gargantuan carry costs associated with holding the VXX, the following idea came to mind: if a long futures strategy was always losing money, why not turn the strategy on its head? Carry could be used as a source of return, rather than a cost. Carry strategies have always been popular in low interest rate environments and the post-GFC period was no exception.

Most of the time, these strategies generate a positive return. However, this "gift" comes at the cost of intermittent large losses. In any case, the nearly insatiable demand for carry led to the creation of the XIV and SVXY in 2010 and 2011, respectively. The XIV and SVXY are inverse VIX ETNs, whose benchmark is based on a rolling short position in short-term VIX futures. We will generally speak of the XIV in the present tense, although it was discontinued after the events of February 2018.

The XIV and SVXY were constructed to capture what the VXX loses in terms of carry by delivering something close to $-1X$ the return of the *SPXVSTR* on a daily basis. Even on the relatively rare occasions where the futures term structure was in backwardation, an investment in the XIV or SVXY could easily be profitable. Backwardation implied that front month volatility was unusually high. If conditions stabilized, the spot VIX would decline, dragging VIX futures down along with it.

We observe that XIV and SVXY are not strictly required to create a short position in the VIX. An investor who is too small to trade standard VIX futures can just short the VXX directly, rebalancing from time to time. If the VXX dropped, more shares could be sold to maintain the same level of exposure per $100 of equity. Conversely, if the VXX rose, some of the existing short position might be covered. However, given the rising demand for short VIX futures exposure, VXX supply was insufficient to support it. As US equities continued to rise, short volatility strategies became vastly more popular than long ones. There were simply not enough shares to borrow.

Another factor driving the growth of inverse ETNs was simplicity, at least from an operational standpoint. Many investors consider outright shorting to be dangerous. While a static long position that loses money shrinks in dollar terms, losing short positions automatically grow in size. The GameStop saga in early 2021 showed exactly how much damage outright shorting can cause. Even when fundamentals are weak, an asset can rise far more than anyone would have predicted. There are really no limits to the move, as options dealers hedge and short sellers scramble to cover their positions. At the extreme, these agents can turn into forced buyers at any price.

In any case, the benchmark underpinning an inverse VIX ETN automatically resets to $1X$ leverage, based on the settlement price at the end of each day. It manages risk for the end investor in a rudimentary way. Rebalancing on a daily schedule is sub-optimal, given the tendency of the VIX to mean revert over time. In Chapter 3, we demonstrated that levered and short products generally perform below expectations when the underlying asset is mean reverting. However, daily rebalancing allows ETN providers to offer a product with limited liability. In other words, investors can never lose more than their initial investment in an inverse ETN.

These factors explain the strong flows into the XIV and SVXY from inception to the Volmageddon (Fig. 4.12).

To repeat, NAV growth was fueled by a combination of outsized performance and steady investor demand for more units to buy. A few individuals with modest experience who made "millions" in the short VIX futures trade acted as billboards for the strategy. We are not trying to criticize these investors too much. We simply observe that performance chasing tends to improve outcomes in the short term, while increasing extreme downside risk.

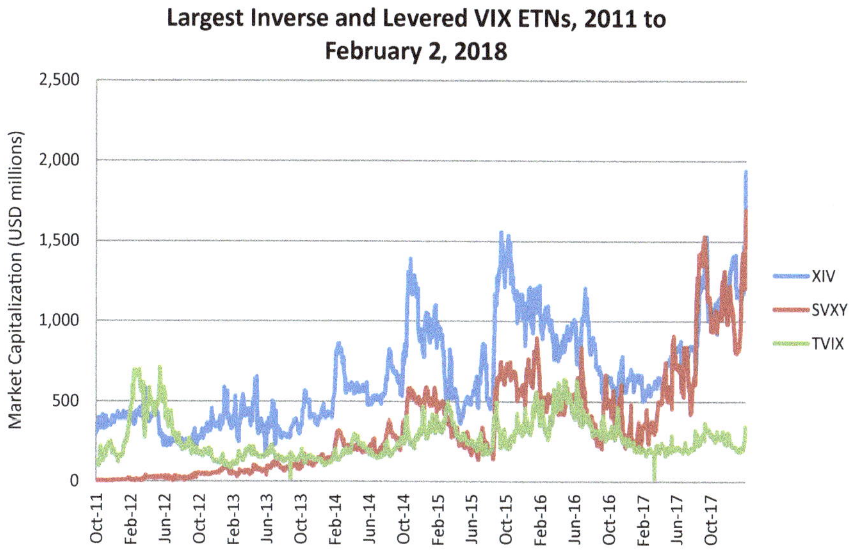


**Fig. 4.12** Performance chasing leads to dangerously strong asset growth for inverse VIX ETNs in 2017

## The Pre-conditions for a Crisis

By the end of 2017, matters had come to a head. The conditions for a mammoth spike in the VIX were firmly in place. A spring can only be pushed so hard before uncoiling. While the exact timing of a spike was inherently unpredictable, a decent-sized initial move in front month VIX futures was bound to set things in motion. This random shock would feed into the network, forcing leveraged and inverse VIX ETN providers to react in size. In a vicious feedback loop, network activity would invariably push the VIX even higher. Forced covering in scale threatened to drive the XIV and SVXY toward bankruptcy, without any change in the real economy.

It remains to specify what these pre-conditions, or "market tremors", were. https://sixfigureinvesting.com/2019/02/what-caused-the-february-5th-2018-volatility-spike-xiv-termination/ offers a detailed and accurate overview of the problem. We recommend consulting this article as a supplement to the material below. Following a theme that is repeated throughout the book, market tremors can often be found in the vicinity of dangerously designed and bloated investment strategies.

- **Rapid growth in inverse VIX ETNs.** In January 2018, inverse and leveraged VIX ETNs accounted for roughly $5 billion in AUM. Overwhelmingly, inverse ETNs were the growth area among the two.

- **High levels of investor complacency.** After an extended "risk on" phase in 2017, front month VIX futures were trading at extremely depressed levels. In December 2017, for example, the average closing value for the front month contract was 10.95, well below its 10 year trailing average of around 18. On February 2, 2018, shortly before the Volmageddon, $UXG8$ (the front month February futures contract) closed at 15.62. This was low enough to cause damage given a decent sized initial spike in volatility.
- **Dangerous incentives for providers.** With an annual fee of around 1.5%, inverse VIX ETN providers alone were collecting fees at a run rate of nearly $40 million per year. In other words, they were incentivized to continue gathering assets without regard for capacity. Even assuming that VIX ETNs accounted for 90% of open interest in VIX futures, it is likely that they would have continued managing the product as usual.
- **Low volatility implies large position sizes.** With front month futures at 15.62, inverse ETNs had to maintain a short position of around 64,000 contracts per $1 billion of equity in order to replicate the benchmark. (Recall that the contract multiplier for standard VIX futures is 1,000. We have ignored the fact that these ETNs blend the two front month contracts for now.) Assuming that all levered long ETNs generated $2 of notional exposure per $1 of equity, they would have to hold around 128,000 contracts per $1 billion of equity to replicate the index exactly.
- **Replicating strategy dominates the market.** In 2017, open interest in VIX futures averaged around 600,000 contracts. Assuming full replication, $5 billion of AUM and a low futures level, inverse and leveraged VIX ETNs would have accounted for over 30% of the VIX futures market!

We can conclude that a garden variety spike in volatility would force massive rebalancing. For example, assume that front month VIX futures jumped by 5 points on an intraday basis. This was *well* within the bounds of believability. $1X$ short and $2X$ levered long ETNs would both have to buy a large quantity of futures to match the leverage of the relevant benchmark on the next day.

We now feel justified in asking the following crucial question. Given the conditions above, how many contracts would need to be bought for a fixed size move in VIX futures, to ensure accurate replication of the index? This topic features in the next section.

## How Many Contracts to Buy, Conditional on a Volatility Spike

Here, we start with a single calculation, before extending to multiple scenarios. For simplicity, our calculation does not consider the fact that the various short-term VIX ETNs trade a mix of the front two VIX futures contracts, rather than the front month alone. We are willing to sacrifice a small amount of accuracy in favor of directness. This assumption slightly overstates the number of contracts that needed to be bought during the Volmageddon. Suppose that, as on the February 2, 2018 close, front month futures are trading at 15.62. Then, the inverse products would need to be short $64,020 = \frac{1,000,000,000}{1,000 \times 15.62}$ contracts **per $1 billion of equity**. If the futures rose by 1 point on February 5, the index would lose $64,020,487 and be left with $935,979,513 of equity.

Notional short exposure would then be $16.62 \times 64,020 \times 1,000$, or around $1,064,020,487. In order to reset leverage to $1 : 1$, $7,704 = \frac{1,078,186,083-935,979,513}{1,000 \times 16.62}$ contracts would have to be bought (Table 4.1).

We can repeat the calculation for an intraday jump of variable size, as in the table below. Note that, if the futures had started at a higher level, fewer contracts would need to have been bought to replicate the *SPXVSTR*. This may explain the recent tendency of VIX futures to spike aggressively from low base levels. We can think about things somewhat more precisely. Assuming that a large spike in the VIX does not depend too much on its current level, the various inverse VIX ETNs are "safer" when volatility is high.

The amount of short notional exposure that has to be covered increases linearly based on changes to the front month VIX futures contract. Observe, however, that the number of contracts to buy increases at a sub-linear rate. This follows from the fact that, the more a futures contract rises, the more a single contract is worth (in notional dollar terms). As a result, we do not need to buy quite so many contracts to generate a level of notional dollar exposure.

The same set of calculations can be performed $2X$levered ETNs, per $1 billion of initial equity. We can see that the **rebalancing requirements are identical** for $-1X$ and $2X$ETNs on the same underlying asset. Table 5.2 is redundant: we have simply included it for purposes of clarification. This simplifies matters, as we do not need to consider inverse and leveraged ETNs separately in our price impact calculations (Table 4.2).

We are now ready to give a more detailed description of the Volmageddon, using the following intraday graph. From the close on Friday, February 2 to around 14.30 EST on February 5, jump VIX front month futures jumped from 15.62 to around 25. After a brief reversal down to 20 or so, it rose to 22.5, before "ripping" to a closing value of 33.23.

Using Tables 4.1 and 4.2 above, 39,152 contracts were required to cover the 6.88 point move from 15.62 to 22.5, per $1 billion of equity. This corresponded to 195,760 contracts to replicate $5 billion of equity, or roughly 33% of the open interest in the entire VIX futures complex!

A buy order of this size was bound to drive front month futures much higher near the close. However, can we quantify *how* much higher the futures

**Table 4.1** Number of front month futures contracts needed to replicate a $-1X$ levered ETN per $1 billion of equity. Previous closing value: 15.62

| 1 day VIX futures move (in % points) | Loss | Equity | Notional | No. of contracts to buy per $1 billion market capitalization |
|---|---|---|---|---|
| 1 | −64,020,486.56 | 935,979,513.44 | 1,064,020,486.56 | 7,704 |
| 2 | −128,040,973.11 | 871,959,026.89 | 1,128,040,973.11 | 14,534 |
| 3 | −192,061,459.67 | 807,938,540.33 | 1,192,061,459.67 | 20,630 |
| 4 | −256,081,946.22 | 743,918,053.78 | 1,256,081,946.22 | 26,104 |
| 5 | −320,102,432.78 | 679,897,567.22 | 1,320,102,432.78 | 31,048 |
| 6 | −384,122,919.33 | 615,877,080.67 | 1,384,122,919.33 | 35,534 |
| 7 | −448,143,405.89 | 551,856,594.11 | 1,448,143,405.89 | 39,624 |
| 8 | −512,163,892.45 | 487,836,107.55 | 1,512,163,892.45 | 43,367 |
| 9 | −576,184,379.00 | 423,815,621.00 | 1,576,184,379.00 | 46,806 |
| 10 | −640,204,865.56 | 359,795,134.44 | 1,640,204,865.56 | 49,977 |

**Table 4.2** Number of front month futures contracts needed to replicate a $2X$ levered ETN. Previous closing value: 15.62. (REDUNDANT)

| 1 day VIX futures move (in % points) | Loss | Equity | Notional | No. of contracts to buy per $1 billion market capitalization |
|---|---|---|---|---|
| 1 | −64,020,486.56 | 935,979,513.44 | 1,064,020,486.56 | 7,704 |
| 2 | −128,040,973.11 | 871,959,026.89 | 1,128,040,973.11 | 14,534 |
| 3 | −192,061,459.67 | 807,938,540.33 | 1,192,061,459.67 | 20,630 |
| 4 | −256,081,946.22 | 743,918,053.78 | 1,256,081,946.22 | 26,104 |
| 5 | −320,102,432.78 | 679,897,567.22 | 1,320,102,432.78 | 31,048 |
| 6 | −384,122,919.33 | 615,877,080.67 | 1,384,122,919.33 | 35,534 |
| 7 | −448,143,405.89 | 551,856,594.11 | 1,448,143,405.89 | 39,624 |
| 8 | −512,163,892.45 | 487,836,107.55 | 1,512,163,892.45 | 43,367 |
| 9 | −576,184,379.00 | 423,815,621.00 | 1,576,184,379.00 | 46,806 |
| 10 | −640,204,865.56 | 359,795,134.44 | 1,640,204,865.56 | 49,977 |

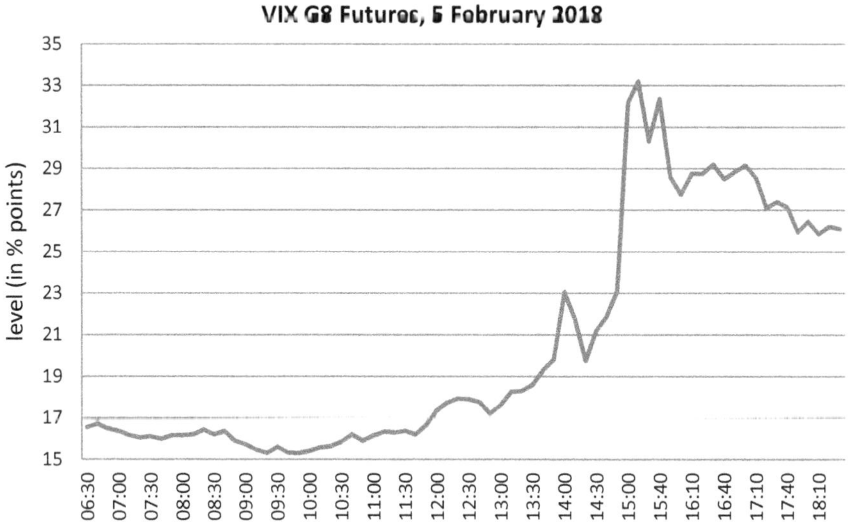


**Fig. 4.13** Re-emphasizing intraday dynamics for VIX futures on February 5, 2018 (*Source* Bloomberg)

were likely to go? This is a challenge that we will face later in the chapter, that distinguishes our book from others that discuss agent-based risk in a more qualitative way. In particular, we will build a rough price impact model that is capable of dealing with very large trades. Before we delve into price impact, however, we need to learn more about a secondary VIX futures order book known as "*TAS*". This supplementary order book was designed to improve market liquidity close to settlement (Fig. 4.13).

## The TAS Order Book

Recall that VIX ETNs are based on quoted benchmarks that rebalance daily, such as the *SPXVXSTR*. These benchmarks are published daily, based on the settlement prices of the relevant VIX futures contracts. Notably, short-term ETNs deliver performance that is contingent on the official settlement prices of the front two futures contracts.

As a result, dealers have an incentive to place buy and sell orders in the Trade at Settlement, or "*TAS*", order book. If they can lock their hedges in at or close to the settlement price, they can minimize drift relative to the benchmark. Following Huskaj and Norden (2014), *TAS* supplements the traditional order book in VIX futures. It allows agents to place bids and offers at or near the official settlement price, without knowing that price is going to be in advance. Orders filled in the *TAS* book allow trading desks supporting an ETN to hedge their risk precisely.

Suppose that we denote the settlement price on a given day by $S$. If one agent placed a buy order for 100 lots 1 tick below $S$ and another agent placed a sell order for 100 at the same level, the orders would cross. A trade would go through at price $S$ minus 1 tick for 100 lots.

The *TAS* database improves liquidity by providing an alternative to aggressive liquidity-taking orders near the 16.15 EST close. In principle, *TAS* leads to a more orderly market, with particular benefit to agents who have to transact near the close. The price impact of a large trade also tends to be lower, given that *TAS* acts as an auction conducted when the market is not moving.

Unfortunately, the *TAS* mechanism works best when it is not absolutely required. Repeating a common theme in the book, structured products, high frequency trading and other technical innovations tend to improve median outcomes for end investors. However, they can create an illusion of safety and liquidity, breeding overconfidence and leading to more extreme negative outcomes. There is no guarantee that unusually large forced orders will find a counterparty. The problem compounds when the largest players, acting as Dominant Agents, all want to trade in the same direction. On February 5, 2018, *TAS* was useful to certain technical traders, at the expense of the larger short volatility strategies that needed it most. ETN providers, in particular, were unlikely to get filled on a collective BUY order of 281,000 contracts in the *TAS* order book. They simply had to hedge in advance of the close. The following graph tracks the intraday move in VIX February 2018 futures through to settlement and indicates a buying frenzy before settlement.

Certain hedge funds and other sophisticated agents were obviously aware that ETNs had significant rebalancing risk. Many were happy to help the process along, buying February and March 2018 VIX futures shortly before the close and waiting for the inevitable follow through. There was likely to be a significant imbalance in the *TAS* order book, skewed to the demand side. As a result, speculators could place sell orders at $S_t$ or even $S_t + 2$ ticks that were almost certain to be filled. This amounted to a nearly riskless in and out trade. By contrast, it was highly unlikely that 281,000 contracts could be bought, even at $S_t + 2$ ticks. The supply of in and out *TAS* sellers was likely swamped by demand from ETN flow desks and other institutional players who needed to immunize against a further VIX spike.

In conclusion, *TAS* improves market function, but cannot handle severe order imbalances near the close. In the next section, we start our quest to build a reasonable price impact function for very large trades. Once we have a handle on expected impact, we can analyze the Volmageddon in more detail.

## Price Impact: Relevance of the Market Microstructure Literature

Initially, we might think of combining various market microstructure studies to measure the impact of a very large VIX futures trade. Bouchaud (2009) offers an excellent survey of the literature. We also refer the reader to O'Hara (1999), who has written a standard reference in the field. Microstructure studies generally focus on two related problems: estimating the price impact of a given trade and developing algorithms to split orders in a way that minimizes price impact.

Both problems require detailed order book analysis. Here, long-standing systematic managers have an advantage. Since they have a lengthy record of orders placed over time, they can collect statistics and decide which algorithms work best. An outsider who only has access to the historical order book for a futures contract, say, will find the order book far more difficult to decipher. For example, it is not easy to distinguish series of small orders placed by different agents from a single larger one that has been broken up into pieces.

Still, it might seem reasonable to apply results in papers such as Zarinelli (2015), which is a curve fitting exercise through futures order book data. This sort of paper would seem to be highly relevant to the VIX problem at hand.

On closer inspection, we can see that the microstructure studies require substantial modification. The trouble is that they rely upon extrapolation. Price impact is usually estimated for small to moderate size orders that go through the market, using a range of regression techniques. Very large trades that go through the market are extremely rare and hence do not receive special attention. On reflection, our massive forced short covering problem bears a stronger resemblance to the available research on "fire sales", which occur in larger size and over longer horizons than the microstructure research can deal with.

However, we will use some microstructure ideas to specify the *ansatz*, or functional form, of the price impact function. The two main choices are square root or logarithmic impact. (Note that fractional power impact, which is also used, lies at the middle of these two extremes.) We will describe what these terms mean by way of example.

Suppose that you want to buy something whose current mid-price is \$100. You place a market BUY order for 10 contracts and are filled at an average price of 100.10. Then, your average trade cost is 0.10, or 0.10% of the previous mid-price. It is the cost to you of executing the trade, relative to the previous print. If price impact follows a square root law, you can then extrapolate what the expected cost of buying a thousand, or any other number of contracts will be. In particular, you are likely to get filled at$100 + \sqrt{1{,}000/10} \times 0.001 \times 100$. This translates to an average price of 101 and a cost of \$1 per contract. You are trading 100 times more than before, at a cost that is $\sqrt{100}$ or 10 times larger. Similarly, if impact is logarithmic, your expected VWAP (volume-weighted average price) will be$1100 + ln\left(1,000/10\right) \times 0.001 \times 100$, or 100.46. More generally, a log impact function implies lower costs for very large trades.

## Price Impact: A Matter of Perspective

Market impact means two different things for an agent who places a trade and someone who simply watches a trade go through the market. We are effectively dealing with price relativism here. Square root and log impact curves only apply if you are the one transacting. In particular, they tell you what your **average** trade price is expected to be, given the size of your trade. An investor who entered a buy order for 1,000 shares with the market currently trading at \$100 might receive the following fill.

Bought 100 @100.20, 250 @100.50, 400 @101.20, 250 @101.50.

Here, the investor paid an average price of \$101 for the trade. Equivalently, trading costs were \$1 per share, or 1% of the previous market price. Assuming a square root impact law, we would then expect a buy or sell order for 10 shares to have $\sqrt{10/1,000} \times 0.01 = 0.10\%$ impact. Similarly, a 4,000 lot order would be expected to cost $\sqrt{4,000/1,000} \times 0.01 = 2\%$, relative to the previous trade price.

Here, we have made the heroic assumption that the *realized* 1% impact on a specific 1,000 lot order is identical to the *expected* impact on a trade of that size. The assumption is in fact too strong and only useful for illustration. In general, we would have to average over many 1,000 lot trades to arrive at a reasonable cost estimate. Price impact for any one trade of fixed size is highly uncertain. It also depends on various time-dependent factors, such as trend and volatility. Are you a liquidity provider or liquidity taker, given recent price movements? Fills are sensitive to the direction and magnitude of short-term price action as an order goes through. Trades that go against the order flow will generally have lower impact than liquidity-taking ones. The cost of buying in a descending market, for example, will generally be lower than usual.

In summary, controlling for path dependence and order splitting when estimating impact is extremely difficult.

The price impact for an **outside** investor is markedly different. You are no longer the one placing the trade. Rather, you have to mark your position to market once someone else's trade goes through. Let us refer to the 1,000 lot buy order example again. Unless prices relax below 101.50, the "impact" of the 1,000 lot order is 1.50 to someone who holds the stock and has to mark it to market. It is a function of the **last** fill level, rather than the average one.

In the case of the Volmageddon, many investors who stayed out of the market on February 5 also suffered catastrophic losses. The existing short VIX exposure (either directly or through an ETN) on their books moved massively against them. VIX ETNs transformed into Dominant Agents (though they always had the potential to do so), taking liquidity without regard to price in an attempt to hedge their risk.

In the next section, we provide some justification for using a square root impact function. The underlying argument does not require any regression methods, which is useful as we try to estimate the impact of extremely large trades by a small number of Dominant Agents.

## Specifying the Price Impact Curve

Most empirical studies, as referenced in Bouchaud (2009), conclude that the expected cost of trading can be described by something between a logarithmic and square root function. This begs the question: do we have to create an internal database of trades to discern the "right" price impact law?

No, we do not want to rely upon regression techniques involving very large quantities of noisy data when selecting our impact function, if possible. Pohl (2017) has proposed an alternative approach, applying something called "dimensional analysis" in physics. The rough idea is that the units on the left and right side of an equation need to match. We can proceed with an example that may be familiar to many. Consider the equation force equals mass times acceleration, as in Newton's Second Law of Motion. If the units for mass and acceleration are kilograms and meters per second squared, respectively, then the units for force *have* to be kilograms times meters per second squared. This quantity is usually referred to as 1 N or 1 "Newton".

Now suppose that, over small enough horizons, the standard deviation of returns scales as $\sqrt{T}$. This is a coarse assumption about the way prices move over time. Recall that $\sqrt{T}$ scaling is characteristic of a random walk (i.e., a Brownian motion in continuous time). This scaling underpins many standard models, such as the Black–Scholes equation. Then, under the assumptions in Pohl (2017), price impact **has** to follow a square root law. There is an equivalence between price action and price impact. Otherwise, the units described in the paper do not line up. The precise argument is not important for our purposes. We can also question the random walk assumption embedded in the paper. However, this approach offers a clear advantage. We no longer have to fit a curve through a cloud of very many small trades, along with one or two large ones. In the curve fitting case, throwing out large values is inappropriate and assuming that small trades are all independent incorrect.

## More Insights into Square Root Impact

We now need to resort to a bit of mathematical notation. Suppose that a trade goes through the market. Its size is $V$, expressed in percentage terms. When dealing with futures, $V = \frac{n}{OI}$, where $OI$ is futures open interest and $n$ is the number of contracts traded. Open interest refers to the total number of contracts, that have been created over time by agents who want to establish long or short positions. For the vast majority of trades, $V$ would be expected to be well below 1%. However, in our "Volmageddon" study, this will not be the case.

Next, let us label the price impact of a trade with size $V$ as $C = C(V)$. As in the previous section, $C$ is the average percentage cost of the trade, rather than the percentage change in the quoted mid-price after the trade has been completed. For now, we are thinking in terms of cost rather than mark to market risk. Square root impact then implies that $C = a\sqrt{V}$ for some constant $a$. This equation is very simple; however, we are faced with a practical problem. We cannot calculate anything solid without specifying the parameter $a$.

Is there anything we can do to circumvent this problem? Intuitively, there are bounds for $a$, beyond which things become silly. The question is whether they are sharp enough. At the left extreme, $a$ has to be larger than 0. $a = 0$ implies no impact at all: prices never adjust to order flow. You can buy or sell as much as you want without dealers changing their quotes. $a < 0$ makes even less sense, suggesting that investors should get rewarded for placing large trades in the market. The buy side would be delighted to hear this, if only it were true. At the right bound, $a \leq 1$. If $a > 1$, a large enough sell order would, on average, drive prices below 0. For example, setting $a = 2$ and $V = 51\%$, we would expect some fills to occur at a *negative* price! Here, the expected cost of a majority SELL order would be roughly 143%, driving the asset price below 0.

Based on recent evidence, it might be countered that negative futures prices are indeed possible. This would invalidate our $a \leq 1$ claim. Let us explore this point a bit further, before dismissing the idea that VIX futures price could dip below 0 in the same way as physical commodity futures. On April 20, 2020, May WTI oil futures amazingly crashed through the 0 bound, reaching an intraday low of −\$40.32 around 14.30 EST.

https://www.institutionalinvestor.com/article/b1lhy2h328jhpt/Inside-the-Biggest-Oil-Meltdown-in-History

*In the minute between 2:08 p.m. and 2:09 .m., 83 futures contracts for West Texas Intermediate light, sweet crude oil, scheduled for May delivery to the oil hub of Cushing, Oklahoma, rapidly exchanged hands at \$0 a barrel. With each contract consisting of 1,000 barrels, this meant that, at least on paper, 83,000 barrels — or 3.5 million gallons of oil — effectively went off the market for free. That same minute, oil prices, encountering little resistance, jack-knifed lower to trade at minus 1 cent a barrel, touching off an unprecedented freefall into negative territory.*

While June was the active contract on April 20 and never crossed 0, markets had entered the theater of the absurd. Negative yields were one thing, but negative prices? The only financial curiosity more remarkable than a negative price would be negative volatility. That would really be something, since it is mathematically impossible for realized variance and hence volatility (which is simply the positive square root of variance) to drop below 0. Given n returns of an asset $r_t$ with average return 0, the variance $\sigma^2$ of these returns is defined by $\frac{1}{n}\sum_i r_{t-i}^2$. Each return is squared before taking an average, implying that $\sigma^2 \geq 0$. Next, since volatility $\sigma$ is defined to be the *positive* square root of $\sigma^2$, it must also be larger than or equal to 0. The VIX is the market's collective estimate of forward realized $\sigma \geq 0$, hence must also be non-negative. Even $\sigma = 0$ is virtually impossible, as it would imply no movement at all in the S&P 500 over the 30 day window that defines the VIX.

Still, it might be argued that spot oil prices in Cushing, Oklahoma (the delivery hub for WTI futures) never went negative, yet the futures did. Here we come to an important distinction: VIX futures are cash settled. There are no storage, insurance or transportation costs associated with delivering a physical commodity. No one needs to be paid to take the VIX off your land and move it somewhere else. More specifically, if you hold a VIX futures contract to maturity, your counterparty does not have to deliver a portfolio of options that replicates the VIX. Rather, there is a simple cash payout, based on the final settlement value. With the VIX, we never wind up with a situation where the cost of delivery exceeds the value of the underlying asset. Cash settlement markedly reduces the (already tiny) odds that VIX futures could go negative at some point in time.

Even if we discard the possibility of negative prices in an actively traded contract, the $(0, 1]$ range for $a$ is far too wide to be useful. For a large order, e.g., with $V = 20\%$, the following diagram shows the wide range $C(V)$ can take as a function of $a$. Naturally, the equation $C = a\sqrt{V}$ implies that cost depends linearly on our unknown parameter (Fig. 4.14).

In our attempt to quantify the price impact of a large trade, we need to narrow things down much further. One idea would be to fit a square root curve through the historical order book. Suppose that a trade goes through the market at time$t$. The average of the bid and ask quotes immediately before and after $t$ are given by $m_{t-1}$ and$m_t$. Then, we would regress the change $m_t - m_{t-1}$ against$V$. (Note that $V$ can be normalized in various ways, e.g., Kyle and Obizhaeva (2017) use a short-term measure of market volatility.) $a$ would then be an optimized quantity, based on a regression. However, a bit of thought shows that this approach is ill suited to the "Volmageddon". While very many small VIX futures orders cross the market, essentially *no*

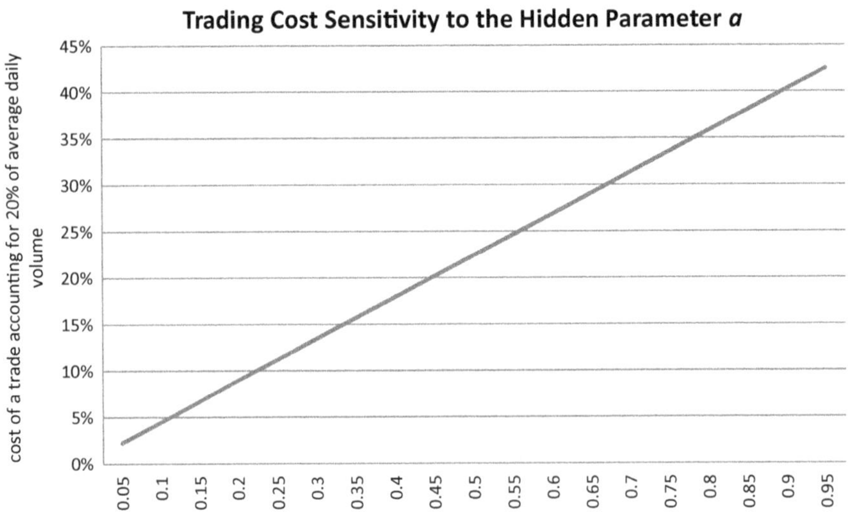


**Fig. 4.14** Cost of executing a trade accounting for 20% of daily volume, based on constant of proportionality in square root impact function

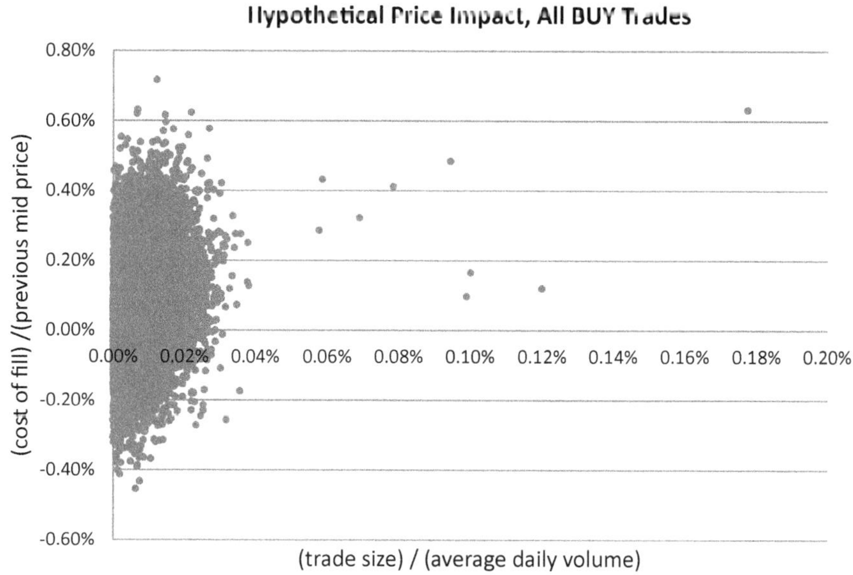


**Fig. 4.15** Curve fitting through historical trades in the order book is fraught with danger (simulated graph)

trades accounting for over 10% of open interest go through. Large trades are rare and invariably broken up into smaller orders. For an outsider studying the order book, it is nearly impossible to tag a sequence of trades to a single buyer or seller. This means that we have to extrapolate from a noisy cloud of small orders to estimate$a$, without any large $V$ data points to latch onto. The following diagram illustrates our core problem (Fig. 4.15).

The question now is whether there is an **indirect** way to estimate the vital parameter $a$. Observe that we only need to have a good handle on $C$ for a single value of $V$ in the equation $C = a\sqrt{V}$. In the next section, we will find such a $V$, drawing from an unexpected source.

## A Surprising Analogy

From a price impact perspective, **forced short covering** in very large size bears a strong resemblance to a **tender offer** during a corporate takeover. Understandably, the reader may have to ponder this idea for a while, but it plays a crucial role in the discussion that follows. Remarkably, the corporate finance literature sheds more light on the impact of fire sales and liquidations than the vast majority of market microstructure studies. This bold statement requires explanation, which we now provide.

A takeover is an attempt to gain managerial control of a company by accumulating a very large number of equity shares. There are a number of reasons why an acquirer may want to take control, which override any potential conflicts within the organization. We can take the perspective of an activist investor. A company might have a great product or service, yet suffer from poor quality controls, excessive input costs and a lack of proper marketing. The list of potential management blunders is virtually endless.

Next, suppose that our target company is exchange-traded. Its stock price might be severely depressed, based on headline numbers (such as earnings) which do not reflect the real value of the enterprise. In other words, a change in management can save the sinking ship. At this point, the activist investor may offer to buy a majority of outstanding shares at a negotiated price significantly above the market. The activist wants control of the company, in an attempt to create even more shareholder value. Meanwhile, senior executives get paid for the disruption.

If the deal is accepted, the percentage paid above the market price is known as a takeover premium. For example, if a given company is currently trading at \$100 and the acquirer buys 50.01% of outstanding shares at a pre-negotiated price of \$125, the takeover premium would be 25%. This premium is the cost of trading 50.01% of shares outstanding in the section above. In other words, $V = 50.01\%$. The exact value of $V$ is of secondary importance. We have simply chosen a number slightly higher than 50%, to designate majority control.

Significantly, tender offers have to be declared to the market. They are in the public domain. Effectively, we are looking at the **telegraphed purchase of a very large quantity of shares.** The intentions of the acquirer are known to other investors. Abstracting the features of the share purchase, we have a situation where.

- a very large quantity of existing supply needs to be bought
- the seller requires compensation for the purchase
- the intentions of the acquirer are known to the market.

Bingo! This situation maps to one where desks supporting VIX ETNs have to buy large quantities of futures after an initial spike.

The next question is a vital one: can we reasonably estimate the cost of taking majority control of a publicly listed company? In other words, we need to specify $C(50.01\%)$. This **boundary condition** will allow us to interpolate the impact of other large trades. We only need to know the expected impact of a single fixed size trade to specify the parameter $a$. Thankfully, the

FactSet Mergerstat/BVR Control Premium Study provides takeover premium data on a regular basis. The "control premium" in the chart below equals the cost of acquiring at least 50.01% interest in shares of the target company. It measures the percentage change in the price paid by the acquirer relative to the marketable share price just before the takeover announcement date (Fig. 4.16).

We can see that the control premium has been stable over this 10.5 year window, ranging from 36.7% in 2019 to 45.5% in 2013. Including the first half of 2020, the average over all years was around 41.8%. Using $V = 41.8\%$ as an input, we can now solve for $a$ in the equation $C = a\sqrt{V}$. In particular, $a = \frac{C(50.01\%)}{\sqrt{50.01\%}} = \frac{C(50.01\%)}{0.71} = \frac{0.42}{0.71}$, or 0.59.

Now that we have a parameterized price impact function, we are nearly ready to estimate the impact of forced rebalancing on VIX futures during the Volmageddon on February 5, 2018. However, we first need to address an important technical issue, which forms the subject of the next section.

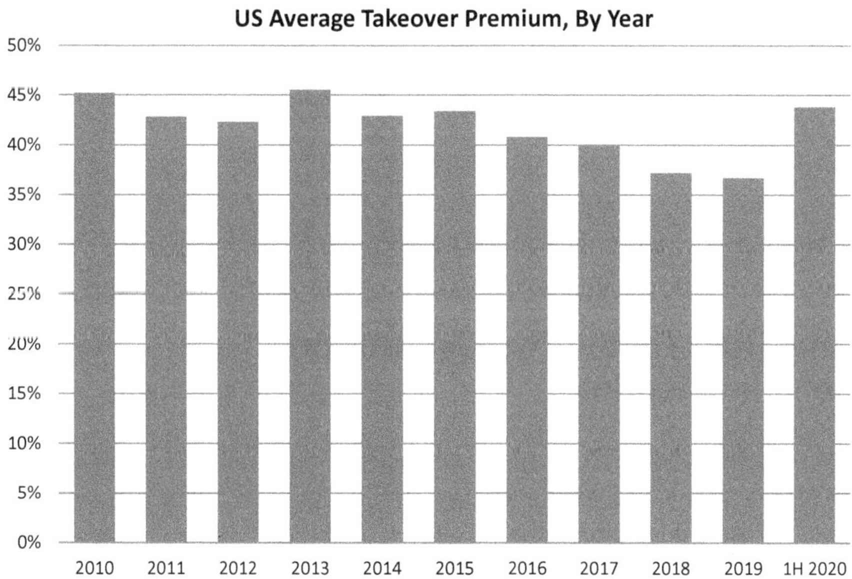


Fig. 4.16 Reasonable stability in the average takeover premium from one year to the next (*Source* FactSet)

## Where Cost and Mark to Market Risk Converge

Admittedly, the analogy between forced rebalancing and the expected premium paid for a controlling stake is an imprecise one. However, it offers significant practical advantages to any approach fits a curve through a large quantity of order book data.

- Parameterization of the price impact function longer depends upon a very noisy regression through a cloud of small orders, followed by extrapolation to estimate the impact of a very large order. Rather, $a$ satisfies an intuitive boundary condition based on very large trades executed in one block.
- Price impact is now **invariant to the frame of reference**. Specifically, $C(V)$ is not only the **cost** of acquiring 50.1% of all shares (or contracts), it is also the **impact** to an investor who needs to mark an existing position to market. The final price, which drives mark to market valuation, equals the average fill price. This follows from the idea that a tender offer is generally accepted at a single negotiated price.
- $V$ is expressed as a percentage of available supply, rather than volume. Shares outstanding and even open interest are stable quantities relative to volume, which can increase dramatically when investors move from greed to fear.

The second point above is crucial, as we do not have to deal with price impact relativism in in the hostile takeover analogy.

## Estimating Follow Through During the Volmageddon

We are finally ready to calculate some concrete risk numbers, using ALGORITHM 2.1 as a guide. Recall that ALGORITHM 2.1 modifies returns generated by the original Mean Field by incorporating the feedback of a Dominant Agent. In particular, we will.

- make an adjusted expected shortfall calculation, in the presence of a Dominant Agent and
- estimate the impact of rebalancing once front month VIX futures hit 23 around 30 min before the close.

We are going to ignore Taleb's (1997) scathing criticism of standard risk measures, such as Value at Risk, for now. Our goal is simply to adjust a known quantity in the presence of feedback. Value at Risk is as good, or bad, as nearly any other statistic that tries to compress uncertainty, in its many facets, into a single statistic.

The closing price for February VIX futures on February 2, 2018 was 15.62. Note that February 2 was a Friday. Regular trading hours resumed on the following Monday, February 5.

With $UX1 = 15.62$, suppose that we estimated VAR at 5 points, with 99% confidence over a 1 day horizon. In other words, on 1 out of every 100 days, $UX1$ would spike to at least 20.62, given a starting value of 15.62.

After a 5 point spike, the various inverse and levered ETNs would have to buy 155,239 futures contracts, or 22% of open interest along the term structure. Setting $a = 0.59$, the expected impact of rebalancing would be + 30% from the new level 20.62, or 6.19 points. This implies that a realistic VAR estimate in the presence of dominant agents should be $11.19 = 5 + 6.19$, over twice as large as one that does not incorporate network effects! In other words, front month VIX futures had a decent chance of reaching 26.89 in a single day given a previous closing value of 15.62.

We have reached the point where we can also estimate follow through in the last hour of trading during the Volmageddon. With $UX1 = 22.5$late in the trading day, the VIX ETN complex needed to hedge exposure with 195,760 contracts, or 33% of open interest. Again setting$a = 0.59$, we wind up with a closing value of$UX1 = 22.5 + 7.58 = 30.08$. Our estimate is reasonably close to the actual closing value of 33.23, even without accounting for other agents in the system!

We conjecture that our model may have slightly understated VIX futures risk because it focused solely on the rebalancing activities of leveraged VIX ETNs. On February 5, 2018, it is likely that other short volatility strategies would have been forced to cut positions as well. In addition, by 3 pm EST, other systems and discretionary traders would have been aware that inverse and leveraged ETNs were going to buy in size. As they bought ahead of ETN orders, these agents would have exaggerated price momentum going into the close. This would have led to an even higher settlement price than our simplified VIX ETN, VIX futures feedback loop model predicted.

## The XIV Goes to 0 on Volmageddon Day

The next two charts highlight the sudden collapse of the XIV on February 5, 2018. First, we have tracked cumulative performance from inception to February 2, 2018 (Fig. 4.17).

Things look entirely different as we inch the time axis to the right (Fig. 4.18).

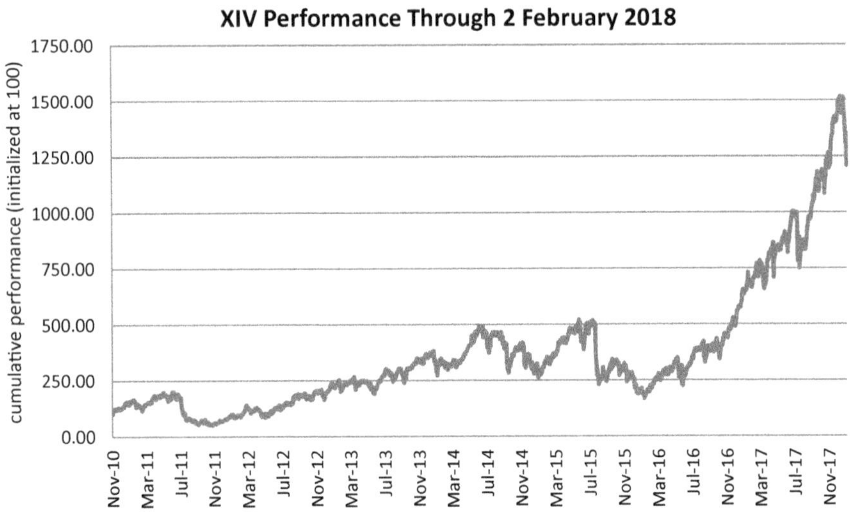


**Fig. 4.17** Inverse VIX ETN performance to February 2, 2018 (*Source* Bloomberg)

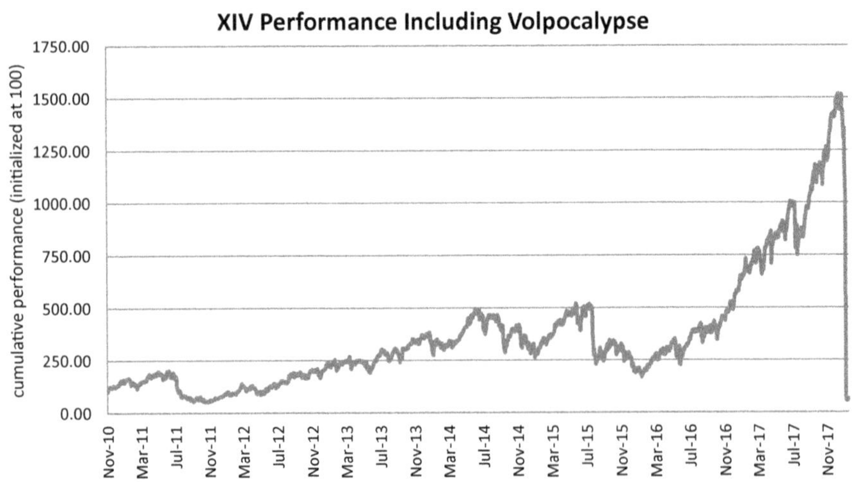


**Fig. 4.18** If one sheep jumps off a cliff, others may follow (*Source* Bloomberg)

Remarkably, the Volmageddon only required a −4.1% down move on February 5! While −4.1% is certainly a large 1 day move, it does not lie at the extreme left tail of the distribution. For example, from January 2011 to May 2020, the frequency of 1 day returns below −4.1% was roughly 0.5%. These sorts of drops should be expected to occur at least once a year.

While the XIV subsequently shut down, the SVXY limped along, ultimately reducing leverage to $-0.5X$, to avoid falling into exactly the same trap twice.

We observe that the main risk to the XIV and SVXY was a sharp spike in the VIX **from a low base level**. This maps to a scenario where the percentage change as well as absolute move in the index is unusually large. With front month futures at 40, rather than 15, the number of contracts that need to be bought after a fixed size jump is much smaller. We can see this in the table below (Fig. 4.19).

If we ignore other network factors (e.g., sharp changes to margin requirements in brokerage accounts) for a moment, it is quite possible that the XIV and SVXY would have survived a 2008-type scenario. This brings us to an intriguing point. A 2008 stress test may have given investors a false sense of security in early 2018. Entering October 2008, these ETNs would have been short relatively few futures per $100 of equity. The front month contract

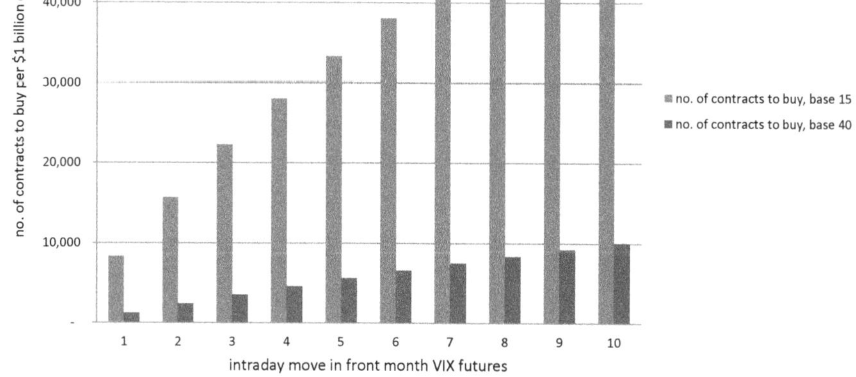


**Fig. 4.19** Fragility of VIX ETN complex is actually *higher* when market volatility is low (parameterization based on FactSet data)

**Fig. 4.20** Shorting VIX futures: disguised risk prior to the Volmageddon (*Source* Bloomberg)

required at least a 30 point jump to destroy all of the equity in the XIV or SVXY.

This decidedly was not the case in early 2018. Volatility compressed to the point where very many contracts needed to be shorted per $1 billion of equity. To repeat, volatility may have been low, but fragility was higher than ever. The size of the inverse ETN complex was growing, largely based on its unusually strong performance in 2016 and 2017 (Fig. 4.20).

As they grew, short ETNs managed to orchestrate the conditions for their own demise by pushing the VIX term structure well below normal. In 2016 and 2017, volatility declined to the point where short volatility. In this sense, the XIV and SVXY created their own Minsky Moment on February 5, 2020.

Given the strong results above, we certainly do not want to end this chapter on a sour note. However, in the interests of completeness, we do need to consider some of the assumptions in our Mean Field—Dominant Agent risk calculations. This is the topic of the next section.

## Strong Conclusions, with a Few Caveats

In this chapter, we are confident that we have improved on standard practice in a crucial way. Namely, we have incorporated agent positioning directly into a risk calculation. Our methods are particularly powerful in regimes where volatility is moving inversely to leverage.

However, need to issue a few cautionary remarks before we conclude this chapter. A long series of calculations are required to arrive at a risk estimate that incorporates Dominant Agents. Each intermediate step carries some estimation error, implying that laser sharp risk calculations are not possible. While our final risk numbers are not sensitive to any one input, we have to accept that the various error terms do add up. We have also made a few simplifying assumptions that are not written in stone. Although standard and theoretically justifiable, we cannot be certain that price impact increases as the square root of order size.

Suppose that impact were logarithmic, instead of following a square root law. Then, the cost of a 30% order, say, would be closer to the impact of a majority 50.01% order than what we predicted. A logarithmic curve is relatively flat for large orders. At a more fundamental level, our hostile takeover boundary condition requires a leap of faith. We proceed by analogy when setting a boundary condition for the price impact curve.

Finally, the various trading desks that support VIX ETNs are not obligated to replicate a reference index exactly. They simply have to deliver the total return of the index at maturity and are incentivized to minimize risk along the way. Hedging can involve a combination of VIX futures, S&P options and S&P futures, in order of accuracy.

Since the VIX formula prices a weighted portfolio of put and call options, S&P futures can be used to hedge some of the delta risk in a VIX ETN. Note that excessive reliance on S&P futures as a VIX hedge is dangerous, though. It cannot account for jumps or sharp changes in investor sentiment. On February 5, a trading desk that dynamically hedged VIX exposure using S&P futures would have had to accumulate an unusually large short futures position. This would have carried significant spread risk when the S&P jumped + 1.7% on February 6, 2018.

In summary, it is generally in the interests of VIX ETN providers to hedge using VIX futures. Accordingly, we have concentrated on this dynamic, rather than focusing on other hedging alternatives that introduce unnecessary complexity to the problem. We have also ignored the extraordinary possibility that a flow desk would choose not hedge at all. A leveraged or inverse ETN that did not hedge VIX futures exposure after a spike would be massively exposed to a continuation of the move on the next day. This could lead to a large trading loss, the sort that finds its way into the newspapers.

In conclusion, we believe that our risk estimates strongly point in the right direction. In the specific case of the Volmageddon, we have improved upon a standard metric such as expected shortfall by a wide margin. In the chapters that follow, we will identify other segments of the market where our methods apply.

# 5

# Liquidity Fissures in the Corporate Bond Markets

Dirt is a Great Respecter of Persons; It Lets You Alone When You Are Well Dressed, but as Soon as Your Collar is Gone It Flies Towards You from All Directions.

George Orwell, Down and Out in Paris and London

## Dangers in the Bond-ETF Feedback Loop

In this chapter, we will move our attention from VIX ETNs to corporate bond ETFs. These ETFs perform a liquidity transformation that verges on alchemy. They attempt to convert a diverse basket of cash bonds into a liquid vehicle with the trading characteristics of a large cap stock.

Crucially, stocks and corporate bonds have entirely different price impact functions. In the land of listed equities, bid-ask spreads move nearly continuously in response to order flow. Under normal conditions, market makers are willing to bid and offer a reasonably large number of shares close to the current spot price. This constitutes low impact. By contrast, bond prices move sporadically. Quotes are generally stagnant until a decent-sized order comes in, at which point prices can jump by a large amount. Screen quotes are frequently wide, stale and importantly, **non-binding**. Dealers are under no obligation to execute at an indicative price. Rather, cash bonds trade through an opaque network of dealers who increasingly act as intermediaries rather than principals. Regulation has discouraged dealers from warehousing positions and thereby clogging up their balance sheets. Major banks and


H. P. Krishnan and A. Bennington, *Market Tremors*,
https://doi.org/10.1007/978-3-030-79253-4_5

specialist bond brokers no longer want to take overnight risk as they facilitate transactions between various agents on the buy side.

As we will discover, dealer risk aversion can create dislocations between the price of an ETF and the NAV of the bond basket that underpins it. In our Mean Field—Dominant Agent framework, ETFs, dealers and ultimately active managers have the potential to increase extreme downside risk in the corporate bond markets.

In Chapter 3, we discussed the "arbitrage mechanism" embedded within exchange-traded funds. When an ETF trades below NAV, dealers are incentivized to buy shares in the open market, deliver them to the provider, receive a representative basket of securities and sell them into the open market for a profit. When it trades above, dealers can theoretically make a profit by delivering the basket, receiving shares and selling them back into the market.

In some sense, this mechanism resembles the "Fed put". If other agents believe that dealers will always step in when a large enough discount develops, they may buy discounted ETFs themselves, reducing the spread between share price and NAV. Dealers then have less work to do. When the arbitrage mechanism works or at least enough people believe it will, the price of an ETF and the NAV of the reference basket is kept in line. However, all bets are off if.

- the securities in the benchmark underpinning an ETF are relatively illiquid and
- there is a large enough random shock to the network.

Here, ETFs that hold relatively illiquid assets, such as corporate bonds, can descend into a toxic feedback loop. We can proceed by example.

Suppose that the shares of a corporate bond ETF drop sharply, based on a technical sell off. There has been a very sharp drop in the broader equity market. In the presence of margin calls, investors are selling whatever "equity" exposure they have and this includes their bond ETFs. The corporate bond ETF is now trading at a $-3\%$ discount to the previously quoted NAV.

Dealers now face a crucial decision. They can do nothing or buy shares of the ETF. If dealers collectively sit on their hands, they are signaling to the market that the arbitrage mechanism is broken. This poses an existential threat to the ETF, as it is no longer tethered to the index. If dealers decide to buy and prices do not quickly stabilize, they may have to take their chances on a share redemption. This requires selling a basket of relatively illiquid cash bonds through the network.

Suppose that there are no ready buyers for these bonds. Selling can only occur at a severe discount. If bond prices overshoot to the downside, the ETF may wind up trading *above* fair value. This is curious, as the ETF caused the problem in the first place, based on its association with other equities. Now, there is a nominal shortage of supply of ETF shares. However, under the wild assumption that dealers decide to deliver bonds back to the provider, the new shares may not find any buyers, causing the toxic loop to continue.

## Framing the Problem for High Yield ETFs

We have chosen to focus on high yield corporate ETFs, as the liquidity mismatch here is particularly glaring. While ETFs only account for around 5% of the US high yield market, their shares trade more actively than the largest and most liquid cash bonds. During normal market conditions, high yield ETFs (along with credit default swaps) give a more accurate description of implied default rates than the prices of cash bonds themselves. However, when the arbitrage mechanism breaks down, high yield ETFs lose their meaning. Indeed, their price fluctuations can actually damage the markets they were supposed to track.

As in the Volmageddon chapter, we can cast the problem in a Mean Field context. The historical distribution of high yield bond returns (possibly estimated using a more liquid proxy) is our Mean Field. During a broad and severe equity sell off, high yield ETF suppliers act as Dominant Agents. Here, they have the potential to distort the Mean Field. If nominated dealers decide to redeem shares and receive bonds in return, the modified Mean Field has to account for the prospect of a fire sale in high yield bonds.

Once high yield ETFs reach a certain size, the "true" Mean Field or distribution is likely to have a much fatter left tail than the historical one. The price impact of a fire sale in an illiquid market is likely to produce a very negative outcome for bondholders. However, any change in the distribution is not very easy to model. Specifically, the price impact function for corporate bonds does not take a clean functional form.

Accordingly, our risk estimates will be relatively rough. We choose to sacrifice *faux* accuracy for a reasonable real-world description of the way bond prices respond to large orders. In particular, we will rely upon an informal survey of market participants to estimate the impact of an outsized sell order in the market.

## OOM Estimates for the US High Yield Market

In order to gauge the risks posed by ETFs on the high yield market, we need to make some order of magnitude, or "OOM", estimates. Specifically, we need to compare the market capitalization of the largest high yield ETFs with the size of trades bond dealers can actually handle. Our calculations are based on late 2019 data, before the Covid-19 crisis in February and March 2020. (Note that HPK gave presentations about the dangerous interaction between high yield ETFs and the underlying market at Real Vision and the CQF Institute in 2019. These talks obviously did not incorporate 2020 data.) Our goal is to map the propagation of risk from ETFs to the cash bond market, generating sensible numerical risk estimates.

As of **late 2019**, the US high yield bond market was around $1.25 trillion in size. We have adhered to the convention that a bond falls into the high yield category if its Moody's rating is Ba or lower. (Note that a Moody's Ba rating is equivalent to BB according to Fitch and S&P.) By comparison, high yield ETFs had a market capitalization of roughly $50 billion.

We can safely assume that these ETFs were almost fully invested in 2019, as they are in 2021. A large cash buffer increases tracking error to the benchmark, without offering any advantage to the provider. Therefore, it is fair to say that ETFs held around $50 billion of the US high yield market in 2019. High yield mutual funds were significantly larger, with an estimated $250 billion of assets. To a large extent, the remaining $900 billion or so was held by institutional investors, such as pension funds, sovereign wealth funds and insurance companies.

Most of these longer-term investors do not trade actively. Positions simply sit on their books, with mild variation over time. Bonds roll off and bonds are added. Many institutional agents apply "hold to maturity" accounting standards to their corporate bond portfolios. Barring a material credit event, they mechanically mark their books up from one quarter to the next. Mark to market risk is largely ignored until a default actually occurs.

Given the size and tendencies of the players, the notional size of actively traded issues was only around $500 billion in 2019. In other words, the segment of the market that ETFs had to operate in was significantly smaller than the headline $1.25 trillion number given above. To be fair, institutional accounts with long investment horizons can and often do act as a liquidity backstop during liquidations. However, they typically do not offer immediacy, the ability to act as a liquidity provider on demand. They cannot satisfy mutual fund redemption requests that need to be met in a matter of days.

## The ETF Premium/Discount: A Potential Sign of Instability

Aside from a broad collapse in the credit markets, the real danger is a short-term crash in the equity markets that drags high yield ETFs along with it. The damage is severe enough that spread traders stay out of the market for a while. Then, the premium/discount to NAV has to be managed with primary trades. Once a large dislocation between an ETF and the underlying market develops, serious problems can then develop. If dealers decide to buy shares and take delivery on a basket of cash bonds, the quantity of selling required to normalize the spread may be too hot for the underlying bond market to handle.

Wild swings in the premium or discount of a high yield ETF to NAV are the inevitable outcome. Extreme volatility in the premium/discount graph indicates that an ETF is not functioning properly. It is no longer saying anything about default rate expectations. The following graphs track the spread between HYG, the largest high yield ETF, and its NAV per share. The "HYG" ticker refers to the iShares iBoxx High Yield Corporate Bond ETF. We have divided our time interval into two, based on available data when this chapter was initially drafted and what happened thereafter. We will save the 2020 chart for the next section (Fig. 5.1).

Several features are apparent from this chart, at least over the 2017 to 2019 window.

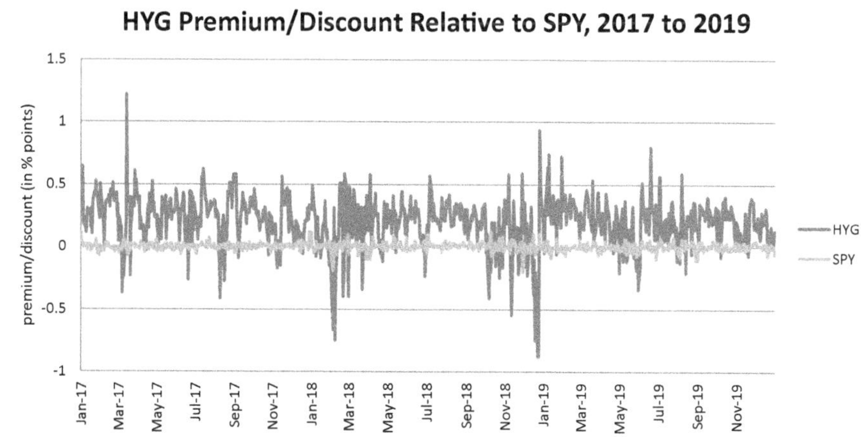


**Fig. 5.1** Comparison of premium/discount levels for a large cap equity and corporate bond ETF over time (*Source* Bloomberg)

- The HYG premium/discount was considerably more volatile than the equivalent metric for the SPY (SPDR S&P 500 ETF Trust). This emphasizes a point we have made previously: ETFs tracking the major equity indices function more smoothly and safely than ETFs that track an illiquid pool of assets.
- HYG usually trades at a premium to NAV. Investors are willing to pay for the liquidity it offers, relative to a basket of cash bonds.
- HYG did trade at a discount greater than −50 basis points during the Volpocalypse in February 2018 and the equity sell off in December 2018. Here, HYG and other high yield ETFs served as a more timely indicator than the cash bond markets. Investors were able to express their bearish views more easily using ETFs.
- Whenever HYG traded at a discount, it rebounded strongly to the upside, typically overshooting its long-term average premium to NAV. Again, movements in the underlying bond market lagged movements in the ETFs that track them. The added premium was probably a function of low liquidity in the underlying market.

HYG generally trades at a discount during "risk off" regimes, where leveraged agents in the network are scrambling for protection. These agents are faced with a choice. They can either sell down their existing positions or try to hedge against further ruin in their portfolios. Shorting a liquid instrument such as the HYG or JNK (SPDR Bloomberg Barclays High Yield Bond ETF) is a sensible option when the cash bond market has seized up.

We can infer that, when the HYG trades at a mild, temporary discount, it generally does provide a useful service. It is a timely arbiter of value. Investors can hedge or express a view on credit spreads through an instrument that is relatively easy to trade. The underlying bond market then has time to adjust, based on what ETFs are signaling. However, a large or persistent discount is far more dangerous than a premium of the same size or duration. As we will find out in the sections that follow, dealers ultimately have to sell high yield bonds into the market to remove the discount. This can have disastrous consequences in a market with no buyers.

Still, we accept that sharp ETF sell offs do not necessarily cause structural damage to the high yield market at large. So long as the premium/discount to NAV is not too volatile, dealers will not have to make large primary market transactions. This requires explanation. A primary market transaction involves the creation of new shares or the retirement of old ones, along with equivalent size trades in the underlying bond market. By contrast, secondary market trades involve the existing float. They do not touch the bond market directly. Historically, the ratio of secondary to primary market transactions has averaged around 5:1.

For example, following an article in ETF Strategy (2019), high yield bond sales in response to ETF outflows only accounted for 3.4% of all primary market trading volume during the Volmageddon in February 2018. This constituted a significant, though somewhat isolated, risk event. Dealers did not have to trade too actively in the cash bond market, even in the midst of −\$1.8 billion of outflows from HYG and JNK. However, this sort of article does not tell the whole story, as it ignores the somewhat unpredictable behavior of other risk-taking agents in the network. The VIX reverted relatively quickly after February 5 and normal market function resumed. Other agents entered the market, anticipating what nominated dealers might do. This likely reduced the amount of primary trading activity required. We can reasonably speculate that if volatility had remained high for a few weeks, high yield ETF selling pressure would have intensified.

## Sketching Out a Danger Scenario

The events of February and December 2018 do not constitute proof that high yield ETFs necessarily improve price discovery in the underlying bond market. Imagine a scenario where the HYG suffers a technical sell off, winding up at a severe discount to NAV. The sell off has more to do with the overleveraged positioning of a few large agents who own bond ETFs than anything going on in the underlying credit markets. Serious problems can arise if the spread remains depressed for a while. A large persistent discount suggests that dealers are either unwilling or unable to trade the spread. Bond market liquidity is insufficient to absorb a large sell order in a reasonable amount of time. The arbitrage mechanism, which underpins bond ETFs, has effectively broken.

Recall that dealers have no obligation to act when HYG or any other ETF is trading out of line with NAV. They merely have an incentive to do so when spreads are wide enough per unit of perceived risk. In a highly volatile market, dealers might conclude that high yield ETFs are simply too dangerous to buy. If they risk share redemption and delivery, they might not be able to sell a mass of bonds into the market in a reasonable amount of time. If indeed there is no arbitrage opportunity, creating a dangerous disconnect between the HYG and NAV. (Readers who have forgotten exactly how the ETF arbitrage mechanism works can refer back to Chapter 3 for details.)

Suppose that certain large agents eventually cover their tactical hedges and reduce their core portfolios. For a time, HYG is likely to trade at a smaller discount, or perhaps even a premium, to NAV. However, if the spread remains extremely volatile, problems can arise. High premium/discount volatility suggests that ETF prices may actually be distorting the prices of the underlying high yield bond market. They are no longer a barometer of default rates, but rather a distortion of them. We might then ask an existential question for standard options pricing models. Does the notion of an "underlying" asset have any meaning when the derivatives market is moving the reference asset as much as the reference asset is moving the derivatives market?

In the next section, we will argue that structural forces have made the HYG, NAV feedback loop increasingly fragile. Jumping ahead to 2021 for just a moment, the problem is not over. While ETF trading volumes have steadily increased, bond liquidity is still significantly lower than before the Great Financial Crisis. This structural disconnect has raised the specter of a future network-driven breakdown in the high yield markets.

## Specifying the Mean Field

Again, the analysis below is based on data available as of **December 2019.** Ignoring network effects for a moment, we can estimate risk in the high yield ETF complex using historical data only. Assuming that the ETF, NAV spread is controlled, it is fairly straightforward to build a baseline distribution of returns for the high yield market. This is our Mean Field. Since HYG is more liquid than its reference index of cash bonds, its historical distribution is a useful proxy for the distribution of the benchmark.

Historical volatility is low, suggesting that this is a "safe" asset. The graph below tracks 1 month trailing volatility for HYG from January 2017 to December 2019. In other words, our chosen lookback period is 3 years (Fig. 5.2).

Realized volatility was constrained below 12%, presumably implying that HYG and the high yield bond market carry significantly less risk than the S&P 500. The next graph reinforces this point by tracking the ratio of S&P 500 and HYG 30 day trailing volatility over the same historical window (Fig. 5.3).

Using a December 2019 30 day trailing estimate of volatility, the Mean Field is not risky at all. 3% volatility translates to a 1 day, 1 standard deviation

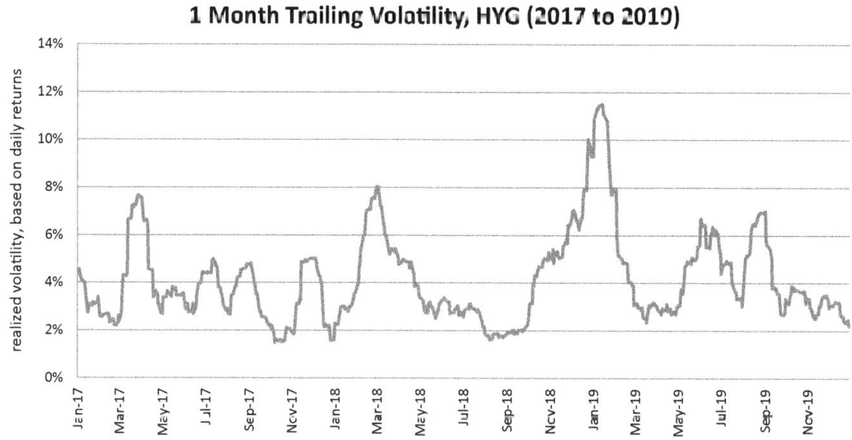


**Fig. 5.2** Realized volatility for the HYG ETF bounded below 12% from 2017 to 2019 (*Source* Bloomberg)

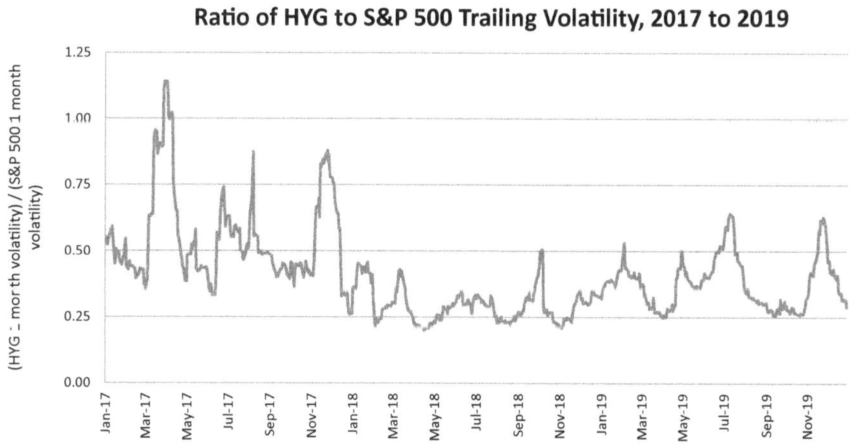


**Fig. 5.3** HYG exhibited far less risk than the S&P 500 from 2017 to 2019. Realized risk giving the green light (*Source* Bloomberg)

move of $\frac{0.03}{\sqrt{252}}$, corresponding to a $\pm 0.2\%$ return. Analogously, a 1 day, 2 standard deviation down move only amounts to around $-0.4\%$.

Even if we shock our volatility estimate, risk levels remain modest. For example, suppose that we decide to take a more defensive stance and set HYG volatility to 10%, near the upper end of its 3 year trailing range. Still, a 2 standard deviation down move only translates to a $-1.3\%$ loss over the course of a single trading day. Simply looking at the data, without imposing any structure on the distribution of historical returns, the worst 1 day return for HYG from 2017 to 2019 was −1.04%.

However, as we will see in the sections that follow, technical factors can drive an individual equity far more than a naïve Value at Risk calculation on a corporate bond proxy would suggest. Over intraday horizons, individual stocks and ETFs lose −5% or more with surprising regularity. As soon as we link a basket of corporate bonds to a security that trades like an individual stock, we have to allow for much larger random shocks than the ones experienced in the data set above.

## Dominant Agents in the Corporate Bond ETF Space

ETF providers and dealers are two of the main Dominant Agents in a composite market consisting of high yield bonds and ETFs. (We will later discover that mutual funds also have the power to distort the Mean Field over longer horizons.) As we will find out, corporate bond ETFs have a complex lead, lag relationship with the underlying benchmark. In the meantime, dealers play a similar role to options market makers. Through their trading activities, they usually manage the spread between an ETF and the reference index. However, we must not assume that dealers are always going to keep prices in line. During severe "risk off" phases, they may well step out of the market entirely.

Once an ETF starts to trade at a large persistent discount to NAV, serious problems can arise. A breakdown in the spread can be the result of dealer risk aversion in an illiquid market. These agents may simply refuse to buy and redeem shares, as redemption requires taking delivery and selling a large basket of bonds into an opaque and illiquid market. An ETF trading well below NAV is no longer acting as a proxy for the high yield bond market. The Mean Field derived from an ETF's historical price series no longer offers a meaningful description of corporate bond risk, as the ETF has become untethered from its benchmark. Once investors lose confidence that an ETF is delivering the exposure they want, the game is over. They are likely to take their money out. In turn, an ETF experiencing severe enough outflows will eventually have to liquidate.

By contrast, if dealers do decide to buy and redeem a large number of shares, the Mean Field has to be significantly modified. The left tail of high yield bond returns increases, based on the impact of large SELL orders into an illiquid cash bond market.

## Forces Driving an Extreme Discount to NAV

In 2019, we speculated about technical factors that could cause a high yield bond ETF to break down. Once we realized that HYG could start behaving like a tradable stock, without direct reference to a basket of cash bonds, things became clear.

*Note* we will see how our various scenarios played out during the Covid-19 crisis at the end of the chapter.

Over short horizons, individual equities can and do crash from time to time. Overzealous positioning is usually the cause. Fundamentals generally do not play much of a role over time scales less than a few months, suggesting that a broken ETF can trade well below fair value for a while. As momentum strategies have come to dominate the market, the frequency of crashes in individual equities is higher than before. This follows from the idea that agents who trade in the direction of a trend accentuate intraday price movements in a non-linear way. Given that they trade on equity exchanges, high yield ETFs are almost by definition vulnerable to a momentum-driven intraday crash. We emphasize that this vulnerability is a function of equity market structure rather than what is actually inside the ETF.

Once we started to think of HYG risk in the context of individual equity risk, a −1.3% downside risk estimate for HYG seemed far too optimistic. A simple cross-sectional example illustrates this point. In December 2018, the S&P 500 dropped −9.18%. Risk levels were high but not very extreme, with the VIX peaking at 36.20 on December 26 and closing the month at 25.42. Even during the steady bull market from 2013 to early 2018, volatility reached higher levels in August 2015 and February 2018. Nevertheless, in December there were roughly **500 instances** of a stock or ETP hitting a downside intraday circuit breaker. This is an astoundingly high number when we consider that there are less than 5,000 stocks and 2,500 ETFs listed on the major stock exchanges, respectively. (We accept that the same securities may have gone limit down on multiple occasions, but this does not negate the point.)

Sometimes, an equity security hits a circuit breaker simply because other stocks in the same leveraged portfolios are in free fall. This was the motivation for our "Two Asset Base Case" example in Chapter 1. In addition, if a correlated cluster of stocks is selling off, statistical arbitrage funds sometimes take a view on correlation by selling the security against the cluster. Once short-term trend followers jump in, a security can crash in the virtual absence of fundamental news flow.

Alternatively, we can imagine a scenario where a crash in oil prices might cause HYG or JNK to hit downside circuit breakers. These ETFs have consistently held a large percentage of debt issued by energy companies. Assuming that HYG or JNK has an intraday trading halt without recovering quickly, we can map the potential impact on the cash bond market.

This brings us to a question that requires some domain knowledge. Where are the circuit breakers set for bond ETFs such as the HYG and JNK? Once we find out, we can estimate the "reasonable worst case" impact of a trading halt in high yield ETFs on the underlying bond market. We will investigate this topic in the next section.

## Limit up and Down Thresholds for Various Securities

Here, we will use our knowledge of circuit breakers to size an initial shock in the high yield ETF complex. Our source for the discussion that follows is ( ).

**Circuit breakers** are trading protocols set by exchanges. They aim to slow down trading after a very large intraday move in a given security. To repeat, their objective is maintaining an orderly market. Once a circuit breaker is hit, the relevant security stops trading. An auction is subsequently held to reset the price, before regular trading resumes.

Most securities on the major US stock exchanges fall into one of two categories: **Tier 1** and **Tier 2**. Tier 1 securities are generally ETFs tracking a broad-based index, with a market price above \$3. By contrast, Tier 2 securities are ETFs on a narrow reference index, are individual stocks, or trade at very low prices. Since a Tier 2 security carries relatively high idiosyncratic risk, its price is allowed to move further from the previous day's close before trading is halted. In theory at least, Tier 2 securities can do less damage to the overall equity market. In particular,

- Tier 1 circuit breakers are set at 5% above and below the previous day's closing price
- Tier 2 circuit breakers are twice as wide in either direction, at 10% above and below the previous close.

We can describe circuit breakers in slightly more technical terms. Readers who are more concerned with the main discussion points of this chapter can proceed to the next paragraph. Suppose that the previous day's closing price for a Tier 1 security is given by $P_{t-1}$. We are currently in the middle of day

$t$'s session. If a designated market maker either places a bid at $1.05 \times P_{t-1}$ or an ask at $0.95 \times P_{t-1}$ and does not pull the quote within 15 s, trading is suspended. This agent is issuing a signal that order flow is completely unbalanced. There are no sellers or buyers, respectively. The market maker is pressing the pause button to avoid getting run over by one directional order flow. Once a halt occurs, quotes are collected until both the bid and ask fall within the $\left[0.95 \times P_{t-1}, 1.05 \times P_{t-1}\right]$ band. This constraint reduces the odds of an immediate gap move once the market reopens.

HYG and JNK have Tier 1 classification, given that the reference benchmark contains over 1,000 bonds. Accordingly, circuit breaker bands are set 5% above and below the previous close. This is not to say that either ETF is diversified enough to protect capital during a credit event. Rather, the implication is that exposure to idiosyncratic single company risk is small.

We have now reached the point where we can size an initial downside shock to high yield ETFs. −5% is justifiable, as it accurately incorporates downside limits set by exchanges before trading is halted. We emphasize that, while limit down moves do not occur every day, they are not very rare. During the sort of highly volatile month that occurs every few years, stocks and ETFs in fact go limit down with surprising regularity. The odds of a randomly chosen security hitting a downside circuit breaker on a random day were close to 1% in December 2018. In months where the VIX peaked above 40%, we would expect this frequency to be much higher.

Given the downside thresholds for Tier 1 securities such as HYG and JNK, we want to understand the implications of a −5% drop in these ETFs on the underlying bond market.

## Deciding How Many Shares to Buy

After an intraday −5% move, dealers have to estimate how many shares to buy in order to arbitrage the ETF, NAV spread. This is complex if not intractable, as it involves two interacting price impact models.

The first step involves estimating the impact of buying a certain percentage of outstanding ETF shares. How much will a purchase of fixed size move the price? Since ETFs functionally trade as equities, with the same microstructure, an **equity impact curve** is appropriate for them. Dealers then need to gauge the impact of selling an equivalent dollar quantity of bonds into the high yield market. This is a **bond impact** problem.

Ideally, if the share purchase is sized correctly, dealers should make a reasonable profit and the ETF should approach fair value. This would restore the ETF's role as a useful proxy for the high yield bond market.

We can proceed with a more concrete example. For simplicity, suppose that we normalize the prices of HYG and JNK to \$100 on the close of a given day. On the next day, suppose that these shares make an air pocket move to \$95. No trades have gone through the cash bond market, so we cannot reliably mark down the high yield index. It is highly probable that the "true" benchmark value is somewhere between 0% and −5% lower than the previous print. However, we cannot be much more specific than that.

As we have stated above, the ETF sell off might be driven by a liquidation in equity space, rather than a fundamental change in perceived default risk. For example, S&P 500 futures might be in free fall. Certain agents in the network (such as statistical arbitrage funds) are selling other securities and ETFs purely based on their historical correlation to the S&P. In this case, the basket of bonds held by the provider might still have fair value close to \$100 per share.

Dealers who believe that the various high yield ETFs have overshot fair value are incentivized to take the following steps.

- Buy an appropriate quantity of shares in the open market.
- Return these shares to the index provider in exchange for a representative basket of high yield bonds.
- Sell the cash bonds through the dealer network for a profit.

As in Chapter 4, our default assumption is that the ETFs in question follow a square root impact law. ETFs are functionally shares, so an equity price impact law seems reasonable. We justified this choice without recourse to any curve fitting, as in Pohl (2017). Then,

$$(average\%costpershare) = a\sqrt{\frac{(highyieldETFsharestraded)}{(highyieldETFsharesoutstanding)}}$$

Using the same takeover premium argument as in Chapter 4, we can set $a = 0.59$. Recall that this is based on the historical premium paid by agents who acquire a majority stake in a publicly traded company.

We can then calculate the number of ETF shares needed to move the price by a specific amount. Using the equation above, we can see that this quantity is proportional to $(average\%costpershare)^2$, as in the graph below. Using data from 2019, we have made an order of magnitude assumption that the total size of the US high yield ETF market is \$50 billion (Fig. 5.4).

The graph above is indicative of trouble. Even though nothing has gone through the bond market, dealers have no incentive to pay anything close

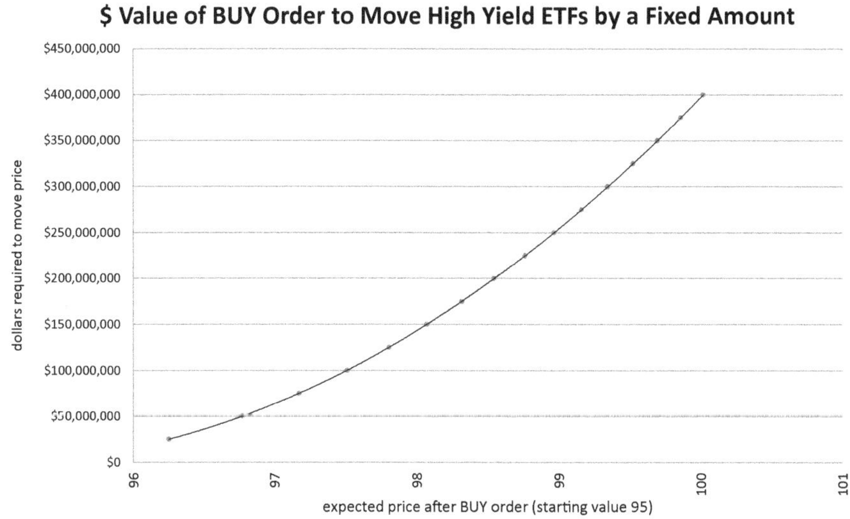


**Fig. 5.4** Large $$$ required to push the price of an equity or ETF by only a few percent

to $100 per share for the HYG and JNK. The number of shares required to do so converts to a sale that is too large for the bond market to digest. For example, dealers would have to buy roughly $400 million of shares to push ETF prices from 95 to 100. In the current regulatory climate, dealers are generally reluctant to hold orders larger than $2 million or so for an extended period of time. After taking delivery, they would effectively have to go into fire sale mode, dumping $400 million of high yield bonds into the market. The credit markets would likely seize up under the weight of this trade.

In practice, dealers might take a more cautious approach, incorporating restricted bond liquidity into their calculations. Again, we can proceed by example. Suppose that dealers buy just enough shares to force the market to 98.5. This still turns out to be a dangerous relative value trade. Price impact is $\frac{(98.5-95)}{95}$, or roughly 3.68%. With $a = 0.59$, 0.39% of outstanding shares would allow dealers to execute a block BUY order at 98.5. This translates to a $195 million share purchase.

Once the dealer receives bonds through a primary market transaction with the ETF provider, an immediate buyer has to be sourced for a basket of $195 million of junk. Hedge funds are likely to be cautious, requiring a discount of −5% or more before they step in. As we will soon find out, corporate bond prices tend to jump by a large amount when lumpy orders go through the market. Moreover, deep value managers are unlikely to buy the entire basket, as they tend to focus on individual securities in their research.

From the standpoint of a buy and hold ETF investor, we need to face a sobering fact. Once HYG, JNK and other high yield ETFs start to trade at a severe enough discount to NAV, arbitrage loses its meaning. It is unclear where the reference index should be trading, hence how badly mispriced the spread is. Immediate bond liquidity is likely to be low, conditioned on the spike in equity volatility.

Once price impact is taken into account, these ETFs might still be mispriced, but there is no safe way to compress the spread. The implication is that nominated dealers are unlikely to act aggressively during a severe sell off in the high yield ETF complex. It is simply too risky to close the spread with a large trade in a volatile market. If dealers refuse to act for a while, the structural linkage between an ETF and its reference index is vulnerable. This is problematic: once an ETF's share price loses permanent contact with the benchmark, agents seeking high yield exposure have no reason to buy it. As we have observed above, liquidation is the inevitable outcome for an ETF that no one wants to own.

Before we can estimate the impact of an ugly technical ETF sell off on high yield, we need to justify our assertion that the bond market would be unable to absorb a large SELL order in a volatile market. This is the topic of the next section.

## Contraction in Dealer Balance Sheets

In the early 2000s, commercial banks took progressively more principal risk, with net exposure peaking in 2007. Balance sheet constraints were modest, allowing banks to take large quantities of credit and duration risk. The freedom to pile on positions with positive carry was not entirely bad. In particular, banks acted as shock absorbers whenever large SELL orders went through the market. They were prepared to buy at a reasonable discount and warehouse distressed securities, while sourcing liquidity in the market. To repeat, they provided a fairly reliable bid to the bond market when the buy side needed to unload positions.

The current situation, however, is markedly different. Banks have been steadily divesting their corporate bond exposure since the Lehman crisis. According to a Bank of International Settlements article (2014), aggregate fixed income risk across primary dealers dropped by over −60% from 2008 to 2012. (Here, risk was defined in Value at Risk terms.) The Dodd-Frank Act in 2010 was a watershed moment in terms of protecting depositors and reigning in bank speculation. However, these protections came at a cost. Banks were

**Fig. 5.5** Dealers focused on reducing balance sheet risk post-GFC (*Source* Federal Reserve Bank of New York)

only able to repair their balance sheets by stepping out of their role as principal buyers. The following graph emphasizes this point, using historical data from the New York Fed (Fig. 5.5).

Recall that primary dealers are typically large banks that trade directly with the Fed. We have used a rolling 3 month average of aggregate dealer net positions to smooth the data. We observe a steady decline in corporate bond exposure as banks have reduced their principal risk. Within the high yield sector, we are limited by the data, which only goes back to 2013. Still, we can see a trend consistent with the corporate bond space at large. With the exception of a moderate blip in 2016, dealers have been increasingly reluctant to expose themselves to Ba credit risk or lower (Fig. 5.6).

One consequence of this trend is beneficial to the financial network, as we have observed above. The commercial banking network has become less vulnerable to a shock coming from the corporate bond sector. This implies, at least, that an exact repeat of the GFC is unlikely. Balance sheet contraction may have reduced profitability, but it has increased safety within the banking network. Dealers have relatively modest exposure to duration and credit risk. However, the reluctance of banks to act as principals has pushed risk into other areas of the financial network. With corporate issuance at record levels, other agents have absorbed the residual risk. Electronic customer-to-customer transactions have picked up the slack somewhat, as agents can source liquidity directly. However, the liquidity in this arena can dry up completely during periods of market stress. Without dealers who are committed to intermediating trades, they are not reliable.

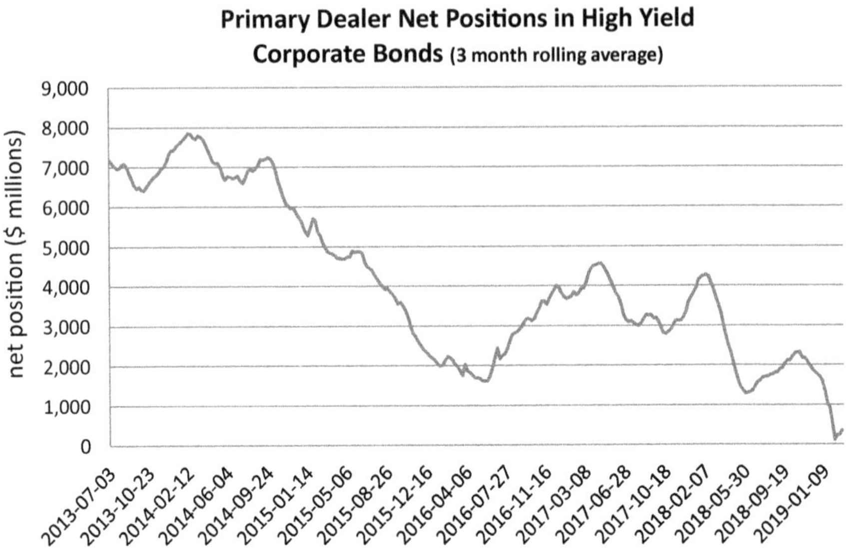


**Fig. 5.6** Dealer high yield exposure also on the downtrend (*Source* Federal Reserve Bank of New York)

We can conclude that, since the Great Financial Crisis, liquidity in the corporate bond market has declined precipitously. Dangerously, this decline has coincided with record levels of lower grade corporate bond issuance. Many companies have issued bonds as a cheap financing vehicle to repurchase their stock, without investing in long-term projects. This has obviously benefitted corporate executives, without adding anything to the real economy. While BBB corporate bond issuance has reached record levels, US high yield issuance has also increased strongly over the past decade (Fig. 5.7).

Assuming a moderate shock, causing credit spreads to widen, it is unlikely that dealers would have a large appetite for high yield debt. Outstanding supply is too large, relative to balance sheet constraints.

## Interpreting the Order Book Data Correctly

Readers who are not interested in technical issues surrounding the historical order book for corporate bonds can safely move on to the next section.

We have drawn from an interesting article by Perotta and Jenkins (2016) in this section. Suppose that an agent wants to buy or sell a corporate bond. The agent calls a trading desk. The desk might give some "indicative" quotes, based on where similar bonds and credit derivatives have been trading. However, these quotes are non-binding. The dealer has no obligation

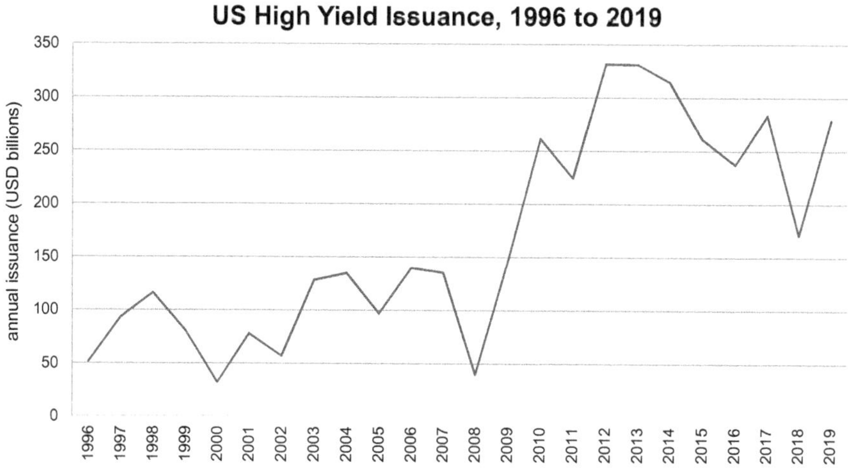


**Fig. 5.7** While dealers step out of the market, high yield supply increases (*Source* SIFMA)

to transact at those levels. In addition, available liquidity cannot be inferred from the width of the quotes. There may be no depth to the market, no size around the bid and ask. In turbulent markets, dealers may pull their quotes entirely for a while. They are likely to wait until they can gauge demand from long-term buyers, such as pension funds and insurance companies. This makes it very difficult to estimate what the impact of an order might be.

One approach would involve gathering historical time and sales data and estimating impact from there. Various databases, such as TRACE, give a detailed record of trades that have gone through the bond market. However, they do not turn out to be very useful indicators of expected impact. The following example serves to clarify things. Suppose that a fund manager wants to sell \$10 million of a single bond issue whose duration is 10 years. In the absence of price impact, the bond is worth around 200 basis points over, or 2% higher than an equivalent duration Treasury bond. Prices are generally quoted in yield, rather than dollar, terms. Recall that 1 basis point is equal to $\frac{1}{100}$ of 1%, or 0.01%.

The fund's internal execution trader asks for a quote, which the dealing desk does not immediately deliver. It is unwilling to warehouse the position before finding a buyer. In other words, the dealer has chosen to act as an agent rather than principal. Instead, it shops the trade around. Finally, an agent is identified, who agrees to pay 210 basis points over for \$10 million of debt. This is a discount of 10 basis points to theoretical value. If the original fund manager is willing to take the offer, the dealer might then engage in two trades that would appear directly in the TRACE database. Here is a sample pair of fills.

BUY \$10 million @ 213 bps over
SELL \$10 million @ 210 bps over

Observe that the BUY order is really a fragment of a single trade that includes the SELL order as well. It briefly transfers ownership from the fund manager to the dealer, as a buyer has already been identified. The SELL order then moves the bonds from the dealer to the end buyer.

Judging from the ledger, we could easily be fooled into thinking that the price impact for this \$10 million trade was only 3 basis points. This is false. In practical terms, only one trade has taken place, with 10 basis points of impact before costs. The 3 basis point spread merely acts as a commission to the dealer. It severely underestimates the impact of a \$10 million order into the market. A much larger trade might have an even lower commission, in percentage terms. We might then see two orders of the following form.

BUY \$100 million @ 242 bps over
SELL \$100 million @ 240 bps over

The dealer is effectively offering a fee discount for volume. This categorically does not mean that a \$100 million sale has lower impact than a \$10 million one. Impact for the large sell order is 40 bps, rather than the 2 basis point commission taken by the dealer.

## A Survey Approach to Estimating Impact

Since the historical record of transactions is not very useful for estimating the impact of large orders, what else can we do? In the absence of quality data, a reasonable alternative is to **ask the experts**, namely portfolio managers who actually transact in low quality and distressed corporate bonds. In this spirit, we conducted an informal survey of three highly experienced hedge fund managers. Each manager has served as a principal at a high yield focused hedge fund for at least 20 years and hence has participated in several credit cycles. We took the view that the buy side would give a more risk conscious estimate of impact than an agent on a dealer trading desk.

One of the survey participants offered an interesting perspective, based on his experience as the managing partner of a large convertible arbitrage fund. It is not hard to understand why. The convertible bond market is somewhat insular, with specialist players. Significantly, it is prone to large-scale liquidations every few years. Arbitrageurs are Dominant Agents in the convertible bond market who face the same structural problem as dealers for bond ETFs. While they help control the spread between two related assets, one liquid and the other illiquid, they also require that the spread does not become uncontrollably volatile. While convertible managers typically hedge their niche bond exposure with liquid equities, dealers try to manage the linkage between an equity-like structure and a basket of underlying bonds. Both agents serve to keep prices in line during normal market conditions, but are vulnerable to large dislocations when risk levels spike. Outflows from convertible arbitrage funds can be damaging to the underlying market.

We can now summarize the results of our conversations. Significantly, each manager gave the same rough price impact estimate in each of two different scenarios. We will follow from the examples in the "Deciding How Many Shares to Buy" section above. Assuming that \$400 million of high yield bonds were dumped into the market, the **expected price impact was around −10%**. This corresponds to the case where dealers buy enough shares to push the prices of high yield ETFs back to \$100. Under the more modest assumption that \$195 million needed to be liquidated in short order, **expected impact was closer to −5%**. \$195 million might not seem much relative to the size of the high yield market. However, recall that it is the marginal buyer or seller, rather than the hold to maturity investor, who moves prices around. To repeat, price discovery occurs at the margins.

## Toxic Leakage into Mutual Funds

So far, we have converted a −5% limit down scenario for the high yield ETF complex into a potential −5% to −10% drop in the relevant bond indices over the course of several days. This is likely to cause selling in other segments of the bond market. We can move along the chain of dependencies, to mutual funds. These potential Dominant Agents are roughly $5X$ the size of the high yield ETF market.

Given that many funds passively track an index, we might hope that active high yield managers, at least, could serve as a price backstop. After a sharp technical sell off, they might act as a discount buyer of debt. Once prices stabilized, dealers could then re-enter the market, without fear of contagion. The arbitrage mechanism would push ETF prices back in line with NAV and things would function as intended again. Unfortunately, a 2017 paper by

Goldstein, Jiang and Ng (2017) casts doubt on this idea, based on investor outflows from bond funds during crisis periods. We will refer to this paper as **GJN** in what follows.

For equities, there is some evidence that value funds provide a reliable bid during a sell off. This has at least been true historically. Many of these agents like to buy into price weakness, on the assumption that fundamentals change far more slowly than prices. As the theory goes, future returns have an inverse relationship to the current price of a security with reasonably stable cash flows. In other words, high returns in the present are borrowed from the future. A value manager who holds excess cash entering a sell off can selectively buy stocks from the bargain bin. (Note that this approach ignores the idea that there is feedback between market prices and fundamentals. In other words, it assumes that markets do not exhibit much reflexivity.)

However, we must realize that mutual funds deploy capital in the larger context of investor flows. In a bear market, value managers who have experienced significant redemptions may have to liquidate positions that are trading at a large discount and may have high prospective returns. Positions simply have to be cut across the board. This brings us to an important issue. Is there a quantifiable relationship between trailing fund performance and flows? If investors redeem too aggressively from underperforming managers after a short-term sell off, these managers will no longer have enough cash to absorb selling pressure in the market. If anything, they may have to sell into weakness to meet redemptions, pushing prices down further.

**GJN** uses a variety of regressions across a large number of funds to show that the flow-performance relationship is qualitatively different for bond and stock funds. In particular, bond funds tend to suffer from relatively large outflows when then underperform the broad benchmark. In practical terms, it is less dangerous for an active equity manager to add to losing positions than for a bond manager to do the same. The bond manager is simply more vulnerable to investor behavior.

Investors tend to be performance chasers across all asset classes. Funds with positive realized alpha attract assets, while underperforming funds suffer redemptions. The question then becomes, does under or outperformance have a larger absolute impact on flows? In concise terms, what is the typical "flow-performance" relationship? A more nuanced question is whether the general shape of the flow-performance curve varies across asset classes. Empirically, as in Chen, Goldstein and Jiang (2010), it turns out that there is a **convex relationship for equity mutual funds**. (We remark that some convexity is lost for mutual funds that trade relatively illiquid equities.) Outperforming equity funds were rewarded more in terms of flows than underperforming funds were punished. In other words, +1% of alpha relative to the benchmark attracted more assets than −1% of alpha lost. The following graph qualitatively summarizes their results, without direct reference to the data (Fig. 5.8).

However, there is more to this story. It turns out that flow-performance curves are both regime and liquidity dependent. Prevailing risk conditions have an impact on investor behavior. In particular, flow-performance curves lose their convexity and hence become less favorable to fund managers during bear markets. This is consistent with experience. Credit tends to be tight during market downturns and investors are capital constrained. This makes them less likely to add to funds that are performing relatively well and more likely to redeem from underperformers. In addition, if certain agents fear that others are likely to redeem, they may choose to sell themselves. This is based on the idea that, after fund managers sell assets to meet redemptions, the market value of their portfolios will be lower than before. Capponi, Glasserman and Weber (2018) have developed an explicit model for the non-linear feedback loop between redemptions, changes to NAV and further redemptions. This leads them to suggestions for distributing costs across existing and exiting investors, as a mechanism for stabilizing the cycle.

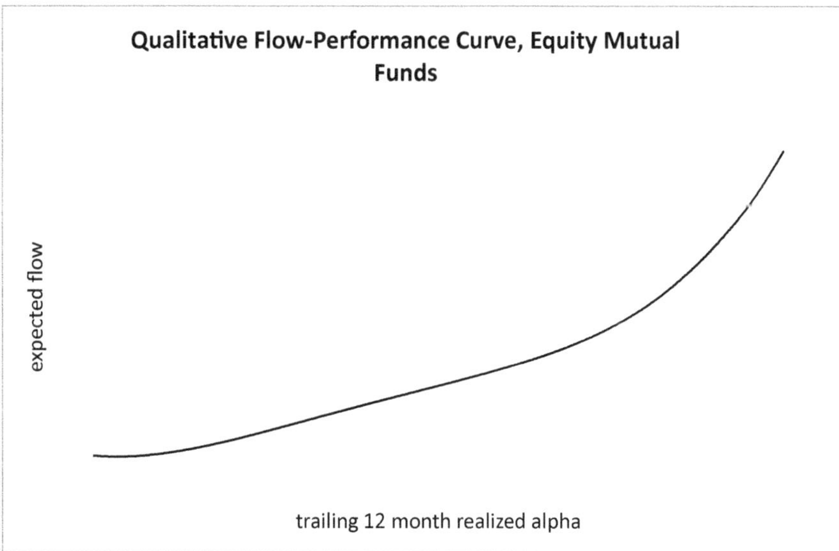


**Fig. 5.8** Typical flow-performance curve for equity mutual funds, based on historical data

## Flow-Performance Curves for Bond Funds

While flow-performance curves for equity funds are convex (especially during calm market regimes), the situation is worse for mutual funds that invest in fixed income securities. Here, averaged across all regimes, the flow-performance relationship is negatively convex. Managers who underperform their broad benchmarks lose assets at a disproportionate rate. Using options jargon, an investor in a bond fund is short gamma to the fund's realized performance. The options description is appropriate, as a short gamma profile is nearly always associated with left tail risk. Investor behavior increases the odds of an extreme event in the corporate bond markets (Fig. 5.9).

"First mover advantage" is usually cited as the reason for negative convexity in corporate bond flows. Investors worry that if they wait too long, they will have to bear the cost of redemptions from other agents in the network. In an illiquid market, even moderate outflows can cause prices to drop quite significantly. This can lead to further underperformance and another round of redemptions at an even lower price level.

Negative convexity for corporate bond funds is particularly apparent when broad market volatility is high. In calm regimes, the flow-performance curve is fairly linear. Following **GJN**, we can characterize a calm regime by tight credit spreads or, as in our case, a low VIX level. When credit spreads are tight, investors do not require much compensation for bearing default risk.

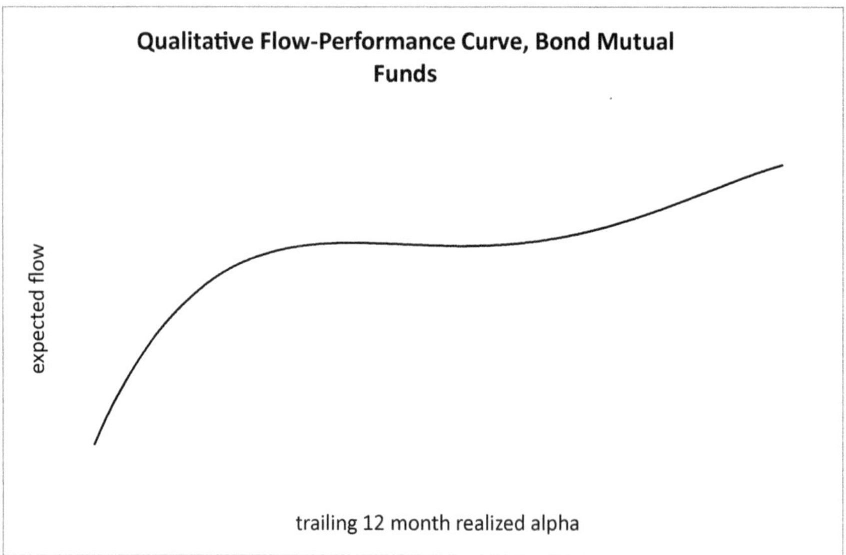


**Fig. 5.9** Convexity flipped for bond mutual funds

Similarly, a low VIX implies that investors are not too concerned about downside equity risk. The demand for insurance is modest. A low VIX implies that investors are not unduly constrained and can bear liquidity risk more easily.

We will restrict ourselves to the VIX as a risk indicator in what follows. The idea of using the VIX as a single conditioning variable might seem a bit strange. After all, it is an equity-based risk indicator and we are trying to analyze flows for bond funds. However, following Bao (2011), bond illiquidity has a strong historical correlation to equity index volatility. If anything, the overlap between S&P volatility and broad market liquidity has increased over time. As described in Coldiron, Lee and Lee (2019), S&P E-mini futures are the premiere risk-taking instruments in modern markets. When investors want to increase exposure, they buy them. Conversely, when investors need to hedge equity, currency or credit risk, E-minis are the easiest contracts to short.

Roughly speaking, the flow-performance curve for bond mutual funds in low VIX regimes is linear. GJN demonstrate this empirically, using over 20 years of data for a wide variety of corporate bond funds. It seems that, during quiet regimes, investors are not unduly worried about short-term underperformance from their active bond managers. The probability of contagion is considered small.

However, problems arise when equity volatility is higher than normal. Then, the flow-performance curve becomes concave. A high VIX suggests two related things: investors are scared and bond liquidity is low. First mover advantage is particularly important during bouts of market volatility, given the high impact of selling bonds into a market with no nearby bids. Mutual funds that maintain low cash balances or hold relatively illiquid bonds are most severely impacted. When volatility is high, each investor is worried about what the network of other investors will do. This serves to make the situation worse, in the same way that a bank run can occur when depositors are worried about withdrawals from other depositors. Waves of selling can turn into a self-reinforcing death spiral if initial redemptions drive prices down to the point where other investors decide to redeem.

We emphasize that price impact is the differentiator between equity and bond flow-performance curves. We have already discussed how regulatory changes have conspired to make the US corporate bond market more fragile than previously. Dealers still account for a large percentage of available liquidity, yet these very same dealers are increasingly risk averse. In a turbulent market, these agents may pull their quotes entirely for a while. The tendency is to wait until they can gauge demand from long-term buyers, such as pension funds and insurance companies.

From a technical perspective, we next need to estimate the size of redemptions from high yield mutual funds after a −5% drop in HYG, JNK and related ETFs. However, we will leave that to the next section, after reviewing where things stand so far.

In the two pronged decision tree below, a US credit event or a technical crash in high yield ETFs sets things in motion. Once these ETFs start to trade at a meaningful discount, dealers have the choice between redeeming shares and doing nothing. We can see that, in either case, potential damage to the junk bond market is large. A toxic feedback loop is also possible between bond prices and mutual fund outflows.

DECISION TREE 5.1

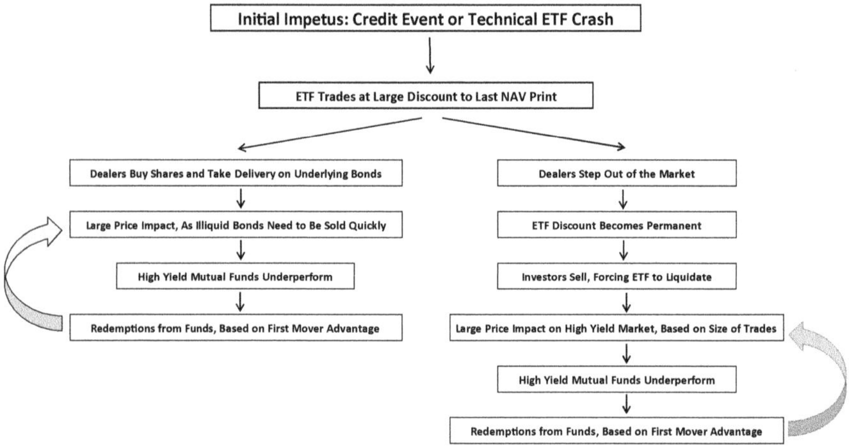


## Quantifying the Relationship Between Performance and Flows

We are now ready to characterize the dependence of bond mutual fund flows on their recent performance. The **GJN** methodology requires two econometric models, where the results from the first model act as inputs to the second.

We can call these **Model 1** and **Model 2**. Model 1 is a straightforward linear regression that estimates rolling fund alphas over time, relative to an appropriate benchmark. Model 2 is effectively a semi-parametric regression. It estimates the dependence of flows on performance for funds with variable liquidity in different market regimes. In particular, Model 2 tests the hypothesis that underperforming illiquid funds in high volatility regimes suffer from unusually large outflows. The slope of the regression line restricted to this scenario is especially steep. This forces the unconditional flow-performance curve to be concave. By "unconditional", are referring to the flow-performance curve that averages across all funds and all regimes, whether alpha is positive or negative.

We need to introduce some notation to explain the **GJN** method more accurately. Suppose that there are $n$ corporate bond funds within a certain category, in our case the high yield bond market. Note that passive mutual funds are included in the **GJN** study, but ETFs are not.

We can set $r(i, t)$ as the return of fund $i$ in month $t$. Given $n$ funds in our high yield category (as above), $i$ ranges from 1 to $n$. We want to measure the alpha $\alpha(i, t)$ of fund $i$ and see how the flow $f(i, t)$ depends on its realized alpha $\alpha(i, t)$. In **GJN**, $\alpha(i, t)$ is estimated using a 2 factor regression against the Vanguard Total Bond Index and CRSP value-weighted market returns, respectively. These are proxies for the broad US bond and equity markets, respectively.

Following **GJN**, each regression has a 12 month lookback window and uses monthly returns. In particular, Model 1 takes the following form.

$$\begin{aligned}\left(fund\ i's\ return\right) = {} & alpha \\ & + \left(i's\ sensitivity\ to\ bond\ index\right) \\ & * (bond\ index\ return) \\ & + \left(fund\ i's\ sensitivity\ to\ equity\ index\right) \\ & * (equity\ index\ return) + residual\end{aligned}$$

The "sensitivities" in the equation above are the estimated coefficients in a linear regression. When the Vanguard and CRSP indices have a low trailing 12 month correlation, these sensitivities roughly correspond to index betas.

In **GJN**, alpha is a fund's monthly, rather than annualized, excess return at a specific point in time. If $\alpha(i, t) > 0$, then fund $i$has beaten the hybrid Vanguard, CRSP benchmark in the past year. Conversely, if $\alpha(i, t) < 0$, then fund $i$ has underperformed in the past year. The set of $\alpha(i, t)$'s form a crucial input to Model 2.

A second set of regressions is needed to map realized alphas $\alpha(i, t)$ onto net flows $f(i, t)$. This constitutes Model 2. Calculating $f(i, t)$ is mildly complicated, as a fund's growth from one time step to the next varies both as a function of flows and performance. A fund can grow by receiving an inflow or posting a positive return. Accordingly, we need to adjust for performance when calculating how much new investment a fund received in a given month. In particular, if share class $i$ has return $r(t)$ in month $t$, then the calculated flow from month $t-1$ to month $t$ is given by,

$$f(i,t) = NAV_t - NAV_{t-1} \times (1 + r(t))$$

If $f$ is positive, fund $i$ received net inflows in month $t$. Conversely, if $f$ is negative, it received net outflows for the month. Note that each pair $(i,t)$ is treated as a separate observation. We are regressing cross-sectionally across funds as well as over time.

Under the assumption that the flow-performance relationship is non-linear, we cannot justifiably estimate an equation of the form

$$flow = flow = beta \times (12\ month\ trailing\ alpha) + residual$$

A single regression would force inflows for outperforming funds and outflows for underperformers to be symmetric. **GJN** uses various indicator variables to control for risk regime, fund type and whether alpha is negative or positive. (An "indicator" variable takes the value 1 if a fund satisfies a certain condition at a certain point in time and 0 if it does not. It allows us to perform regressions on different subsets of the data within a single larger regression.)

We effectively wind up with a scenario-dependent set of linear regressions that generate a non-linear flow-performance curve. This may sound very complex, but the reader need not worry about the exact specification of Model 2. In rough terms, **GJN** conduct a separate regression for each of the following 8 states (Table 5.1).

For example, state 1 imposes the following three binary conditions at a given time $t$

- each fund has positive realized alpha

**Table 5.1** Possible states for a given fund in a given risk regime

| State | Alpha | Risk condition | Relative fund liquidity |
|---|---|---|---|
| 1 | positive | risk on | high |
| 2 | positive | risk on | low |
| 3 | positive | risk off | high |
| 4 | positive | risk off | low |
| 5 | negative | risk on | high |
| 6 | negative | risk on | low |
| 7 | negative | risk off | high |
| 8 | negative | risk off | low |

- each fund holds relatively liquid assets
- the prevailing risk regime is calm, or "risk on".

Restricting ourselves to state 1, we can estimate a linear flow-performance curve. More generally, within any state $i$, there is a corresponding regression line. It is reasonable to assume that the slope of each regression line is positive: an increase in alpha should lead to higher expected net flows, once we control for risk regime.

## Expected Outflows in State 8

State 8 is particularly relevant to our discussion, since we want to analyze severe downside scenarios that are at least somewhat predictable. After a limit down move in high yield ETFs, followed by a bond fire sale, we are likely to find ourselves there. Let us review the conditions that determine state 8, in the context of our problem. Once HYG and JNK start to trade at a persistent discount, we want to explain why,

1. High yield bond funds are likely to be illiquid relative to a "typical" or median bond fund
2. the VIX is likely to be higher than average
3. high yield bond funds are likely to have negative realized alpha (relative to the appropriate benchmark) for the month in which the risk event occurs.

1. holds, irrespective of market conditions. High yield bonds are a relatively illiquid segment of the bond market. (We have applied the **GJN** methodology a bit liberally here: the authors define liquidity both as a function of underlying asset liquidity and reserve cash holdings. We have ignored the percentage of assets held in cash in our analysis.) There are relatively few natural buyers, as many funds that take external money are restricted from holding non-investment grade securities. Condition 2 also has high statistical probability. Given a very sharp sell off in high yield ETFs, the VIX is likely to be higher than usual. Either we are in the midst of a technical equity crash or a credit event. Either event is likely to raise the fear index within the financial network. Recall that benchmark credit spreads and volatility reliably move together when market conditions deteriorate.

It remains to show that nearly all high yield bond funds are likely to have negative realized alpha in our scenario. Condition 3 might not be obvious, as each high yield fund has its own $\alpha(i, t)$. Roughly 50% of all high yield funds are likely to outperform a high yield benchmark, gross of costs. However, the choice of benchmark in **GJN** plays a defining role in determining the sign of each alpha. The problem is set up in such a way that, during market downturns, alpha is likely to be negative for the vast majority of high yield funds.

Recall that $\alpha(i, t)$ is based on a joint regression against the Vanguard Total Bond and CRSP value-weighted equity indices. The lookback window is 1 year, at monthly frequency. Significantly, there is not much overlap between the chosen benchmark and a typical high yield bond fund. If a high yield benchmark had been used, we would expect a roughly even split between funds with positive and negative alpha. Our situation is markedly different.

During a sharp sell off, the hybrid benchmark is unlikely to lose much. The Vanguard Total Bond Index has a large weight in Treasury securities, which have traditionally performed well during flight to quality events. (We realize that it is possible that Treasury yields will rise during the next systemic crisis, but are concentrating on downside risk scenarios in our decision tree.) The pie chart below serves to clarify things (Fig. 5.10).

Observe that roughly 2/3 of the notional value of the Vanguard index consists of bonds backed by the US government. These have provided reliable protection for several decades. If Treasuries continue to act as they have since the 1980s, they are likely to rally during the $-10\%$ downside scenario for cash bonds that we have described. Given its large weight in Treasuries, along with negligible exposure to high yield debt, the Vanguard Total Bond benchmark in **GJN** has every chance to be up in month $t$.

The equity component of the benchmark requires more thought. We accept that the CRSP value-weighted index is likely to be down in the midst of a sharp credit sell off. However, the beta of a high yield bond fund to the CRSP index is likely to be less than 0.4 in advance of an unexpected air pocket move in month $t - 1$. We can see this in the following graph (Fig. 5.11).

Assuming that high yield bond funds have a modest equity beta going into an ETF flash crash, the hybrid benchmark in **GJN** is unlikely to be down much in month $t - 1$.

If history is a guide, the Vanguard Total Bond Index has a positive expected return in State 8. While the CRSP equity return in month $t - 1$ is likely to be negative, we are multiplying it by a small regression coefficient. This dampens its impact on the hybrid benchmark return. We wind up in a situation where high yield bond funds have dropped by an average of $-10\%$, while the expected benchmark return is close to 0%. Supposing performance

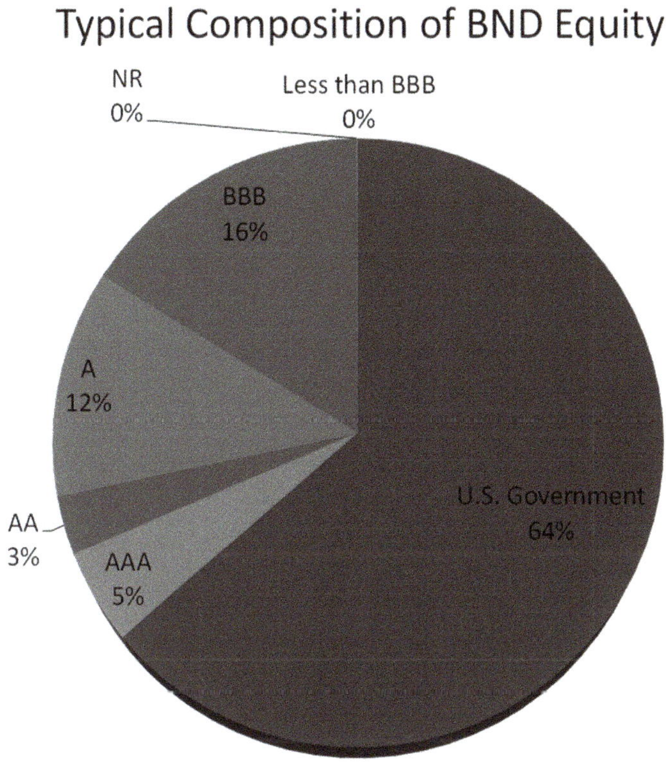


**Fig. 5.10** The benchmark BND ETF largely consists of US government and highly rated corporate bonds (*Source* Vanguard)

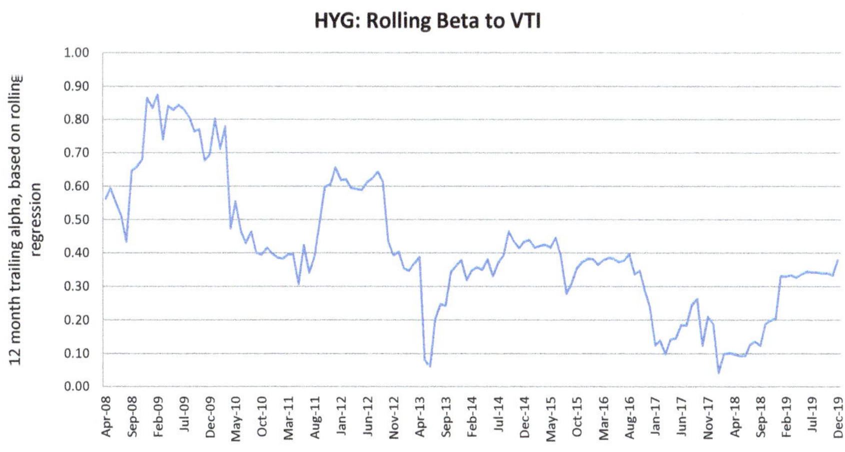


**Fig. 5.11** In quiet regimes, HYG has a modest beta to equities (*Source* Bloomberg)

in line with the benchmark from months $t - 12$ to $t - 2$ and $-10\%$ underperformance in month $t - 1$, a typical high yield fund would have generated $-\frac{10}{12}\%$ or $-0.87\%$ of monthly alpha $\alpha_{t-1}$ over the past year. This negative alpha estimate does not include fees and is based solely on underperformance in month $t - 1$.

We can now use $\alpha_{t-1} = -0.87\%$ as an input to measure expected high yield mutual fund outflows in State 8. Referring to **GJN** again, 1.44 is the estimated beta in the equation

$$flow = beta \times (12\, month\ trailing\ alpha) + residual$$

given above, for funds in State 8. This implies that each $-1\%$ of incremental negative alpha estimated in month $t - 1$ is expected to generate $1.44 \times (-0.01) = -1.44\%$ of outflows during month$t$. This "1.44" estimate is one of the main results in the paper. In our case,$\alpha_{t-1} = -0.87\%$, rather than $-1\%$. This means that we should expect $1.44 \times (-0.0087) = -1.3\%$ of outflows after a $-10\%$ ETF induced sell off in high yield bonds. $-1.3\%$ maps to roughly \$3.14 billion of redemptions from high yield mutual funds. This is a very large number. Even if fund managers decide to draw down their cash balances, it is likely that \$2 billion dollars or more of high yield paper would have to be sold into the market to meet redemptions.

The managers we surveyed estimated that the impact of a \$2 billion high yield bond sale over the course of a few weeks would be around $-5\%$. Note that mutual funds can be more patient than dealers when unwinding large positions. Still, this translates to a nearly $-10\% - 5\% = -15\%$ total decline, based on a credit event or more surprisingly, a purely technical sell off in high yield ETFs!

It is possible to extrapolate all sorts of doomsday scenarios from here. Given the sharp increase in BBB debt over the past several years, over \$3 trillion of securitized debt would be vulnerable. The market would be forced to reprice risk at the investment, non-investment grade boundary. This would increase financing costs for companies that are already heavily indebted and might trigger a credit crisis. However, since this scenario is beyond our current modeling capabilities, we will leave further speculation to the reader.

## Postscript: Tackling the High Yield Bond—ETF—Mutual Fund Feedback Loop During the Covid-19 Crisis in Q1 2020

Let us rewind the clock to February 2020. Once investors realized the implications of lockdowns on economic growth, equities sold off violently and credit spreads spiked from a low base level. The following graph tracks the "spread to worst" of a representative basket of US high yield bonds relative to equivalent duration Treasuries. The spread to worst represents the lowest yield differential investors can capture if a given bond does not default. It accounts for the fact that issuers can retire callable bonds early, changing the effective yield to maturity (Fig. 5.12).

Using DECISION TREE 5.1 as a guide, we can specify that an exogenous event triggered the mega spike in high yield spreads.

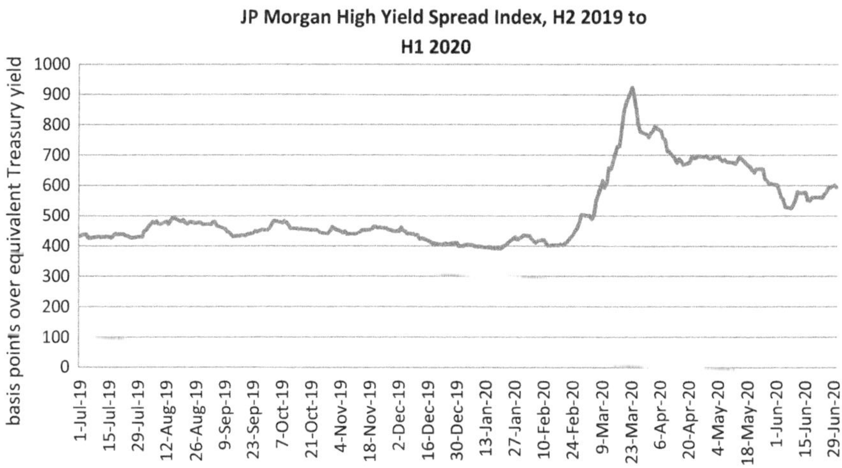


**Fig. 5.12** Jump in high yield spreads during the Covid-19 crisis (*Source* Bloomberg)

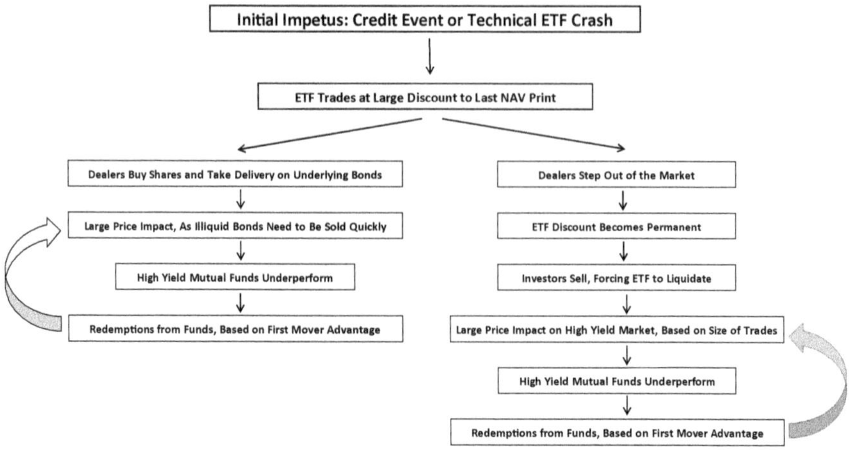


High yield spreads reached a peak of 9.23% on March 23, from 4.03% on February 17. As expected, HYG and JNK started to trade at a significant discount as spreads peaked. On the previous trading day (March 20), HYG traded at a −1.27% discount to NAV. JNK was sputtering even more badly, trading at a −1.60% discount. Nominated dealers were obviously in risk averse mode, reluctant to "arbitrage" the discount in a highly illiquid market.

HYG and JNK net flows were dangerously skewed to the downside. Note that we have taken a 10 day trailing average of combined flows in the graph below. In the worst 10 day window, roughly **$6 billion** (or 10 * $600 million) was taken out of two ETFs whose assets add up to roughly $30 billion (Fig. 5.13).

Operating with a slight lag, high yield mutual funds also suffered from large outflows.

As of March 23, the odds of a technical crash in a major high yield ETF were unusually high. We have already mentioned that there were over 500 instances of a stock going limit down in December 2018. From March 1 to March 20, 2020 alone, nearly **6,000** circuit breakers were hit. Under the conservative assumption that 50% of these were limit down events, roughly 200 circuit breakers were hit on a typical trading day! Many of the scenarios we had discussed in 2019 were playing out.

It is likely that the Federal Reserve was alarmed by many of the same indicators we have described above. On March 23, they took a drastic measure, announcing that they would **directly** buy investment grade corporate bonds and ETFs. (Open market purchases of corporate bonds and ETFs obviously have a more reliable impact on spreads than ordinary Treasury purchases. Buying Treasuries has a more indirect impact on credit spreads and equities. We discuss the usual transmission mechanism in Chapter 7.) From there, the

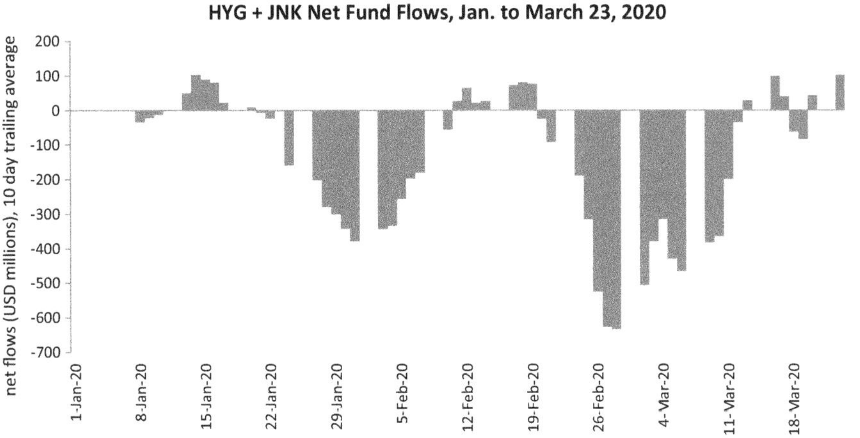


**Fig. 5.13** Rolling 10 day average of high yield ETF flows, early 2020 (*Source* Bloomberg)

floodgates opened. Dealers and mutual funds in the investment grade space now had access to a willing buyer with a theoretically unbounded balance sheet. VCIT and LQD, two of the largest corporate bond ETFs, popped + 5.4% and +7.4%, respectively, on March 23 alone.

While the Fed did not announce its intentions toward high yield bonds, investment grade bond purchases clearly reduced the pressure on dealer balance sheets. By March 27, HYG and JNK were trading at a significant premium (+2.09% and +1.24%, respectively) to NAV. They had resumed their roles as leading indicators, suggesting improved credit market conditions.

Had the Fed not intervened directly in the credit markets, we suspect that HYG and JNK would have fallen into a destructive feedback loop. Recall that, once dealers buy shares at a discount to NAV, they have to sell bonds into an illiquid market. This can cause bond prices to overshoot to the downside. Investors with long credit exposure may then be inclined to hedge by selling more units of HYG, forcing HYG back to a discount.

We can see from the graph below that dealer risk aversion generally increases as a function of market volatility (Fig. 5.14).

After March 23, net flows to HYG and JNK became strongly positive, as we can see in the next graph. Again, we have smoothed the data with a 10 day trailing moving average (Fig. 5.15).

However, conditions in the high yield space remained volatile. From March 20 to April 9 (consisting of 15 trading days), the standard deviation of HYG and JNK's premium/discount to NAV remained roughly 10

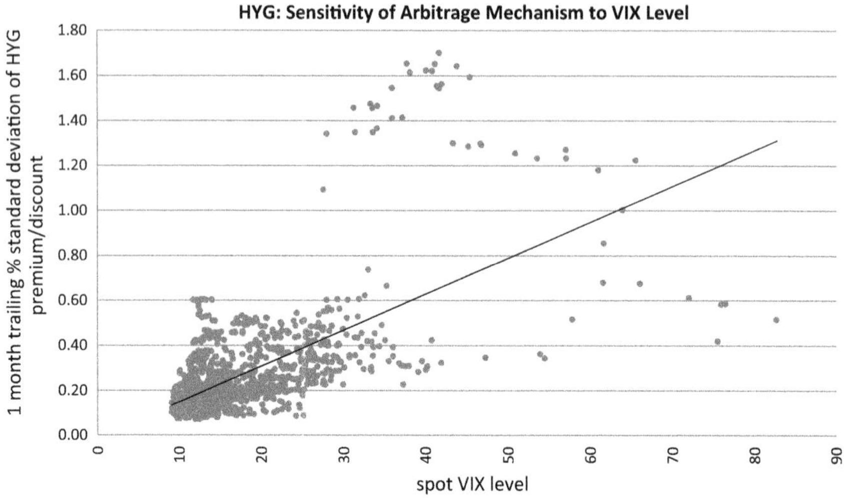


**Fig. 5.14** As the VIX rises, HYG's link to the cash bond market becomes increasingly unstable (*Source* Bloomberg)

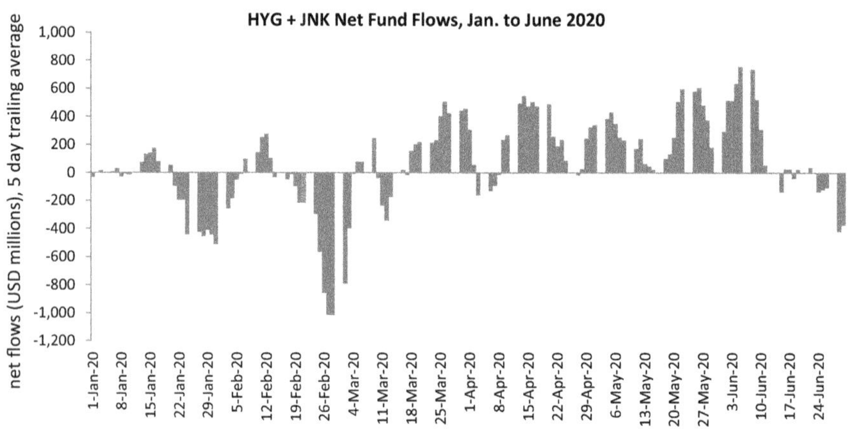


**Fig. 5.15** Money flows back into HYG and JNK once Fed's intentions are digested by the market (*Source* Bloomberg)

times above its 2019 average. The following chart demonstrates this point (Fig. 5.16).

In early April, US high yield mutual funds also suffered significant outflows, again operating with a lag to high yield ETFs.

On April 9, 2020, the Federal Reserve announced that it would increase the size of its corporate bond and ETF asset purchases by over $550 billion.

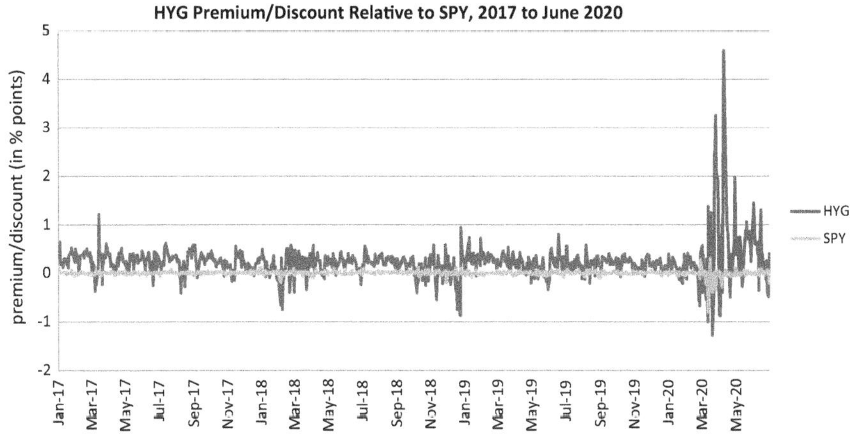


**Fig. 5.16** The alchemy of liquidity fails when investors require liquidity the most (*Source* Bloomberg)

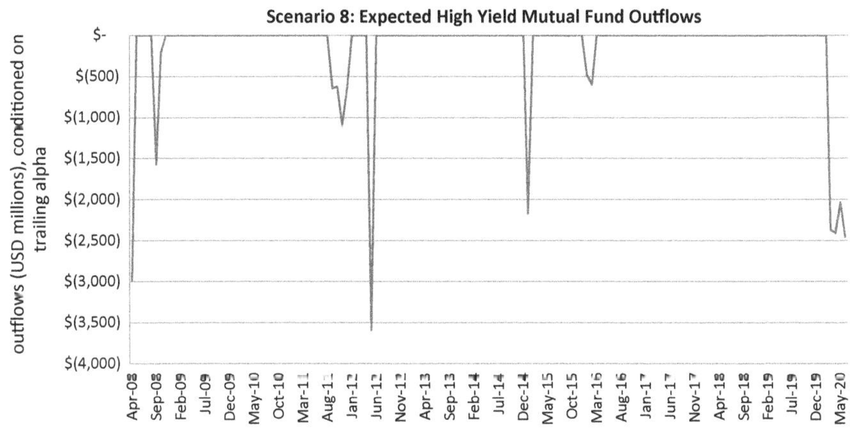


**Fig. 5.17** High yield mutual fund outflow expectations, based on the GJN paper methodology (*Source* Bloomberg)

Significantly, new provisions also allowed for the **purchase of high yield bonds** if they had been downgraded during the crisis.

If the Fed had not taken extraordinary action on March 23 and April 9, our implementation of the **GJN** model would have anticipated additional mutual fund outflows in the **$7 billion** range from April to June 2020. The toxic feedback loop may have continued. The graph below focuses on Scenario 8 (illiquid funds with negative alpha in high risk regimes) outflows from earlier in the chapter. It calculates expected flows on a monthly basis (Fig. 5.17).

Looking into the future, we believe that structural problems in the high yield markets remain. According to order book-related measures, equity liquidity has been dropping sharply over the past few years. A limit down move in HYG or JNK would not require an exogenous shock, as in Q1 2020. The overhang of high yield debt also suggests a bloated market, as we can see from the graph below. The paths taken in DECISION TREE 5.1 are still entirely possible, especially if the Fed chooses not to make direct ETF purchases during the next crisis.

# 6

# Market Makers, Stabilizing or Disruptive?

## Part One: The Corona Sell Off and the GEX

We can provide motivation for this chapter with some informal market commentary. Figure 6.1 tracks the performance of the S&P 500 index from 2011 to early 2020.

We see a steady rise, followed by a very sudden and severe drop starting in February 2020. Going into 2020, US equities and credit had been in a debt-fueled bull market for a full decade. In this context, the February to March 2020 sell off occurred almost without warning. The market ricocheted straight off an all-time high, increasing its speed as it dropped. We can also view things in risk, rather than price, terms.

The options markets (which are thought to incorporate forward estimates of risk) were also unaware of the dangers ahead. Trailing 12 month implied volatility was extremely low across currencies, rates and equity indices going into February 2020. Figure 6.2 demonstrates this point.

Figure 6.3 zooms into the period from December 2019 to March 2020 for the S&P 500. The sharpness of the regime shift is staggering. We observe a market that appears to be riskless in December and January, followed by several weeks of wild two-sided price action within a vicious down trend. Intraday ranges also expanded dramatically.

We accept that the initial slide in late February was caused by an exogenous shock, namely the COVID-19 virus. As US markets finally digested the news, it became clear that the impact of shutting down a significant portion of the economy would be enormous. However, information flow could not explain


H. P. Krishnan and A. Bennington, *Market Tremors*,
https://doi.org/10.1007/978-3-030-79253-4_6

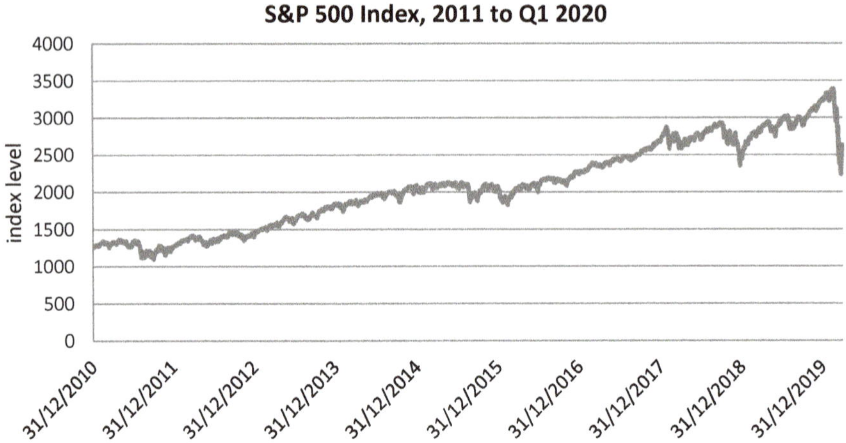


**Fig. 6.1** The S&P 500: positive trend interrupted by a sudden drop in 2020 (*Source* Yahoo! Finance)

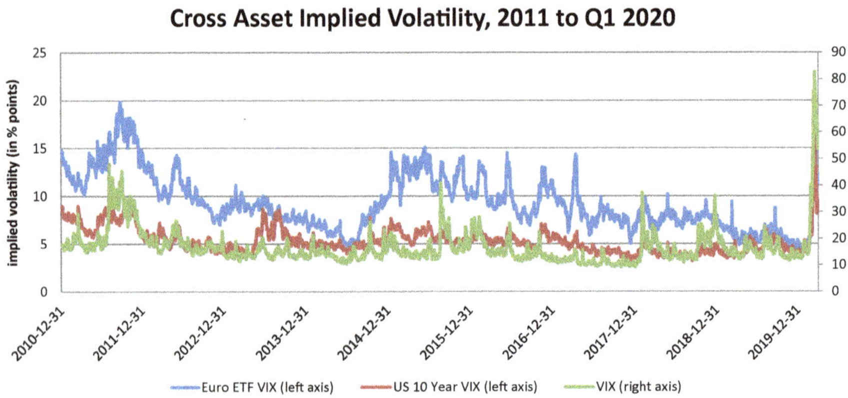


**Fig. 6.2** Cross-asset class volatility depressed in advance of the COVID-19 crisis (*Source* Bloomberg)

the saw-toothed path that the market took thereafter. Figure 6.4, we have plotted the GDP Nowcasts for Q1 and Q2 2020, produced by the New York Fed.

These "Nowcasts" are generated by an econometric model that aggregates a number of widely quoted economic indicators, such as manufacturing surveys, imports and housing starts. Whenever a new data point is released, the GDP estimate for the current and next quarter is updated. For example, suppose that the month over month change in Housing Starts is released on a given day. The new number is 1%, while the most recent forecast was 0%. Relative to the model, this constitutes a +1% surprise to the upside. Next

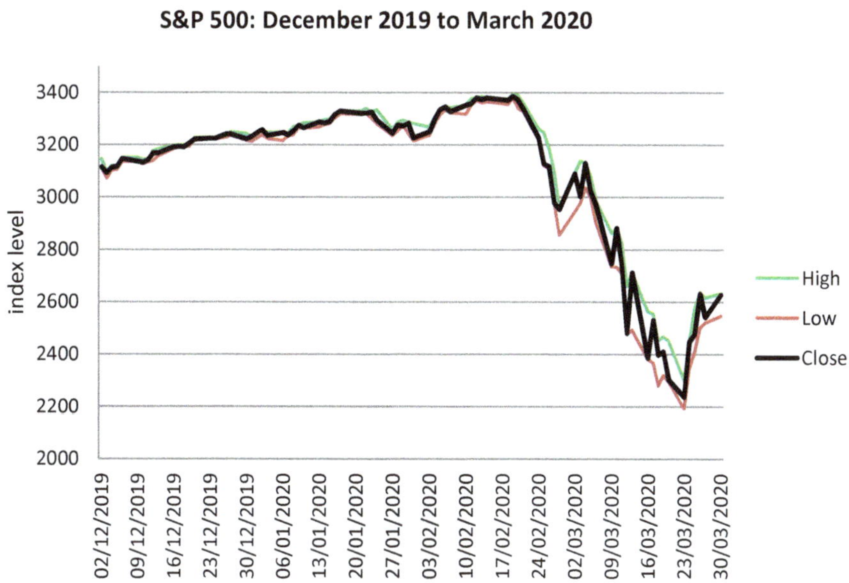


**Fig. 6.3** Violent two-way action in S&P 500 during the February and March 2020 sell off (*Source* Yahoo! Finance)

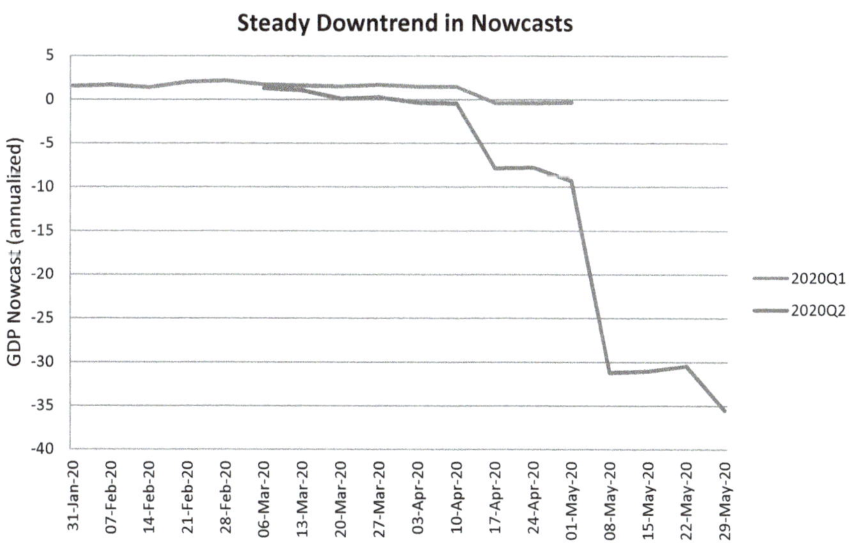


**Fig. 6.4** Nowcasts do not explain sharp reversals during the sell off (*Source* Federal Reserve Bank of Atlanta)

suppose that Housing Starts have a weight of 0.02 in the Nowcast model. The weight of a release, updated periodically, is based on its historical impact. This means that, based on a historical regression, past surprises in Housing Starts had a 0.02 expected impact on realized GDP for a given quarter. Then, the GDP Nowcast would have to be updated by 0.02 * 0.01 = 0.02%. We observe that the Nowcast 1 quarter ahead tends to be more volatile than the current one. The reason for this is straightforward: there is more time for new data to arrive and change the final estimate.

In summary, Nowcasts offer a coherent framework for estimating current economic activity, given the data available. They act as a data compression tool, mapping a large number of releases onto a single measure of economic growth (from one quarter to the next). Returning to the problem at hand, we can see that the Q1 and Q2 Nowcasts only declined at a shallow pace until April 10. This in itself could not justify the severity of the move in the S&P 500 and other risky assets. The Q2 Nowcast only began its precipitous decline after the S&P had started to recover.

It might be argued that, given the lockdowns, the market was able to predict a collapse in growth a month or two ahead of time. Market folklore suggests that markets are able to discount future outcomes quite effectively and this may well have been the case in March 2020. However, even given perfect forecasting ability, knowledge of the Q2 Nowcast could not have explained the violent down *and* up moves observed in early March. To repeat, the volatility of information flow was not enough to explain the volatility in market prices. Something else was clearly at work.

This brings us to an alternative hypothesis: perhaps the S&P 500 was moving inversely to the incidence of new COVID-19 infections? We might then be able to justify the wild gyrations in the S&P 500, based on the idea that the index was loading onto a single factor that was also highly volatile. Unfortunately, this hypothesis fails to agree with the data. We can see that the incidence of new infections followed a reasonably stable and predictable path in the US. This path was consistent with what was observed in Europe and other open societies.

Exponential growth in the early stages of an epidemic, followed by curve flattening, was characteristic of the various pandemics that had occurred throughout history. The path should not have been entirely surprising to investors.

All of this implies that we need an alternative explanation for the wild oscillations witnessed in early March 2020. While the initial drop in February was COVID-dependent, we would argue that *positioning* (one of the twin heralds of risk specified in the introduction) was a likely factor in the

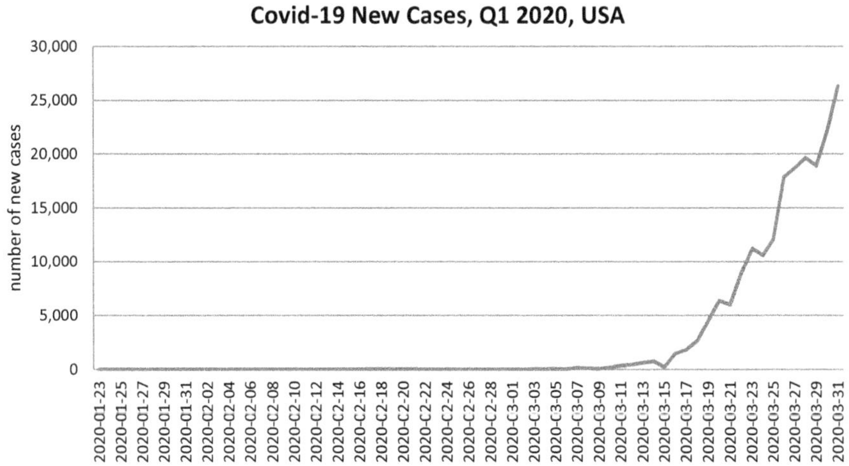


**Fig. 6.5** Fairly smooth increase in spread of virus (*Source* ourworldindata.org)

extremely jagged path equities took in March. Dealers became the dominant players in an unstable market, as we will see in the sections that follow.

## Institutional Demand for Bond-Like Equity Structures

The more we understand about the volatility regime preceding the COVID-19 crisis, the easier it is to explain what happened in February and March 2020. This requires some clarification, which we provide in the next two sections. Aside from localized scares in August 2015, February 2018 and December 2018, the VIX was unusually depressed from 2013 to 2019. Interest rate volatility was also exceptionally low, which we observed in Fig. 6.5.

To repeat, volatility was in an extended bear market. This was a function of structural changes to the market and buoyant investor sentiment.

- In a world with near 0% government bond yields, investors craved other sources of return.
- Selling options was an obvious way to capture premium over time.
- Given a stable market, the time decay on a short options strategy acted as a proxy for income.
- In a self-reinforcing feedback loop, low volatility increased investor confidence, creating even more demand for short volatility exposure.
- The so-called Fed put also acted as a license for excessive risk-taking. The idea was that, if conditions did start to destabilize, Central Banks would

inject liquidity into the system. At the extreme, they would buy corporate bonds and even equities directly, as a last line of defense.

While many investors sold options or VIX futures, an even larger number tried to capture carry in less direct ways. Many institutions increased their allocation to global equities, in an effort to increase expected returns. Defined-benefit pension funds, for example, had absolutely no chance of hitting a 7% return target with a buy and hold portfolio of government bonds. The only alternative was to increase their weighting to asset classes that (through capital appreciation) offered at least some hope of a higher return.

Many institutions favored equity index "collars", in an attempt to convert equity longs into bond-like structures with higher return potential. A "collar" combines a long position in an asset such as the S&P 500 with a protective downside put and short upside call, as in Fig. 6.6.

For the purposes of clarity, we will restrict ourselves to collars on the S&P 500 for now. A typical structure might involve selling 1 month calls +3% above the current index level, while buying an equivalent number of 1 month puts −5% below. Assuming that the premium collected from the calls equals the premium paid for the puts, we might call this a "costless" collar. Downside protection is financed by selling calls. This requires a lower net cash outlay, while reducing the profit potential for the strategy. In the example above, the short call gives away all returns in excess of +3% in a given expiration cycle.

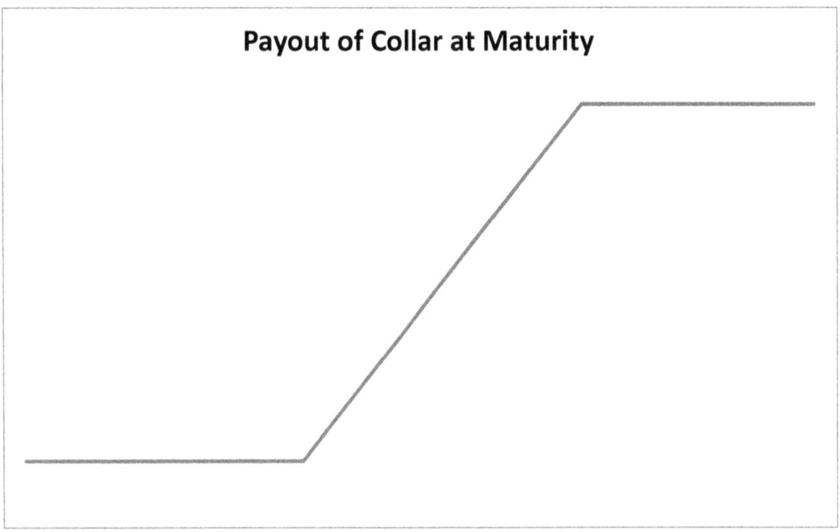


**Fig. 6.6** Payout of a collared position at maturity, beloved by many allocators

At expiration, losses are capped at −5% below the current spot, while gains have a +3% upper bound. This explains the flat payout profile both at the far left and far right of Fig. 6.6.

Index collars allow institutions to tap into some fraction of the equity risk premium, with a hard floor on potential losses. Recall that the equity premium is the expected long-term excess return for investing in the stock market, relative to cash. In theory at least, it is the compensation investors receive for bearing an undiversifiable risk.

For a costless collar, index puts are generally struck further away from the index than index calls. In other words, puts trade at a premium to calls that are an equal distance away from the current index level. (Note that we have made the simplifying assumption the forward curve is flat for the purposes of this discussion.) There are two reasons why puts are relatively expensive.

- In the equity index space, very sharp downside moves ("meltdowns") have historically occurred at higher frequency than equivalent sized positive ones ("meltups").
- There is natural excess demand for downside put protection. Most end investors are net long the market and use index puts to bound their losses over a fixed time horizon.

This brings us to an important point. Electronic market makers and bank dealing desks take the *opposite* side of net customer flow. When institutions and retail investors initiate BUY orders, open interest rises and market makers wind up with new short positions. Conversely, when investors SELL, market makers add long options positions to their books. By taking the other side of customer trades, market makers offer liquidity to the market. They facilitate the vast majority of trades that go through the market. Options market makers typically manage their residual risk by "delta hedging", i.e., buying and selling the underlying index, to reduce their net exposure. We will explain this dynamic later in the chapter.

Market makers adjust to one-sided customer flow (BUYS or SELLS) by moving their quotes around. During periods of heightened fear, they require more compensation (in the form of options premium) when selling insurance. Index puts become more expensive, increasing the steepness of the implied volatility skew. (Recall that, as implied volatility rises, the premium embedded in a given option also increases.)

Given that institutions like to buy index puts and sell calls, we can characterize aggregate market maker positioning as in Fig. 6.7. On an unhedged basis, options market makers are naked short puts and long index calls. For

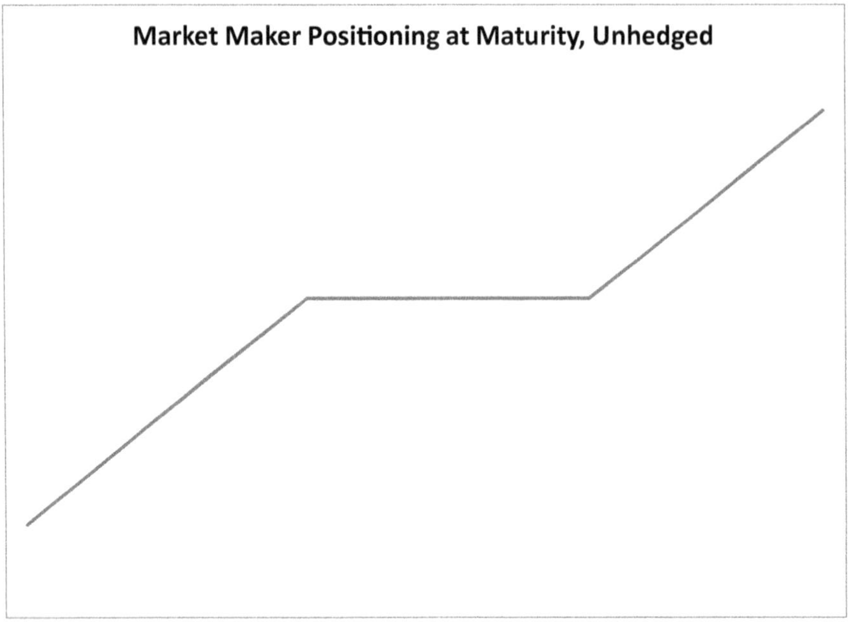


**Fig. 6.7** Options market maker exposure given institutional demand for collars

simplicity, we have mapped all downside puts and upside calls onto a single strike, respectively.

When the S&P 500 is trending up, the call side of the payout curve dominates. Since the puts are locally out of play, options market makers are effectively long gamma in this zone. These agents can monetize volatility by trading around call strikes, but do not have to act very aggressively. After a sell off, however, market makers can be highly disruptive: they have to trade aggressively in the direction of the recent trend to avoid extreme losses in their trading books. This requires a deeper understanding of delta hedging dynamics, which we describe in the next section.

## The Impact of Dealer Hedging on Price Action

We have already described how many institutional investors like to layer options over an existing long position. Options reshape the payout curve to match their perceived objectives. In the collar structure above, investors actually truncate the range of outcomes that they face. Collars reduce upside and downside risk, implying that the net position does not need to be managed actively.

For dealers, however, the situation is far different. Here, positions need to be dynamically hedged, either to monetize volatility or control downside risk. **There is no structural long in the first place.** A dealer who takes the other side of a collar has a long call, naked short put position. That is it. If markets sell off rapidly, an unhedged dealer trading book can be wiped out. Options market makers generally cannot afford to take large losses. In summary, these agents face a combination of open-ended risk and limited cash and collateral to meet margin requirements.

Delta hedging is a standard approach to minimizing price exposure. While it is the first line of defense, it is vulnerable to large jumps in the underlying. As we mentioned casually above, delta hedging involves dynamically buying and selling units of the underlying to reduce price exposure of a portfolio of options. For example, a dealer in S&P futures options would typically trade in and out of S&P futures as a risk mitigation strategy.

A bit of basic options theory is in order, just for reference. The *delta* of an option is its sensitivity to small changes in the underlying. For example, consider a "50 delta" call with strike $K$ on a futures contract that is trading at price $F$. In this context, $F$ is the underlying. The call currently has price $C$. Suppose that the futures $F$ moves by a small amount $\varepsilon$ (the Greek letter "epsilon"), starting at $F$ and winding up at $F + \varepsilon$. Fixing all other variables, such as volatility and time to maturity, the call should then be worth $C + 0.5\varepsilon$. In other words, the price of a 50 delta call moves half as much as the underlying index, assuming that the index move is small. Similarly, the price of a 10 delta call would move 10% as much as the underlying and so on.

The same rule applies to puts, though with opposite sign. If the futures $F$ moves by $\varepsilon$, a 50 delta put with initial price $P$ will be worth $P - 0.5\varepsilon$. Observe that puts lose value when the underlying goes up, hence the sign change.

This brings us to a more concrete example. Suppose that a market maker sells 1000 50 delta S&P E-mini futures calls to a customer. The market maker is unlikely to already own these calls, so will have to take on a short position. Hedging requires buying 500 futures against the calls. Then, the position will be locally hedged. It is not hard to see why. (Note that a 1 point move in S&P E-mini futures is worth $50 per contract.)

- Suppose that the futures contract is currently trading at $F = 3000$ and it ticks up by $\varepsilon = 1$ point to 3001.
- Then, the 100 short calls would be expected to lose $-0.5 * 1000 * 50 * 1 = -\$25{,}000$.

- However, this loss would be offset by a gain of +500 * 50 * 1 = +$25,000 on the long futures hedge.
- Similarly, if the futures traded down by −$1, the +$25,000 gain on the short call position would be neutralized by a −$25,000 loss on the 500 long futures. (Naturally, it would have been preferable not to have hedged in this scenario, but this can only be said after the fact!)

For larger moves in the underlying, we can no longer assume that an option's delta is fixed. The change in an option's delta as a function of small changes in the underlying is known as *gamma*. This means that a futures hedge needs to be adjusted over time, based on its current level of gamma. In the example above, 500 long futures will not hedge a 100 point move in the S&P very accurately, as delta will have changed along the way.

Given these preliminaries, we can analyze the specific case where institutions are long collars on the S&P 500. Market makers (or dealers) have the opposite position in puts and calls. Unhedged, we characterized the composite structure as a risk reversal in Fig. 6.7. However, it is fair to assume that market makers *will* hedge against adverse price movements in the underlying. Their "edge" consists of repeatedly buying at the bid and selling at the ask, along with payment from the exchange for providing liquidity to the market.

It might reasonably be asked, what does all of this have to do with positioning risk, Mean Fields and Dominant Agents? Have we veered far away from our original objective? The answer is no: we are developing the necessary background to test a hypothesis. We want to show that, in specific circumstance, options market makers can turn into Dominant Agents. When they are long or short a large amount of gamma, dynamic hedging can have a disproportionately large impact on the distribution of underlying returns. Figure 6.8 is instructive.

As before, we have mapped all puts and calls onto a single strike, respectively. In practice, market makers have exposure to a range of strikes above and below the current spot. However, gamma can still concentrate in specific regions of the payout curve. These typically correspond to strikes where the level of options open interest is high. The delta profile for a risk reversal is always positive and falls within the range 0 to 1. In visual terms, we can think of delta as the slope of the payout curve at a given point. This implies that a market maker always needs to be short some number of futures as a hedge, though this quantity is variable.

For clarity, we have broken the payout curve into regions $A$ through $E$ in the diagram above. We have also restricted ourselves to the payout at maturity.

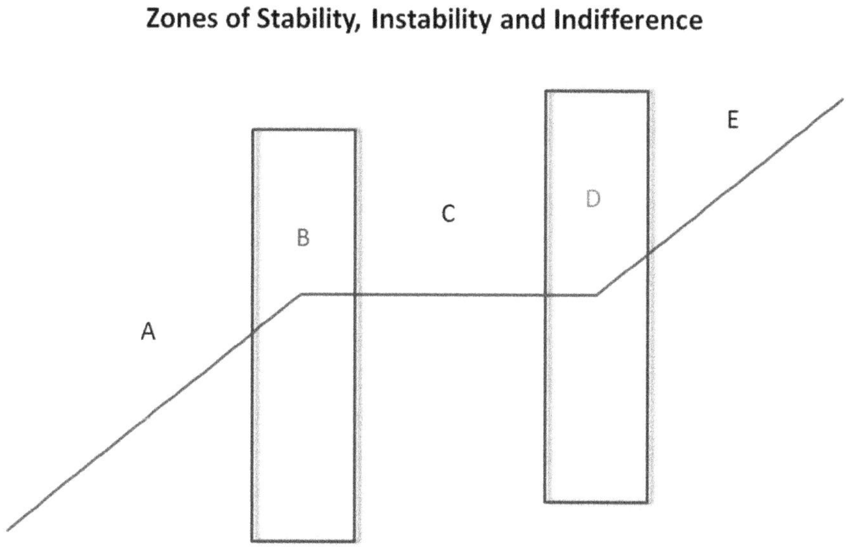


**Fig. 6.8** Conditional impact of market maker hedging, based on index level

This accentuates the gamma risk in a typical market maker's book. In regions $A$ and $E$, delta does not is close to $+1$, without much variation. An accurate hedge would involve selling nearly 1 futures contract for every short put in $A$ and every long call in $E$, respectively. Region $C$ has a relatively constant and low delta and hence does not require much hedging at all. $A$, $C$ and $E$ are conceptually similar in the following sense: dealers can maintain a relatively static hedge so long as the underlying futures contract does not drift into another zone.

Regions $B$ and $D$ are more interesting. Here, dealers need to rebalance their hedges dynamically. At the extreme, these agents can dominate the market as they rebalance. The magnitude of "gamma" is high in both regions. In other words, delta hedge ratios are highly sensitive to small changes in the underlying. If dealers maintain a fixed hedge here, they can get badly hurt if prices move in the wrong direction. Betting on direction is not a game many market makers can afford to play.

While both $B$ and $D$ have high curvature, $B$ is concave while $D$ is convex. $B$ acts like a source, pushing nearby prices away, while $D$ is a sink. From the perspective of an options market maker, these two regions require entirely different delta hedging strategies. Market maker gamma is positive in zone$D$: the payout curve is a smile rather than a frown. Delta increases rapidly as the underlying moves through the strike from below and decreases at a nearly equal rate when it drops from above. This induces strong mean reversion around the strike. Market makers need to buy dips and sell rallies in the underlying futures contract. They buy dips to reduce their short futures hedges below the strike, as delta has decreased. Conversely, moving above the strike, the delta of a risk reversal increases and dealers need to sell more futures to compensate.

Figure 6.9 summarizes open interest for March S&P E-mini futures options on 24 February 2021. This date carries no special significance, but is representative of recent positioning. We observe that interest tends to be highest for strikes that are a multiple of 50. Investors typically like round numbers when they set their stop orders or buy options. More importantly, we can see that call open interest is relatively high for all strikes above 3800, while put open interest increasingly dominates below. Zone *D* corresponds to the 3900 to 4000 range in March S&P E-minis, while the danger Zone *B* seems to be in the 3400 to 3650 range.

Dealer hedging patterns give us some insight as to why S&P volatility tends to decrease in a rising market. It is *not* simply a matter of investor complacency, though sentiment clearly plays a role in both "risk on" and "risk off" states. Rather, if the market rises enough in a given options expiration cycle, it passes into region *D*. At this point, market makers will be trading strongly against the trend to manage the deltas in their options books. This

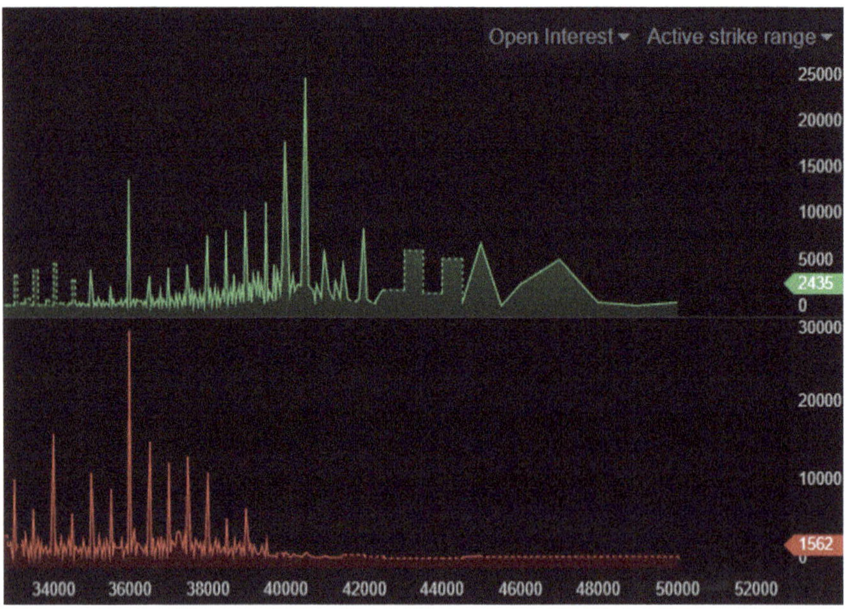


**Fig. 6.9** Using options open interest to infer where the various regions might be (*Source* CQG)

can act as a strong stabilizing force, compressing volatility near strikes where there is a large amount of open interest. Observe that, when there is a large amount of open interest at a given call strike, market makers are likely to have a larger position to hedge.

By contrast, $B$ is the danger zone, both for market makers and for end investors who are long the market. Until recently, most investors have been unaware of the impact options market makers can have when forced to hedge. This can be to their detriment in zone $B$. Dealers have substantial negative gamma in $B$. If prices approach the various put strikes that they are short, they have to sell hard into weakness to neutralize directional exposure in their books. Valuation is of no concern to an intermediary. It is simply too risky to sit back when the market is threatening to fall into zone$A$. Each time dealers SELL, prices are likely to drop further, forcing another round of hedging. Cascading dealer sell orders can cause an "air pocket" move to the downside, in a pernicious feedback loop. (It is worth mentioning that some open interest is *not* held by dealers, either on the long or short side. Rather, these contracts represent offsetting positions held by institutions, asset managers and other agents. We have made the simplifying assumption that the net effect of their hedging and rebalancing activities does not offset the impact of dealer rebalancing.)

Given that cascading sales in the S&P are not an everyday occurrence, we admit that this is not the whole story. The market ecosystem is more diverse than that. At some point, other agents might decide to buy in zone $B$. These might be countertrend traders or longer-term value investors. Buyers might also step in if external news flow becomes more positive. Then, dealers with negative gamma profiles will serve to exaggerate the rebound. In particular, as their long deltas decrease, they will have to buy significant quantities of futures to cover their shorts. The price impact of these BUY orders is likely to push the market higher.

Using the framework developed in Chapter 2, we can reformulate the problem in Mean Field terms. Suppose that $H$ is our best estimate of the distribution of 1 day forward S&P 500 returns, in a zone where market makers do not have to rebalance their hedges. We might, for example, be in Zone $C$. For the time being, there is no Dominant Agent. Then, the distribution of returns might look something like the blue line in Fig. 6.10. Volatility (here represented by the width of the distribution) is fairly low. Next, assume that a random shock pushes the S&P into Zone $B$, where market makers are short gamma. Then, the prospect of dealer hedging will widen the distribution $H$ as in the red line below.

For simplicity, we have assumed that both distributions are symmetric. There is no negative skew: large negative jumps are no more likely than equally-sized positive ones. This is not strictly correct, but useful for the purposes of illustration. Even blended normal distributions can understate risk substantially. Our aim was to isolate the impact options market makers can have when forced to hedge aggressively in the direction of a short-term trend.

Initial down *and* up moves are exaggerated when market makers act as Dominant Agents in Zone $B$. To repeat, Dominant Agent activity stretches the distribution of 1 day returns.

More generally, we are faced with a different distribution $H^*$ depending on which region we start in. We have already explained why market makers can have a destabilizing influence in $B$. Far from expiration, or within Zones $A$, $C$ and $E$, their influence is relatively low. Finally, in region $D$, market makers act as stabilizing agents. Here, they are net long gamma: their short downside puts are far away relative to the current futures price. Delta hedging in $D$ involves buying dips and selling rallies around the call strike. This has the effect of compressing volatility around the strike. In the following graph, we can see how these Dominant Agents affect the range of outcomes within Zone $D$. We emphasize that, if prices jump outside this zone, options market makers will no longer act as a stabilizing force. In other words, Figure 6.11 only gives a local description of outcomes.

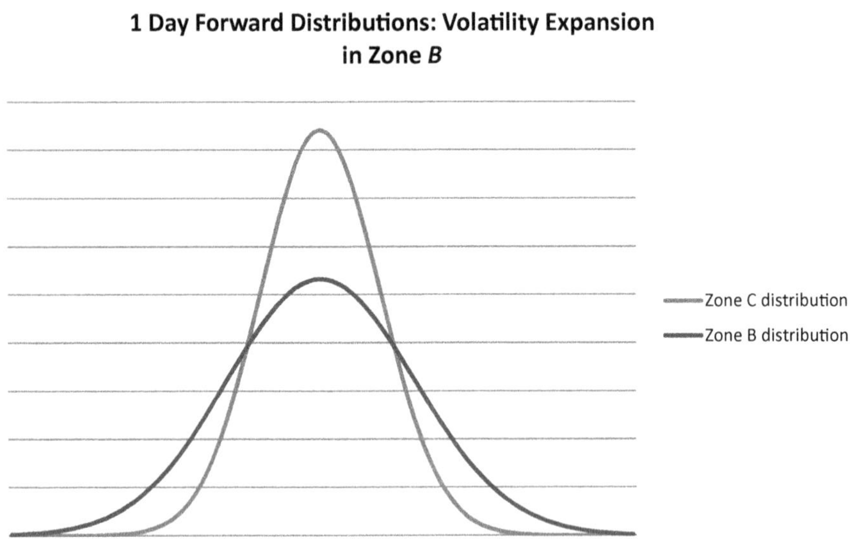


**Fig. 6.10** Characterizing the forward distribution based on current index level relative to options open interest

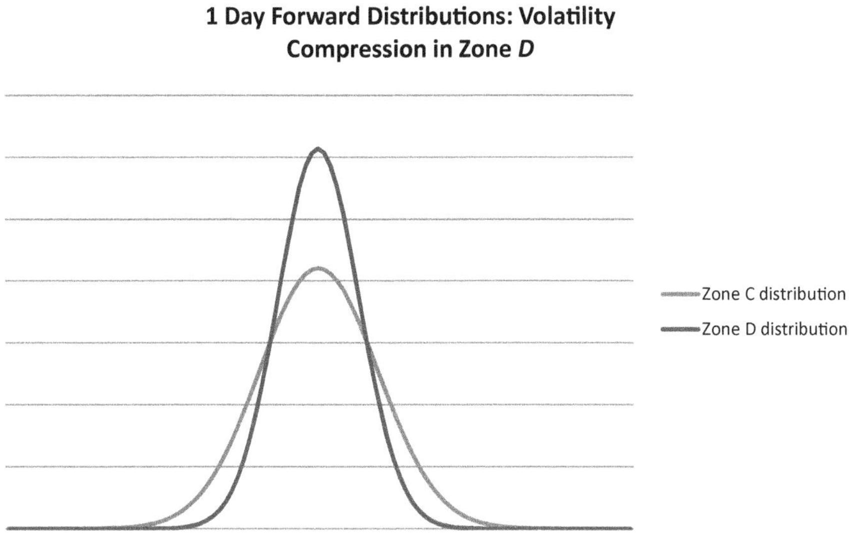


**Fig. 6.11** Near call strikes with high open interest, market makers act as a volatility dampener

To repeat, options market makers compress volatility in region *D*, while increasing the amplitude of price fluctuations in *B*. This serves as a dual roadmap for

- the upward trending, low volatility regime for the S&P 500 entering mid-February 2020
- the sharply down move in late February and early March 2020, with frequent outsized reversals.

We can think of the problem in the following way: the S&P 500 crashed into *B* after spending a very long time in *C* and *D*. Within *B*, very large swings were inevitable, as market makers were forced to dynamically hedge their short index puts. In the next section, we will introduce an index known as the "GEX", in an attempt to quantify net gamma exposure over time. The GEX will be useful in the statistical analysis that follows.

## Aggregate Gamma Exposure and the GEX

SqueezeMetrics (squeezemetrics.com) has created two indices that give valuable information about dealer positioning in the US equity markets. In our opinion, the developers of these indices (whoever they might be) have deep insights into the market making space. The Dark Index, or "DIX", establishes a connection between short interest in individual stocks and forward returns. While the DIX is very interesting, we will focus on the "Gamma Index" or "GEX" in the discussion that follows. Note that the DIX and GEX are the two headline indices produced by SqueezeMetrics. The "GEX" gives a daily estimate of net gamma exposure for S&P 500 options market makers. It is measured in US Dollar units of net gamma, according to Eq. 6.1.

$$\mathrm{GEX}_t = \sum_{K,T-t} 100(-OI_{\mathrm{put}}(K, T-t)\gamma_{\mathrm{put}}(K, T-t) + OI_{\mathrm{call}}(K, T-t)\gamma_{\mathrm{call}}(K, T-t)) \tag{6.1}$$

Here,

- $OI_{\mathrm{put}}(K, T-t)$ is the number of open contracts for a put with strike $K$ and time to maturity $T-t$.
- $\gamma_{\mathrm{put}}(K, T-t)$ is the amount of gamma per contract for puts with strike $K$ and time to maturity $T-t$. Once we know the price of a given option, we can calculate gamma using the Black–Scholes equation.
- Similarly, $OI_{\mathrm{call}}$ and $\gamma_{\mathrm{call}}$ give the open interest and gamma for each call in the options chain.

Recall that an options chain consists of all listed options contracts on a given underlying asset. Open interest tends to be highest for "out of the money" options, namely puts with strikes below the current index level and calls with strikes above. There are a few technical issues involved in calculating the GEX, which we have buried in an endnote to this chapter. These details are not necessary for understanding the main concepts in this chapter.

In words, the GEX estimates the net amount of gamma that options market makers are exposed to at any point in time. The GEX makes the simplifying assumption that customers are buyers of S&P index puts and sellers of calls. This generates the "collar" structure we described earlier in the chapter. Options market makers, as liquidity providers, have the reverse position. This explains the minus sign in front of the first term within parentheses in Eq. 6.1. Since puts and calls both have positive gamma, a *short* put position contributes negative gamma to a market maker's payout curve. When the put terms in Eq. 6.1 dominate (as in Zone $B$ above), market makers will tend to be net short gamma. The amount of positive call gamma in their books is not enough to offset the negative put gamma in their books. Accordingly, in Zone$B$, market maker delta hedging is likely to exaggerate S&P index moves in both directions. From a trading standpoint, it is possible to improve upon the GEX by pinpointing strikes where dealers are short the most gamma. These strikes constitute Zone B: if the index enters this zone, it is likely to be more volatile than usual.

## Potential Hotspots for the GEX

The GEX has some properties that require further investigation. When the S&P is trending higher, the GEX also tends to be high. We are not too far from the low volatility zone $D$. The puts that investors own are likely to be far out of the money, implying that their gamma $\gamma_{\text{put}}(K, T-t)$ is low. This means that the $-OI_{\text{put}}(K, T-t)\gamma_{\text{put}}(K, T-t)$ terms are small and the $+OI_{\text{call}}(K, T-t)\gamma_{\text{call}}(K, T-t)$ terms dominate in the GEX calculation above. In words, a rise in call gamma pushes the GEX higher. After a sell off, however, puts contribute more to the GEX, as the index moves toward the put strikes. Assuming that investors have bought enough puts in anticipation of a correction (equivalently, put open interest is high), we wind up near the danger zone$B$. In this scenario, the GEX tends to be lower than usual and indeed can be negative.

Now that we have come to grips with the GEX formula, we can graph it over time (Fig. 6.12).

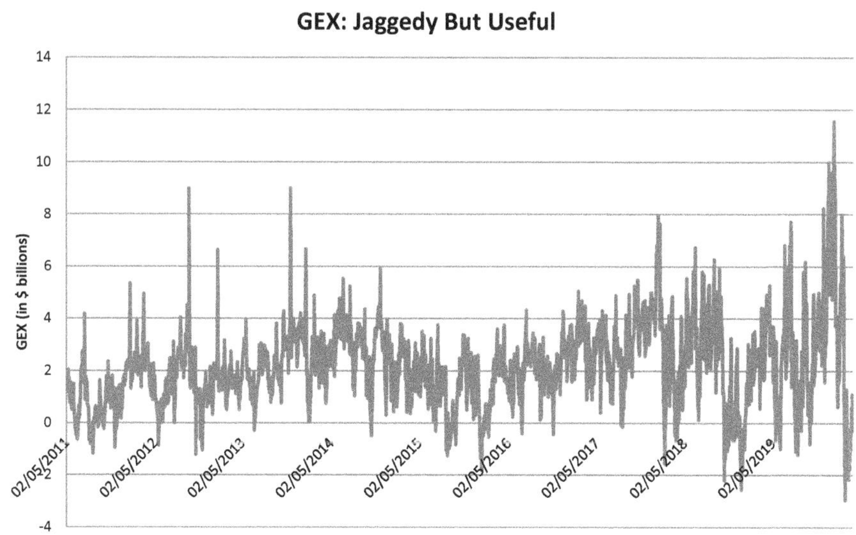


**Fig. 6.12** Historical time series for the GEX (*Source* squeezemetrics.com)

We observe that the index is skewed above 0. The GEX never becomes very negative, relative to its maximum positive value. This is largely a function of the way gamma depends on implied volatility. In rising markets, volatility generally declines. After an extended rise, it tends to be low. The combination of rising prices and declining volatility serves to push downside puts further out-of-the-money (OTM). When S&P 500 implied volatility is 15%, a put with strike 10% below the index is effectively further out-of-the-money than in a regime where implied volatility is 30%. The probability of reaching the strike is lower in the first case.

Very low delta options have virtually no gamma, implying that all of the meaningful terms in the equation for $GEX_t$ are positive. Meanwhile, calls whose strike is close to the spot pick up gamma over time. This drives the index higher. Conversely, after a significant decline in the S&P 500, volatility invariably spikes. This reduces the amount of gamma supplied by at-the-money (ATM) puts, while keeping OTM calls in play. Rising volatility levels preserve the gamma embedded in OTM calls. Figure 6.13, we can see that gamma becomes more evenly spread, with a lower peak, as volatility increases. In other words, the GEX does not have to be very negative to signify danger.

A 0 GEX implies that dealers do not have to rebalance their hedges much at all. They are no longer playing a stabilizing role in the S&P futures market. More dangerously, these agents will act in a highly destabilizing way if the GEX drops any further.

Statistically, it turns out that a high positive value for the GEX indicates relative safety. Market makers are compressing price swings as they rebalance

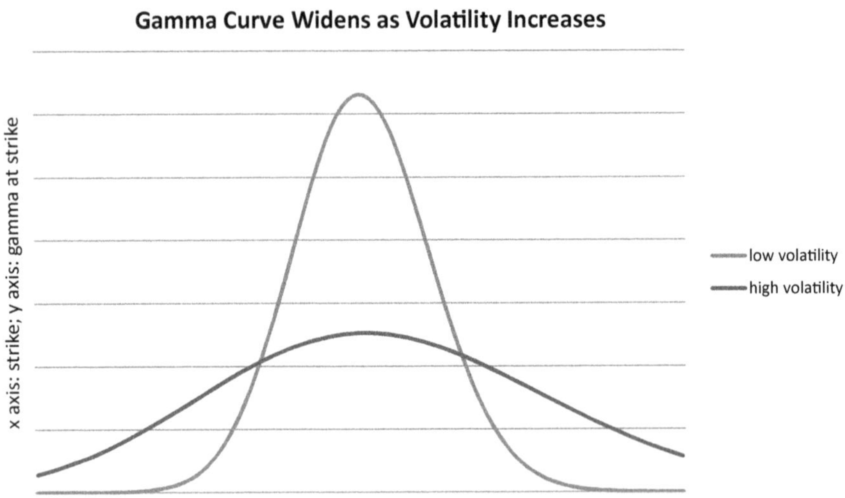


**Fig. 6.13** Dealer exposure is not only level but volatility dependent

their deltas. By contrast, the fallout from hedging when the index becomes modestly negative can be surprisingly large.

As a cautionary note, we observe that the graph is quite volatile. This sharply reduces its effectiveness as a long range forecasting tool. If we plan to hold a position in the S&P for 6 months, say, we cannot rely on an indicator that is highly volatile from one expiration cycle to the next. Still, the GEX can be very useful for flagging potential distortions in the market over horizons of a few days. In the next section, we will explore this idea further.

## Statistical Properties of the GEX

Now that we have described the main features of dealer hedging, we can sensibly analyze the data. The following scatter plot relates the GEX value on day $t - 1$ to the S&P 500 return on day $t$. In other words, we are using the GEX to characterize index returns one day ahead (Fig. 6.14).

We can see that the dispersion of 1 day returns increases sharply as the GEX crosses 0 from the right. The GEX is acting as a powerful short-term risk forecast. Note that there is a reasonably high incidence of large positive as well as negative returns when the index is low. This implies that the GEX is a more useful predictor of uncertainty than direction. As we can see in the next graph, Fig. 6.15, outsized returns in both directions tend to cluster. (We accept that there is insufficient data to draw a very strong conclusion about the clustering of outsized moves.) Successive returns are connected by straight lines in the graph. More specifically, a +5% day is more likely after a recent

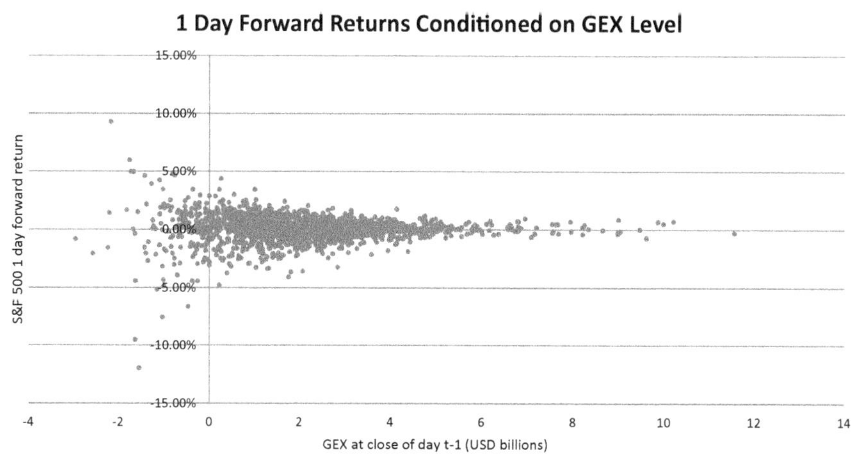


**Fig. 6.14** High dispersion of 1 day forward returns when GEX is relatively low (*Source* squeezemetrics.com, Yahoo! Finance)

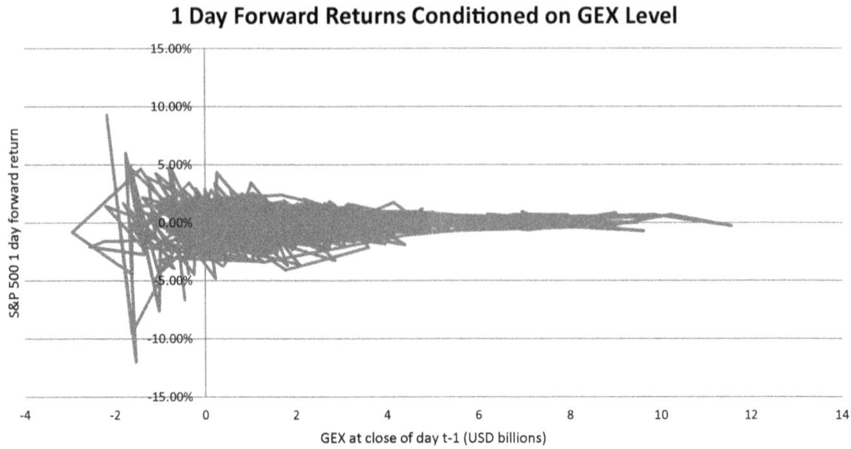


**Fig. 6.15** Outsized returns tend to occur in sequence when the GEX is low (*Source* squeezemetrics.com, Yahoo! Finance)

−7% day than after a quiet stretch. This set up offers a qualitative description of S&P dynamics in March 2020, as we will see at the end of Part 1.

Relating the GEX to 5 day forward returns, we see a similar, though noisier pattern. This is to be expected as the GEX by its very nature is a short-term risk indicator (Fig. 6.16).

We observe that large 5 day downside moves occur quite often when the GEX is low but still positive. In other words, the GEX does not have to be extremely low for bad things to happen over the next week. We can infer

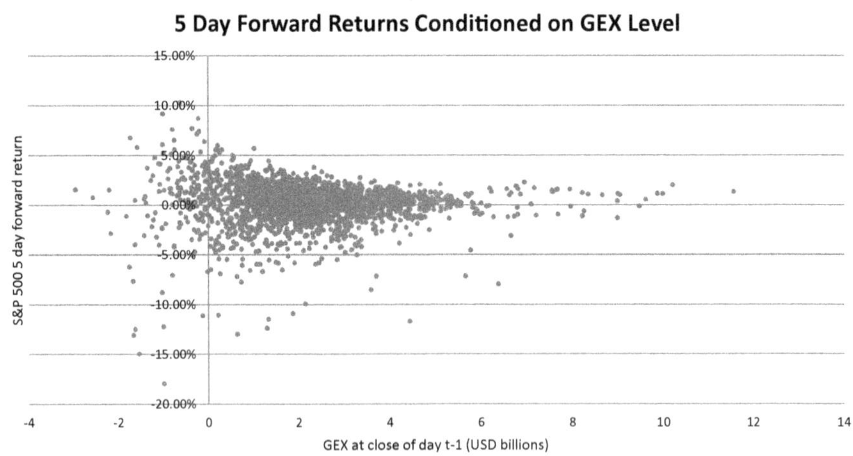


**Fig. 6.16** The scatter plot becomes noisier as we extend the forecast horizon (*Source* squeezemetrics.com, Yahoo! Finance)

what the mechanism might be. When the GEX is at +$1 billion, say, dealers are short puts that are still somewhat out of the money. Positive gamma on the call side slightly outweighs the negative gamma derived from puts. If the market drops from there, gamma will pick up rapidly on these puts, driving the GEX lower. This increases the odds of a sharp second leg down, given that dealers will have to sell futures mechanically into a falling market.

Over 15 day horizons, even more structure is lost. The next chart is relatively noisy. This should not be a surprise, as the impact of dealer hedging is relatively short-lived. A down trend has more time to build, progressively pushing the GEX lower, until market makers are forced into the market. Over long enough horizons, reasonably high GEX values can precede major sell offs. The S&P can move from Zone *C* or even *D* into *B* before flushing out (Fig. 6.17).

We observe that, even though the cloud of 15 day forward returns is less orderly than before, it still contains some interesting structure. Most large *positive* jumps in the S&P 500 occur when the GEX starts at a low level. These correspond to short squeezes that are exaggerated by market maker hedging. When speculative shorts cover or buyers come back into the market after a sharp sell off, market makers need to buy futures to stay hedged. The impact of dealer hedging can push the market to other critical levels, where momentum traders start to buy.

While trend following strategies overtly trade momentum, other products implicitly trade in the direction of recent price moves. The size of the global momentum trade is much larger than many investors might imagine. For

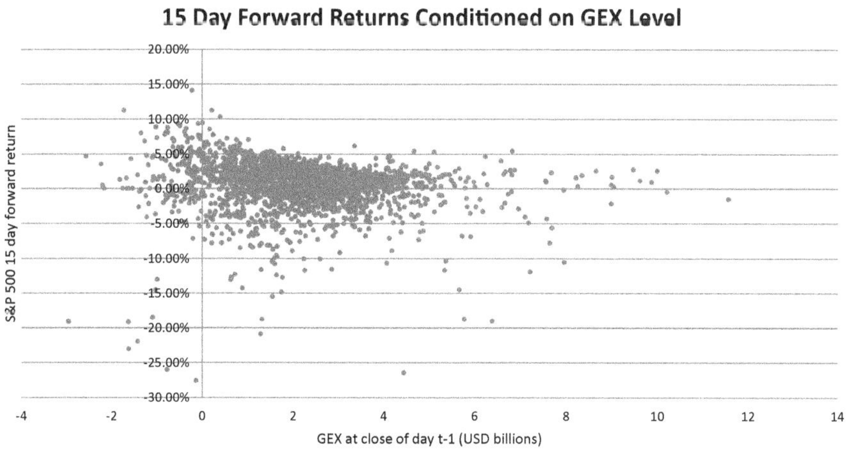


**Fig. 6.17** Over 15 day forward horizons, more structure is lost (*Source* squeezemetrics.com, Yahoo! Finance)

example, volatility control funds tend to be sellers into severe short-term weakness and buyers when conditions stabilize. These agents act more slowly than options market makers, but can be pulled into the market if risk conditions change sharply enough. This requires some explanation. Volatility control is a strategy that targets a fixed level of volatility by varying its cash reserve over time. It is a momentum strategy in disguise, given the strong negative correlation between equity index returns and realized volatility. Suppose that an S&P 500 fund has a 10% volatility budget. If realized S&P volatility over some period is 10%, the strategy would be fully invested. For every $100 in the fund, there would be $100 of notional exposure to the S&P. However, if the market sold off and volatility jumped to 20%, 50% of the S&P position would have to be sold to hit the 10% target. An exaggerated sell off would likely push realized volatility higher. This would force volatility control funds to sell units of the S&P, regardless of valuation, amplifying the down trend. We wind up with a stronger version of Goodhart's Law: when a somewhat useful risk measure becomes a rigid target used by too many agents, it can have destabilizing effects on the financial network.

As we extend the forecast horizon, we need to take more agents into account in an attempt to explain the path prices have taken. This complicates things considerably and implies that the GEX adds the most value over multi-day, rather than multi-week, horizons.

## Incremental Value of the GEX

We have seen that the GEX gives important information about positioning and the distribution of forward returns. However, many of the same things could be said about the VIX. A high VIX also predicts a relatively wide distribution of forward returns, including large relief rallies. It also reflects aggregate investor demand for insurance. This raises an important question: Does the GEX encode any useful information over and above the VIX? In this section, we will show that the GEX does indeed have additive value. It acts as a useful adjunct to the VIX, e.g., in the context of a 2 factor regression.

The next two charts mimic the charts in the previous section, with one exception: we now scale S&P forward returns by the spot VIX. Scaling allows us to see what the GEX can add on its own. We want to decide whether the quantity of open interest at various strikes reveals something more than the level of implied volatility at those strikes. More formally, suppose that $GEX_t$, $P_t$ and $\sigma_t$ are the values of the GEX, S&P 500 and VIX, respectively, at time $t$. We want to use the GEX to characterize $n$day forward, VIX adjusted returns.

Strictly speaking, $\sigma_t = \sigma_t(n)$ depends on $n$. The range of outcomes for an asset with fixed volatility widens over time, hence $\sigma_t$ is increasing in $n$. This means that we need to scale the VIX by the length of our forecasting window. Assuming that there are 365 calendar days in a year and, as in a standard Brownian motion, volatility scales as the square root of time, $\sigma_t(n) = \frac{\sigma_t}{\sqrt{\frac{365}{n}}}$. (Note that there are other ways to scale volatility by time that may be superior in a practical trading context. However, our basic argument holds, regardless of the scaling factor we choose. In addition, the rescaling above is the simplest possible.)

In summary, we want to relate $\text{GEX}_t$ to $\frac{1}{\sigma_t}\frac{P_{t+n}-P_t}{P_t}$, which is just a volatility scaled return. To repeat, we have factored out the VIX component of the S&P 500 day$n$ forward return, to see whether the GEX still encodes valuable information. The S&P returns are now in units of standard deviations, as in Fig. 6.18. Note that we have set $n = 1$ below, to isolate 1 day forward returns. We have also restricted our attention to the case where the GEX is below \$1 billion, to see whether the GEX is able to flash a warning signal over and above the VIX.

1 day forward returns are more negatively skewed than a distribution scaled by the VIX would predict. This is not only true for the left tail, but also for moderate downside moves in the 1 to 2 standard deviation range. The options market has not fully priced in dealer positioning risk across a range of put strikes. Investors have not fully absorbed the fact that, if the S&P

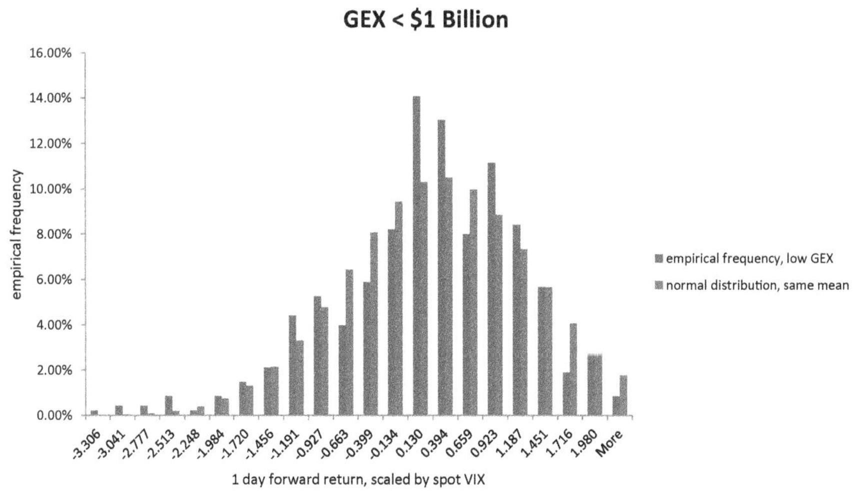


**Fig. 6.18** When the GEX is low, the distribution of 1 day forward returns exhibits severe negative skewness (*Source* squeezemetrics.com, Yahoo! Finance)

declines any further, options market makers will have to sell large chunks of S&P futures. "Potential gamma" risk is large and negative for dealers. The open interest-weighted sum of gamma across all put strikes might not be large now, but it *will be* if the S&P drops much further.

This gives rise to a rough trade idea. Now would be a good time to consider buying some out-of-the-money puts or put spreads, as the market is underpricing downside risk. Put open interest is not directly incorporated into standard options pricing models, such as the Black-Scholes formula, but has an empirical effect on the distribution of forward returns. The following chart supplies more evidence in favor of buying S&P put structures when the GEX is low. We have restricted ourselves to days where the GEX was below \$1 billion and constructed a histogram of normalized 15 day forward S&P returns. This 2+ week horizon gives a long put structure more time to develop, while reducing drag from transaction costs.

Figure 6.19, we divided the return from day $t$ to day $t+15$ by the following quantity: $\frac{\mathrm{VIX}_t}{\sqrt{\frac{252}{15}}}$. Here, $\mathrm{VIX}_t$ is the value of the VIX at the beginning of the period and $\sqrt{\frac{252}{15}}$ is a normalization constant which adjusts for the fact that we are modelling forward returns over 15 trading days and that there are around 252 trading days in a year. (Again, we are making a standard rescaling that may not be the most appropriate one in practice.)

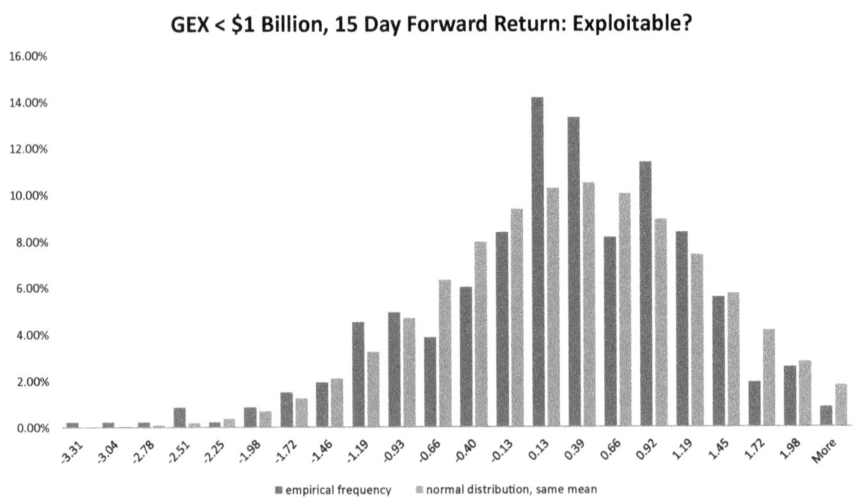


**Fig. 6.19** 15 day forward distribution of S&P returns, scaled by VIX, when GEX is low (*Source* squeezemetrics.com, Yahoo! Finance)

Again, the frequency of returns more than 1 standard deviation below the mean is higher than a normal distribution scaled by the VIX would suggest. To repeat, even after adjusting for implied volatility levels along the skew, the left tail is heavier than normal. Our put or put spread buying idea holds up over 15 day horizons when the GEX is low.

In the next section, we will turn our attention to the COVID-19 crisis of early 2020. Equipped with some knowledge of dealer positioning and the GEX, we will explain why the wild oscillations of the S&P 500 within a sharp down trend were not as shocking as it may have seemed at the time.

## Dealer Positioning and the Q1 2020 Crisis

In this section, we will establish a direct connection between options market maker positioning and the wild, two-way swings in the S&P 500 from late February to early April 2020. Our tool of choice will be the GEX. We accept that our analysis will not be comprehensive. Clearly, other factors contributed to high levels of volatility in the market. The market ecosystem is complex and it is hard to completely isolate the impact of any one factor on prices. However, we can show that price action became significantly more violent when the GEX dropped into Zone $B$ in Fig. 6.19.

Even before 2020, low GEX values were associated with sharp reversals. (Note that the GEX time series only goes back to May 2011.) From this starting date to December 2019, we logged all days where the S&P 500 declined by at least −2%. We then divided sell offs into two regimes, according to whether the GEX was positive or negative after the sell off. The results were quite instructive.

- **Case 1**. Suppose that the S&P 500 dropped by -2% or more on day $t-1$and the GEX was greater than or equal to 0 at the close of trading. Then, the S&P recorded a positive return on day $t$ **56%** of the time. On rebound days, the average return was **+0.87%**.
- **Case 2**. By contrast, suppose that the GEX was negative after a drop of −2% or more in the S&P 500. Then, the day $t$ return for the S&P was positive **66%** of the time, with an average return of **+1.69%** on positive days.

From 5 May 2011 to 31 December 2019, roughly 54% of all 1 day returns for the S&P 500 were positive. This is not very different from the frequency in **Case 1** above. In **Case 2**, however, the frequency and magnitude of rebounds are materially higher. We can speculate why. Assuming that

**Case 2** sell offs were at least partly a function of dealer hedging, they were somewhat technical in nature. A change in fundamentals could not explain the entire move. We can conjecture that statistical arbitrage strategies and other “noise traders” would have been incentivized to buy **Case 2** dips in the S&P 500. These traders take the other side of price moves that are considered to be random, rather than accompanied by fundamental news flow.

Figure 6.20 gives us further indication that non-fundamental factors had a large impact on the S&P 500 in February and March 2020. We can see that, as investors absorbed the impact of large-scale lockdowns, US 10 year constant maturity yields were far less choppy from day to day. Treasury bonds tend to respond to fundamental changes in growth and inflation prospects far more directly than equity indices. We observe a near straight line drop in yields from mid-February to March 9, 2020.

This supports the contention that the sawtooth-shaped move in the S&P 500 was a function of network effects in the equity markets, rather than changes to external news flow.

We can now refer back to the GEX, focusing on situations where

- the GEX closed below $1 billion on the previous day
- during the historical window from 2011 to 2019.

Here, downside risk was high and the average 1 day rebound after a drop of over −2% on the previous day increased by a factor of nearly $2X$.

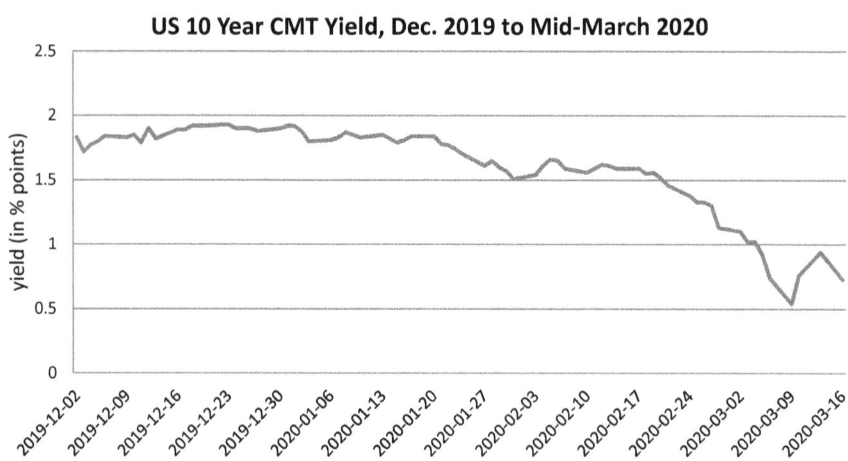


**Fig. 6.20** US 10 year constant maturity Treasury yield, December 2019 to March 2020 (*Source* FRED [St. Louis Federal Reserve Database])

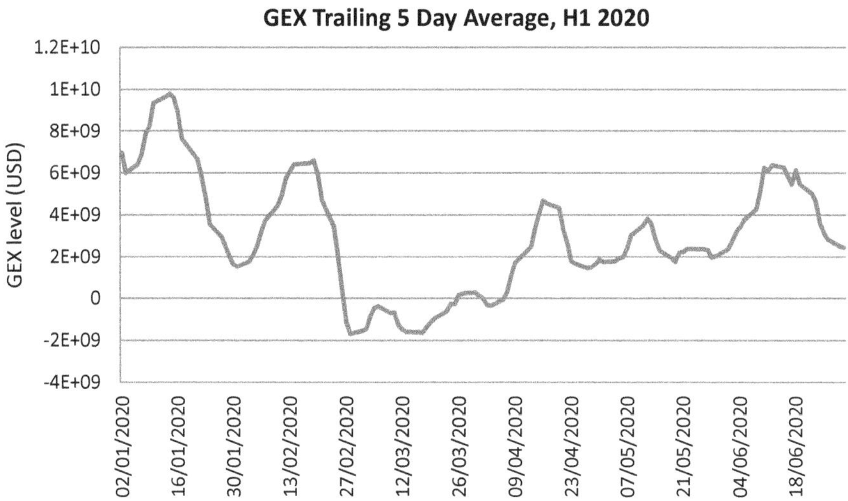


**Fig. 6.21** Smoothed version of the GEX, January to June 2020 (*Source* squeezemetrics.com)

We now have a coherent explanation for the price dynamics that occurred from late February to early April 2020. It should no longer be puzzling that S&P price action became increasingly jagged once the GEX dipped below 0 on February 24, 2020. Figure 6.21 tracks the index in the first half of 2020. This includes the danger interval from late February to mid-April, when the GEX stabilized above 0 again.

This gives rise to the widening envelope of 1 day returns in early 2020 (Fig. 6.22).

We have seen how options market makers can act as Dominant Agents as they delta hedge in the underlying asset. In Part 2 of this chapter, we will analyze a variation of the standard random walk model for asset price returns. The updated model directly incorporates dealer hedging. With the correct parameterization, it turns out that this model naturally generates fat-tailed returns similar to the type we witnessed in early 2020.

## Part 2: A Qualitative Model of Market Maker Impact

*NOTE: This remainder of this chapter is relatively mathematical and can be skipped by readers who want to jump straight to the "Non-Technical Summary".*

We can now analyze and subsequently modify a model that incorporates delta hedging by options market makers. In the original model, hedging

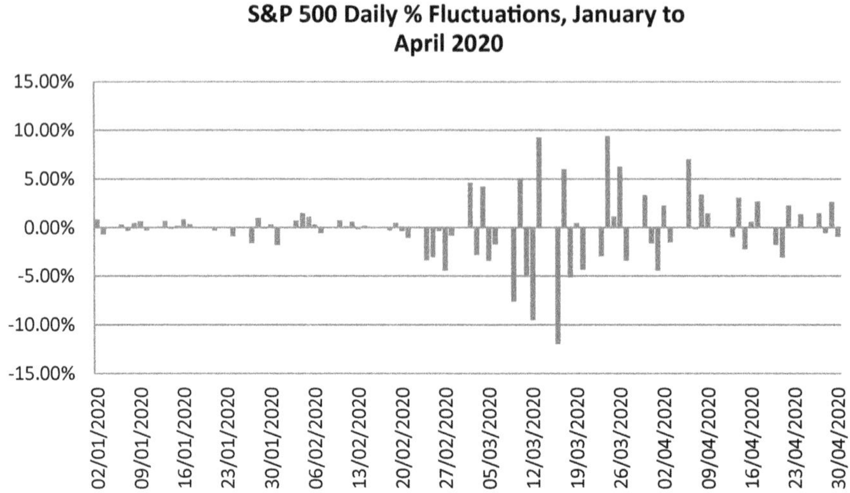


**Fig. 6.22** Low GEX, high dispersion of 1 day returns (*Source* Yahoo! Finance)

acts as a dampening force: close to expiration, it reduces volatility near options strikes. However, if we change the inputs to account for situations where dealers are net short gamma, the same formulation generates extreme volatility and fat tails. As in Part 1, hedging now acts as a strong destabilizing influence.

We will draw upon a model that was initially used to explain a market anomaly called "stock pinning". We can give a bit of historical context to the problem. In the early 2000s, several authors observed that certain stocks had a higher than expected probability of landing near a multiple of 5 on the third Friday of a given month. There seemed to be some sort of gravitational attraction to prices such as 5, 10, 15, 20 and so on. A vital insight was that most of the stocks landing near multiples of 5 also had a lively options market. This could not be a coincidence. Equity options generally also have strikes that appear in multiples of 5 and expire on the third Friday of a given month. There had to be a connection between options trading activity and price action in the underlying stock. In other words, pinning was the statistical tendency for stock prices to land near option strikes near expiration.

As might be expected, traders had been exploiting this tendency for quite some time before the academic papers came out. Ni et al. (2005) produced perhaps the first definitive verification of pinning. They focused their attention on a cross-section of US stocks whose listed options satisfied certain liquidity constraints. Restricting to this subset, prices had a larger than expected tendency to land near a multiple of 5 near settlement. For example,

99.95 was a more likely settlement price than 97.5 given the results of their study.

Ordinarily, we would expect the distribution of settlement prices to be nearly uniform, with 97.5 and 99.95 equally likely.

The mechanism for pinning was initially unclear, at least to the non-dealer community. One conspiratorial idea was that market makers who found themselves short options near expiration were incentivized to push the underlying stock toward the strike with a succession of small trades in the right direction. This would serve to maximize the payout on their short options position. We can consider this idea further. Suppose that a certain stock had been rallying hard over the past few months. There was excess demand for calls, as a speculative upside play. Investors who had come late to the party wanted to participate in the rally, with implicit leverage and bounded risk. This dual objective induced them to buy calls. At the same time, agents who were already long the stock decided to buy puts in size, to protect their gains. Then, dealers (after taking the other side of customer orders) might wind up with a net position similar to Fig. 6.23.

The combined position is known as a short "straddle", struck at 100, say. Unhedged, the profit on a short straddle is highest at the strike. This implies that, if the stock were trading at 99 a few hours before expiration, dealers might try to push the stock toward the strike. Conversely, if the stock were at 101, sell orders on the underlying would be issued, forcing the stock back toward 100.

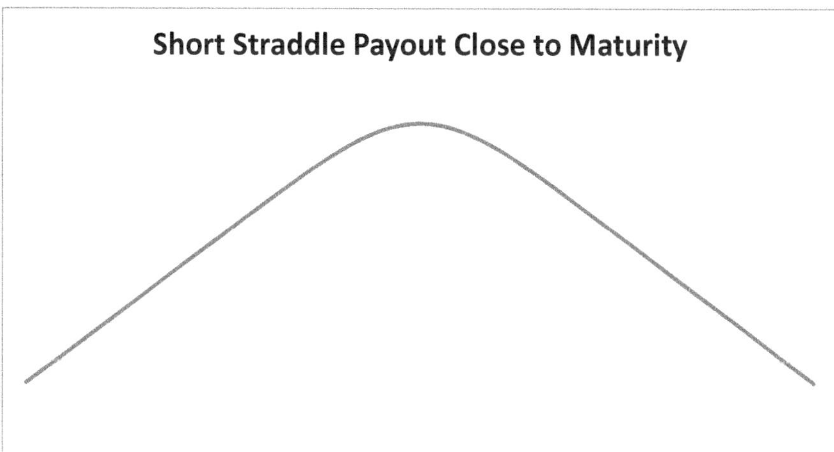


**Fig. 6.23** Payout profile of a short options straddle, close to maturity

Without worrying too much about the pinning mechanism itself, Krishnan and Nelken (2001) used a modified random walk model to describe the price action of a stock that had probability $p$ of getting pinned. This modified "Brownian Bridge" model was then used to reprice options, given the revised path that the underlying might take. While constraining the motion of a pinned stock using an established theoretical model was a decent start, it did not offer a mechanistic explanation as to why pinning should occur in the first place.

Avellaneda and Lipkin (2003) made a conceptual breakthrough by incorporating dealer hedging activity directly into the dynamical model for a pinned stock. Now, pinning was a natural consequence of options market maker risk management practice. In the next section, we will analyze their model in some detail.

## Pinning Arises from Dealer Hedging

Avellaneda and Lipkin's assumptions were contrary to the ad hoc argument above, but in our opinion, offered a more accurate representation of dealer behavior. Avellaneda and Lipkin observed that, every so often, options market makers would find themselves net long options as they took the other side of short volatility customer trades. During the .com bubble and its aftermath, equity volatility was high, allowing investors to collect a large amount of premium from put and call selling. "Buy writes" were especially popular at the time. Investors would sell calls against speculative long positions. These structures capped their upside, but generated income in a regime where many companies did not pay any dividends. More generally, many retail and institutional investors have a bias toward *selling* options on individual stocks. These agents can be characterized as yield chasers, swapping extreme event risk for something that looks like income. As long as nothing very dramatic happens, volatility sellers profit from time decay.

Although we are sorely tempted to do so, we will not pass judgment on short volatility as a dedicated strategy. For now, it is fair to say that supply and demand imbalances can lead to a situation where market makers are left holding a large quantity of options whose strikes are near the current spot price. In other words, they are carrying a lot of long gamma exposure. It may be that these options are theoretically cheap, as dealers automatically lower their bids when investors are keen to sell volatility. In other words, market makers expect to be paid a premium for bearing risk. However, warehousing large positions (even at a discount) can be dangerous. These agents typically have strict risk limits, as their core business relies upon repeatedly capturing the bid/ask spread. To repeat, market makers want to generate a predictable return by selling at the ask and buying at the bid, again and again, while hedging away any residual exposure.

Whenever dealers absorbed flow from premium seeking investors, they would accumulate long options positions. Options market makers automatically take the opposite positions from their customers. On an unhedged basis, dealers would actually benefit from large moves in the underlying. As a corollary, it would be counterproductive to push prices toward the strikes they were long. This would effectively reduce their payout at maturity. The payout curve might look something like a *long* straddle, as in Fig. 6.24. This is a reflection of Fig. 6.23 around the horizontal axis: the payout is diametrically opposed to the one that would appeal to conspiracy theorists. Dealers would be net long various puts and calls, in varying amounts.

Hedging the deltas in a long straddle involves **buying** shares when the underlying drops and **selling** shares when it rises. It is implicitly a contrarian strategy. Close to maturity, hedge ratios fluctuate more than usual. Gamma is high near the center strike. Dealers have to buy dips and sell rallies more often and/or in greater size. The impact of these trades compresses volatility near options strikes with a large amount of open interest.

In this context, pinning arises naturally from the hedging activities of dealers, rather than from price manipulation close to options settlement. Occam's razor applies: the simplest possible explanation is at least equally correct, as it does not involve market maker shenanigans. In the next section, we provide details of Avellaneda and Lipkin's original model.

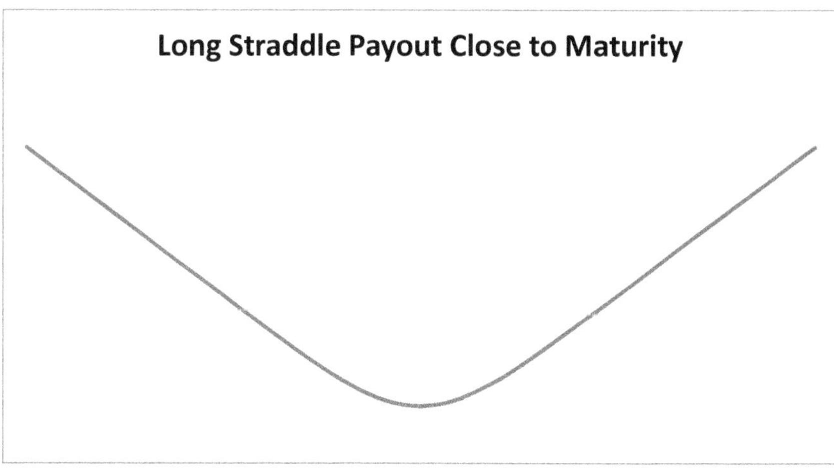


**Fig. 6.24** Payout profile of a LONG straddle, close to maturity

## Discrete Time Pinning Model

Introductory finance textbooks usually make the default assumption that stock returns are normally distributed over all time horizons. We can describe things a bit more precisely. In continuous time, the logarithm of price evolves according to a Brownian motion. For readers who are uncomfortable with basic stochastic calculus, we will focus on a discrete time version of their model in what follows. This serves our purposes in any case.

Suppose that $P(t)$ is the price of a certain stock at time $t$. According to standard theory (which underpins the Black–Scholes equation), the probability-weighted range of outcomes for $\frac{P(t+T)-P(t)}{P(t)}$ has a normal distribution for any time increment $T > 0$. Note that $\frac{P(t+T)-P(t)}{P(t)}$ is just the percentage return in price from one time step to the next. We can simulate paths for $P$ by breaking time into small partitions $\Delta t$ and writing an equation that describes its movement from time $t$ to $t + \Delta t$.

In particular, setting $r(t) = \frac{P(t+\Delta t)-P(t)}{P(t)}$ to be $P$'s return from $t$ to $t + \Delta t$, we can write $r(t) = \mu \Delta t + \sigma \sqrt{\Delta t} \xi$. $\mu$ is the drift and $\sigma$ is the volatility of $r$. The drift is the "expected" or average return from $t$ to $t + \Delta t$. Here, $\xi$ is a normally distributed random variable with standard deviation 1 and mean 0. While we know the distribution of $\xi$, we do not know which random value will be drawn at any given point in time. In other words, $\xi$ creates the uncertainty in any given path.

The drift term $\mu$ can be interpreted in various ways. Assuming that we have no idea what $P$'s expected return should be, we can reasonably set $\mu = 0$. This generates a directionless random walk, similar to the path a drunken sailor might take on the way back to his or her hotel. In options pricing models, such as Black–Scholes, $\mu$ is replaced with something called the "risk neutral" drift. Here, $\mu$ only depends on interest rates and volatility $\sigma$. Remarkably, the true drift does not have any impact on the fair value of a put or call. Following Mehrling (2005) and Derman (2003), this was a remarkable insight that has at least some of the qualities of a genuine scientific discovery.

We can now say something about Avellaneda and Lipkin's interpretation of the drift term $\mu$, when a stock is pinned. In a market dominated by dealers who have significant gamma exposure and have to hedge, the drift changes over time. The impact of hedging creates somewhat predictable price action, which invalidates the random walk assumption above.

Using the framework developed in Chapter 2, the original distribution $H$ can be transformed into a non-normal distribution $H^*$ in the presence of options market makers. Non-normality is induced by a variable drift term. These agents have the potential to turn into Dominant Agents when they have a large quantity of options on their books and have to hedge. Gamma can grow either as a function of movements in the spot or jumps in the quantity of open interest at various strikes.

Avellaneda and Lipkin (2003) provide a technique for simulating the modified distribution $H^*$, by making the drift $\mu = \mu(t)$ variable in the equation $(t) = \mu(t)\Delta t + \sigma\sqrt{\Delta t}\xi$. This is their technical adjustment for the presence of market makers as a Dominant Agent. More specifically, the drift depends on how aggressively and in what direction dealers have to rebalance their hedges. Instantaneously, $r(t)$ is normally distributed at any time $t$. However, the variable drift term alters the distribution of returns over any horizon longer than $\Delta t$. In the original pinning model, the drift $\mu(t)$ is assumed to have the following properties.

- $\mu(t)$ is proportional to the amount of open interest at the strike closest to the current price $P(t)$. Here, open interest is expressed as a percentage of average daily trading volume for the underlying stock. It is not given in absolute terms. The more options dealers are long, the more shares are required to hedge. Open interest includes puts and calls at the nearby strike. Both open interest and volume are expressed in units of US dollars.
- The drift $\mu(t)$ is also proportional to the change in aggregate put and call delta from time $t - \Delta t$ to $t$. If delta has gone up, dealers need to sell shares at time $t$ to stay hedged. If delta has gone down, they need to buy at time $t$. This means that $\mu(t)$ depends on the change in options delta, with negative sign.

More formally, we can set $OI$ to be the total options open interest at a given strike $K$, $\langle V \rangle$ as the average daily share volume (measured over some lookback period) and $\delta(t)$ as the sum of put and call delta at $K$. Then, $\mu(t)$ is assumed to be proportional to the quantity $-OI\left(\frac{1}{\langle V \rangle}(\delta(S(t)) - \delta(S(t - \Delta t)))\right)$. This is the key Avellaneda and Lipkin (2003) correction term to the standard model. This term effectively represents dealer "demand for deltas" from one time step to the next.

In reality, $OI$ can change over time. Large changes in open interest are possible even on an intraday basis. However, we will ignore this detail as we proceed, as our results in Part 2 are purely qualitative.

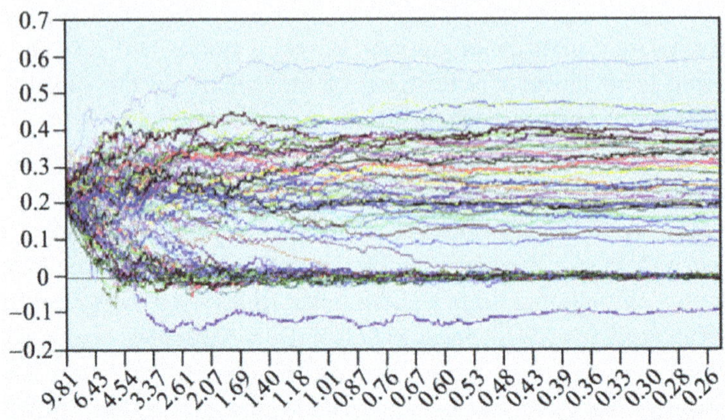


**Fig. 6.25** Simulated distance between a stock and a nearby options strike as maturity approaches (*Source* https://citeseerx.ist.psu.edu/viewdoc/download?doi=10.1.1.146.143&rep=rep1&type=pdf, https://papers.ssrn.com/sol3/papers.cfm?abstract_id=458020)

## Simulated Paths Near Expiration

Using their equation for a stock that might be pinned, Avellaneda and Lipkin (2003) generated a large number of paths close to expiration. We have borrowed the next figure from their paper (Fig. 6.25).

The $y$-axis measures the distance from a strike as time passes. Meanwhile, the $x$-axis tracks the number of days to maturity. Each path starts \$0.20 above the nearest strike. Finally, we observe that the units along the $x$-axis are stretched close to maturity, in proportion to their theta. (There is a technical reason for stretching time close to maturity, which is not important for the purposes of this discussion.) In the simulation above, we can see that the probability of landing near a strike at maturity is much higher than random. The model naturally induces pinning as a function of delta hedging near expiration.

## Generalizing the Model

Avellaneda and Lipkin (2003) focused on stock pinning when setting the drift $\mu(t)$ proportional to the quantity of deltas dealers need to buy or sell to rebalance their hedges. However, there is no reason to restrict their model to pinning. This is an interesting point. The same set up applies to any situation where market makers have a large amount of residual options exposure that they need to hedge.

In other words, the model is highly generalizable. In principle, it should apply to indices and commodity futures as well as to individual stocks. Also, dealers are not required to have to have a long gamma position, where they buy dips and sell rallies around the strike. They can be net short options or even have a hybrid position where they are long certain options and short other ones, without any structural change to the model. In particular, we can apply the assumptions used to construct the GEX in Part 1 of this chapter to Avellaneda and Lipkin's equation and simulate paths accordingly.

Assuming a constant drift term, we know that the distribution of returns is Gaussian: there are no fat tails. Our goal is to test the following hypothesis. Can the variable drift term $\mu(t)$ generate fat tails, even when our volatility input $\sigma$ does not change? Usually, practitioners think in terms of time-dependent volatility, rather than drift, when generating non-normal distributions. However, there is not a hard requirement. If our hypothesis is correct, we can conclude that S&P 500 options market makers can have a highly destabilizing influence on the distribution of index returns over short horizons. They have the power to generate wild oscillations and non-normal distributions. When options market makers dominate the network, the feedback loop between index options and the underlying can be toxic.

We are now ready to fix the parameters in our Monte Carlo simulation, as in Table 6.1. These inputs are merely designed to be illustrative, so that we can test for fat tails.

Note that, in practice, dealers are going to be long and short many different strikes and maturities. For simplicity, we have mapped all puts and calls onto a single strike and fixed the initial time to maturity at 1 month. Still, we believe that we have captured two properties of the S&P options market in a rough but realistic way.

**Table 6.1** Sample inputs for Eq. 6.1, given S&P options market maker positioning

| Initial price | 100 |
|---|---|
| Time step (years) | 0.0040 |
| Volatility | 10% |
| Risk free rate | 0 |
| Short put strike | 92.5 |
| Long call strike | 102.5 |
| Initial time to maturity (years) | 0.1233 |
| Options open interest (% of average daily volume) | 15% |
| Call open interest (% of put open interest) | 50% |
| "Delta demand" coefficient | 1 |

- The put strike at 92.5 is further away from the spot (normalized at 100) than the call strike at 102.5. This reduces the cost of an index collar and is consistent with the various structured products available in the market. Typically, real money investors want to have 0 outlay or receive a net credit if they choose to collar their existing long positions.
- Other agents have simply decided to hedge against moderate downside scenarios using puts, without writing any calls. As a result, call open interest is only 50% as large as put open interest. Not that this assumption only applies to indices and not to individual stocks.

The second assumption is consistent with average put/call ratios observed in the S&P options market.

Intuitively, we should expect to see many paths drift toward the call strike. In this case, the underlying dynamics are similar to stock pinning, over longer horizons. Assuming that the S&P is in a flat to up trend, dealers will find themselves net long gamma. The index will have landed in Zones $C$, $D$ or $E$. Here, dealer hedging activities act as a natural stabilizing force: dips are mechanically bought and rallies sold.

Every now and then, however, a path will drift down toward the put strike. This move toward Zone $B$ would be based on an exogenous risk factor or at least something external to options market making activity. There it has a high probability of slashing through the strike, as $\mu_t$ becomes strongly negative. Dealers rapidly pick up units of short gamma as the index sells off, which amplifies short-term fluctuations, as well as increasing the left tail of the distribution. Figure 6.26, we can see that one path drifts toward the stable "equilibrium" at 102.5, while the other accelerates through 92.5 from above.

The blue path drifting toward 102.5 is considerably more likely than the red one. It is also typical in the sense that volatility declines as expiration approaches. We can think of the blue path as a weaker and longer horizon version of stock pinning. In other words, the median return over a 1 month horizon has a small positive drift and relatively low variation around the drift.

However, for the smaller class of paths that approach Zone $B$, dealer hedging induces negative skewness in the modified distribution. This is bad for investors who are long the S&P 500, as they are carrying more risk than they might think. When a distribution is "negatively skewed", large negative outcomes are more likely than equally sized positive ones. This brings us to another important point. While options market makers can cause exaggerated price moves, their influence is typically restricted to short-term horizons. Once the downside red path drops below 85 or so, gamma drains out of the

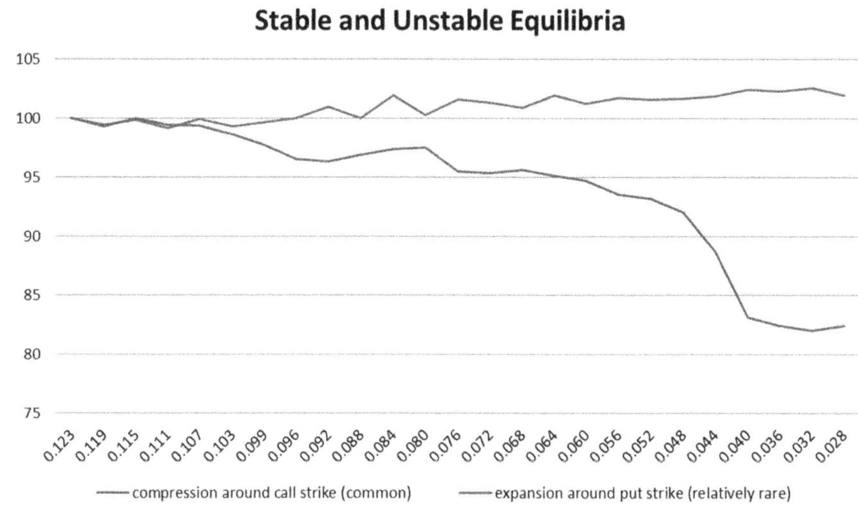


**Fig. 6.26** Call strikes attract a path that originally rises, put strikes create instability for paths that drift far below the initial price

position. The simulated price stabilizes shortly thereafter. Dealers can maintain a fairly static hedge and hence no longer have a material impact on the underlying index. They are neither stabilizing nor destabilizing as we move into Zone *A*. If the S&P is going to continue to drop, other agents (such as trend following futures strategies) will have to sell.

## Statistical Results: Fat Tail Generation and Potential Whipsaws

As we approach expiration in an S&P options cycle with a large amount of open interest, the probability of an extreme 1 day return can increase. This is conditional on the path that the index takes. In the example above, if the price approaches the 92.5 downside strike late in the cycle, dealers will have to manage a large short gamma position. This transforms them from liquidity providers into forced liquidity takers in the S&P 500. The next graph is derived from a Monte Carlo simulation. We have used Eq. 6.1 to generate paths, given inputs from Table 6.1 above. We have plotted the lowest percentile 1 day return across all simulations, based on the time to options expiration (Fig. 6.27).

Assuming that open interest remains constant, the magnitude of the worst percentile return increases by a factor of around 6 as time decreases from 45 to 10 days. (Observe that values along the *x*-axis are decreasing as we

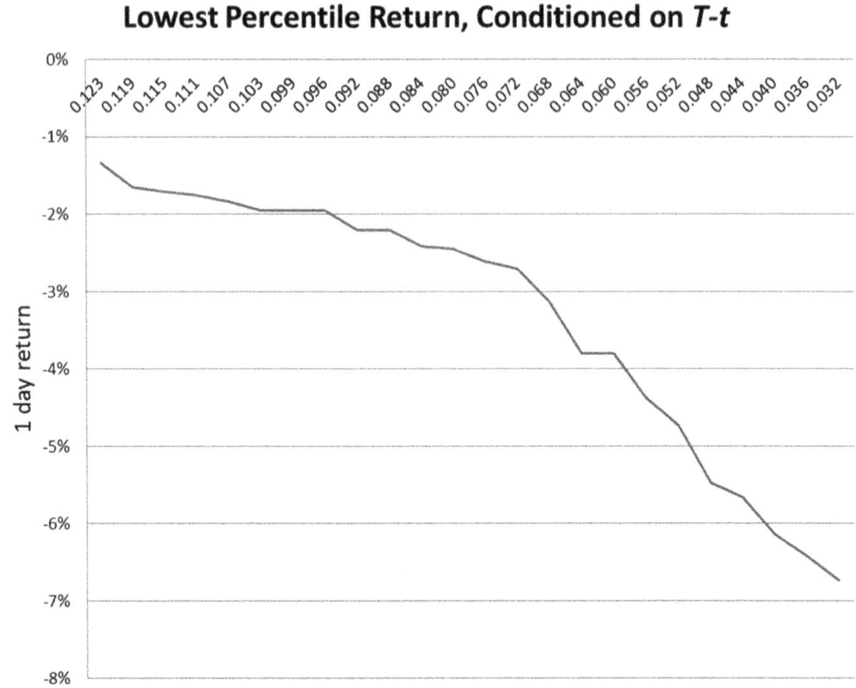


**Fig. 6.27** Simulation of lowest percentile 1 day return as maturity approaches

move to the right.) The exact size of these returns should not be interpreted too literally, as our choice of the constant of proportionality $c$ is somewhat arbitrary. However, the relative difference in bad outcomes is very large, and purely a function of rapidly increasing demand for deltas if the S&P 500 drops early in the cycle. The volatility input in Eq. 6.1 remains constant throughout.

An related feature is that, after a very large 1 day down move, the probability of a nearly equally sized up move increases. Near the 92.5 strike, a random price increase on the following day will force dealers to buy S&P futures in size to maintain delta neutrality. The impact of large-scale covering is likely to drive prices much higher on an intraday basis. Figure 6.28, we have taken the same simulation and replaced the lowest 1% of 1 day forward returns with the highest 1%. We wind up with a near mirror image of the previous chart.

This is the phenomenon we observed in March 2020, where mega down days were followed by huge 1 day relief rallies, in a down trending market. The toy model above explains some of the essential features of the violent sell off witnessed in Q1 of 2020.

We can also gain some insight from Fig. 6.29. This displays the dispersion

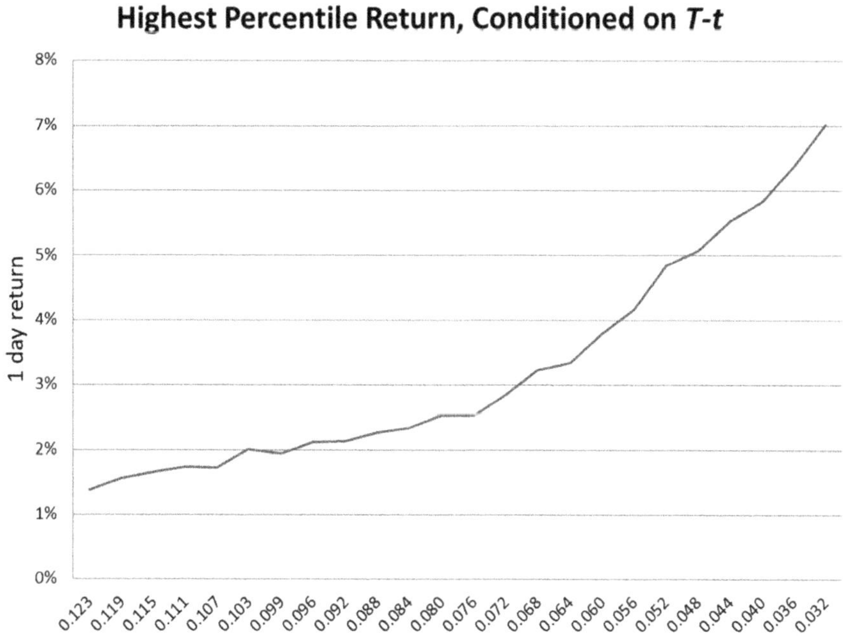


**Fig. 6.28** Highest percentile 1 day return as maturity approaches, using the same set of simulated paths

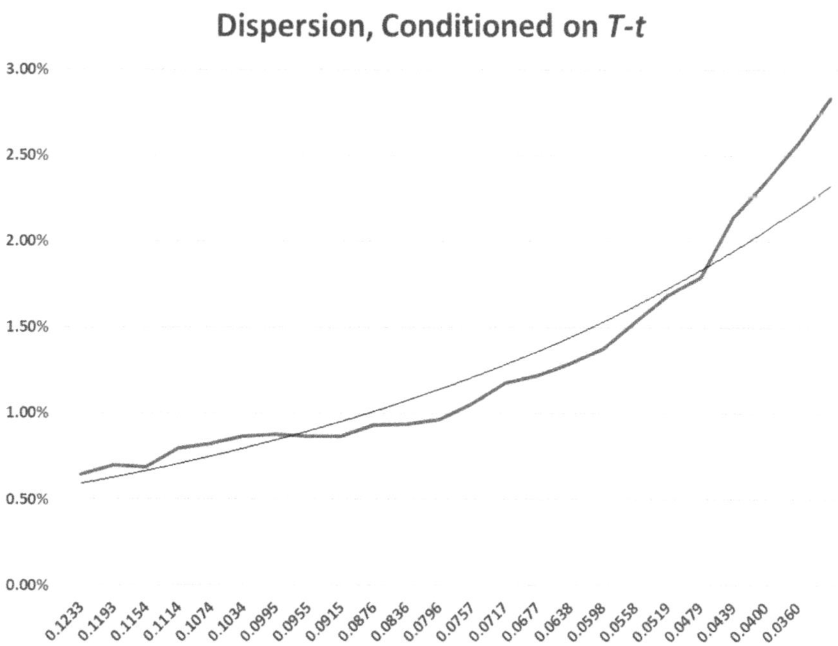


**Fig. 6.29** Dispersion of 1 day returns across simulations, as maturity approaches

of 1 day returns, as a function of time to maturity. Here, "dispersion" is the standard deviation of returns across all simulations for each fixed time to maturity. High dispersion indicates that a wide range of outcomes is possible. As before, time is decreasing along the $x$-axis.

Fitting a parabola through the simulated data, we can see that dispersion increases at a faster than linear rate as expiration approaches. In the absence of dealer hedging, we would expect the graph above to be completely flat. We observe that dispersion is nearly 3X higher with 15 days to maturity than with 45 days to go. Our Dominant Agents are having a significant effect on the distribution of returns as time goes by.

While downside risk is high, outright directional bets can be dangerous when dealers are short a large amount of gamma. The S&P 500 has the potential to make a violent move either up or down. However, we can draw a practical conclusion from our simulation. An investor would be ill-advised to sell short-dated puts with strikes at or below strikes where dealers are short a large amount of gamma. These puts might seem attractive short candidates, based on their rapid time decay. However, the odds of the S&P blasting through the strike from above are higher than the market has priced in. Investors generally do not incorporate supply and demand imbalances into their options pricing formulas. Dealer hedging can have an outsized impact over short-term horizons. As we observed in *The Second Leg Down*, as a general principle, we would rather be a buyer than a seller of very short-dated options. Following Gopikrishnan (1999), the potential for returns in excess of 3 standard deviations is highest over horizons less than a week.

## Non-technical Summary

Investors can glean important insights from large or unusual options activity in the markets they trade. The same reasoning applies to individual stocks, indices and other asset classes, though baseline positioning might be different. When open interest is unusually high or concentrated at certain strikes, market makers have the potential to distort prices. This occurs as a natural consequence of delta hedging, rather than by design. If we know how investors are positioned on aggregate, stronger conclusions can be drawn. For example, the GEX draws on knowledge of how institutions like to use S&P 500 options. In regions where these agents are short options, market makers will be net long. Here, delta hedging by market makers will tend to compress volatility. Conversely, when investors are long options, market maker hedging can cause wild swings in prices.

## Technical Endnotes

Several details are buried in the GEX calculation, which we discuss below.

- S&P options take a variety of forms: E-mini futures options, SPX cash options and options on the SPY ETF. All of these need to be included, with the relevant multiplier adjustments. In particular, E-minis and cash SPX options have a multiplier of 50 and 100, respectively.
- Gamma ($\gamma$) can be measured relative to a one point or percentage move in the S&P 500. This can make a material difference for options on indices whose base level can vary dramatically over time, such as the VIX. While less important for the S&P 500, we assume that standard practice has been followed and gamma is based on percentage changes.

# 7

# The Elephants in the Room: Banks and the "Almighty" Central Bank

And besides all this, there was a certain lofty bearing about the Pagan … He looked like a man who had never cringed and never had a creditor.

Herman Melville, Moby Dick

## Part 1: Central Bank Policy and Forward Credit Spreads

In previous chapters, we identified danger conditions in the VIX, S&P 500 and high yield corporate bond markets, respectively. We found that, in calm market regimes, standard models understated risk in the presence of a Dominant Agent. Significantly, our analysis was validated by realized price moves that occurred shortly thereafter. During the February 2018 Volmageddon, we were able to explain the mega spike in VIX futures reasonably accurately. In the early phases of the COVID crisis, moreover, we used options market maker positioning as an explanatory variable for the extreme sawtooth-shaped price action for the S&P 500. Finally, we managed to predict the magnitude, though perhaps not the timing, of the collapse in high yield ETFs during March 2020.

In each case study, our thought process was relatively consistent and took the following form.


H. P. Krishnan and A. Bennington, *Market Tremors*, https://doi.org/10.1007/978-3-030-79253-4_7

- First, we screened for products and strategies that had grown too large for the underlying market to support. These included ETPs and listed options.
- Next, we estimated the size of a random shock that would force our Dominant Agents into the market.
- Finally, we estimated the price impact of liquidation, rebalancing or hedging by these agents.

We believe that we have made considerable progress with this approach. However, our case studies are not easily generalizable. Each study came with a high barrier to entry, requiring detailed knowledge of the relevant segment of the market. This is a practical limitation and raises an important question. Is it possible to estimate the potential impact of certain Dominant Agents in the market, in a repeatable way, *without* specialized knowledge?

Loosely speaking, we want to avoid having to build a different playbook for every potential crisis. In this chapter, we will find that, by focusing on the banking system, there are rough but repeatable things we can do. What we lose in precision, we make up for in generality. In particular, we will provide some statistical evidence of the following hypothesis: leverage has a measurable impact on equity and credit market returns over medium-term horizons.

We can summarize with two slogans. In the corporate bond markets, a large increase in liquidity (which we will define as we go on) compresses credit spreads. Moreover, for equities, leverage often trumps valuation as a predictor of forward returns.

At this point, we have to make a cautionary remark. The methods in this chapter are *not* suitable for identifying extreme event or "tail" risks. Rather, they characterize median outcomes. Central Bank policy does not deliver an ironclad guarantee that risky assets will never collapse. Our rough statistical analysis can only characterize typical outcomes. Overconfidence in the Fed's ability to support equity and credit markets can actually worsen extreme outcomes by creating a dangerous feedback loop. If investors believe that the Fed will always engage in QE whenever spreads widen and that QE will always put a floor under risky assets, complacency can set in. In turn, excessive complacency encourages even more risk taking in the short-term. The current crisis postponed, speculative risk accumulation can lead to an even greater crisis in the future.

Still, it is possible to show that sufficiently large increases in the size of the Fed's balance sheet have historically stabilized credit and duration spreads. Fed assets, along with interest rates, give a useful if low-resolution view of the availability and cost of credit, as well as the value that equities offer relative to bonds and cash.

## Raw Size of the Banking System

Many investors and market commentators take it for granted that banks (including Central Banks, such as the Fed) have a large impact on asset prices and the broader economic cycle. There is no question that leverage is intrinsic to modern western economies. In the US, for example, the collective size of commercial bank balance sheets is the same order of magnitude as GDP. It stands to rcason that, if all loans wcrc unwound, GDP would collapsc. Ncw projects and businesses generally require significant access to funds.

In this regard, banks are always mega agents in the network. We can start at the top of the food chain, again with a focus on the US. The Federal Reserve Bank system essentially acts as a bank to other banks and hence plays a critical role. However, it differs in one major respect from commercial banks: there are no hard constraints to the Fed's balance sheet. The Fed can buy Treasuries and other assets, increase its balance sheet and debit its cash balance, without having to hold any deposits. Fractional reserve requirements apply to commercial banks only. By contrast, commercial banks have to hold significant cash deposits, which offers some protection against a run on the bank. The following Fig. 7.1 tracks the US dollar value of Fed assets over time. Note that we have converted the y-axis to log units. This makes percentage (rather than absolute) changes in the balance sheet more visible over time. Even after

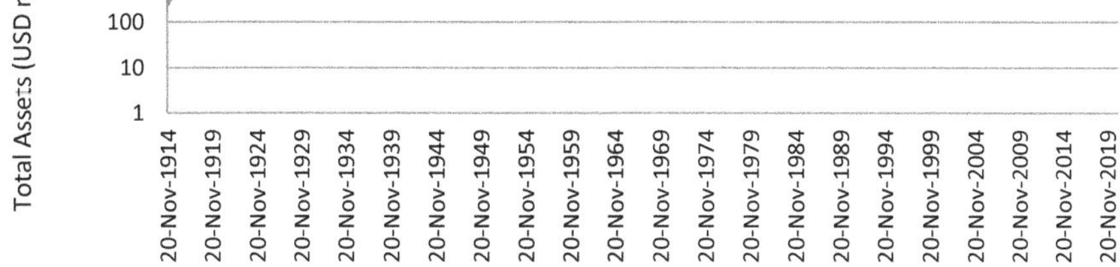


**Fig. 7.1** Fed assets since inception, using a log scale (*Source* Center for Financial Stability, FRED [St. Louis Federal Reserve Database])

log scaling, we can see two nearly vertical spikes in the Fed's balance sheet. These correspond to the massive Quantitative Easing experiments conducted in 2008 and 2020.

On both occasions, the Fed transformed itself from a large but fairly static agent into an entity that tried to dominate the financial network by acting as a buyer of last resort in the Treasury and credit markets. The Fed essentially became the world's largest distressed hedge fund, without the risk of margin calls or investor redemptions.

In a similar vein, we can track the growth of US commercial bank assets. Since there are smaller jumps and a shorter history, we have used an ordinary scale in the Fig. 7.2. Whenever Fed assets spiked, commercial banks were incentivized to lend more, based on an increase in reserves. As the Fed bought securities, banks became more solvent. Accordingly, we see a strong correlation in Fed and commercial bank assets from 2008 to the present. However, had the major banks decided not to lend based on an increase in reserves, the correlation would have been broken. Money supply may have increased, but would have been offset by stagnation in the velocity of money.

Note that this chart understates the full extent of lending in the financial system, by a wide margin. "Shadow banks", such as securities lenders and certain hedge funds, are not included. These entities account for a larger proportion of total lending than before, given tighter regulations on the traditional banking system. Even so, asset levels in the chart exceeded $20 trillion as of Q4 2019.

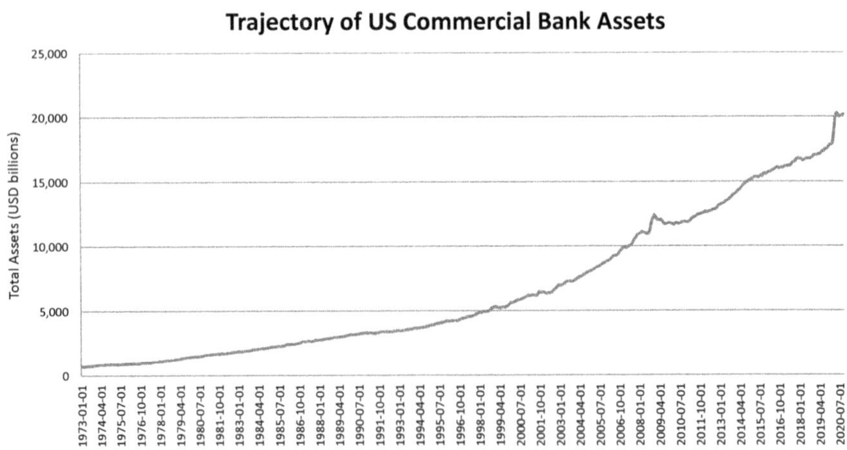


**Fig. 7.2** Jumps occur in similar locations for commercial bank assets since 2000 (*Source* FRED)

It is important to remember that every bank asset is a liability for some other agent in the network. This means that, as bank assets grow, the amount of lending in the financial system also increases. In other words, bank assets track the quantity of dollars borrowed by the real economy, namely corporations, households and the US government.

Given that banks are always large players in the market, the change or trend strength in balance sheet size over time is of interest. If we classified them based on size alone, they would always be Dominant Agents. Using the ideas formulated in Chapter 2, our indistinguishability condition would be continuously violated. No Mean Field would exist and there would be nothing to modify when there was a large-scale change in the amount of credit available in the system. However, recall that we are not applying a strict definition of indistinguishability in this book. The historical distribution of returns is only modified if large agents start to act out of proportion to their normal behavior.

When credit growth slows, companies find it increasingly difficult to raise money. Lenders become wary of default risk, requiring a higher return on capital from borrowers. This pushes credit spreads higher and typically exerts downward pressure on equities. Conversely, as additional funds flow through the banking system to real economic borrowers, two things tend to happen. Investors have more money to invest and companies have an easier time financing their debt. This creates a virtuous feedback loop where access to new lines of credit becomes easier.

## Central Bank Levers

In broad terms, Central Banks have two policy levers at their disposal. (For the sake of completeness, they can engage in second-order policy moves, such as varying the interest paid to banks for excess deposits held at the Fed.) Restricting ourselves to the main instruments of policy, the Fed can

- influence short-term interbank interest rates and
- engage in something called open market operations.

Historically, when the economy showed signs of overheating, Central Banks targeted higher short-term rates. They pulled the first lever above. This increased the cost of overnight financing for banks, creating a barrier to the flow of credit through the system. In isolation, lending became less attractive, as the spread between lending and borrowing rates decreased. Conversely, during a period of sluggish growth, the Fed pushed rates lower, incentivizing commercial banks to borrow cheaply and lend over longer horizons.

With yields close to 0%, the first lever has been more difficult to pull and perhaps is less consequential. Negative rates create dangerous incentives to agents who want to lever their portfolios to the moon. By contrast, raising rates from a 0% base by even a small amount can be destabilizing. The Fed's current lack of wiggle room is apparent in the following Fig. 7.3.

Accordingly, Central Banks have shifted their focus to changing the size and composition of their balance sheets. Open market operations involve buying and selling securities, such as Treasury bonds, from other institutions. In general, direct asset purchases are the most direct way in which the Fed can increase market liquidity. By contrast, Fed asset sales absorb excess cash from the system, reducing the amount banks can lend. Open market operations can also have an impact on the shape of the yield curve, depending on the securities that the Fed decides to buy or sell.

For simplicity, we will restrict ourselves to the US financial system for now. When the Fed buys and sells Treasuries, it changes the composition rather than quantity of assets that other banks hold. We can proceed by example. Suppose that the Fed buys $100 million of Treasury bonds from a primary dealer (i.e., a Fed nominated bank). $100 million of bonds are added to the asset side of the Fed's ledger and $100 million of cash is debited from its current account. The cash appears as a credit on the primary dealer's reserve account, held at the Fed.

At first, this liquidity/duration transformation might not seem to accomplish anything. However, for every additional $1 held in a reserve account, commercial banks can lend a *multiple* of $1 to other agents. More credit

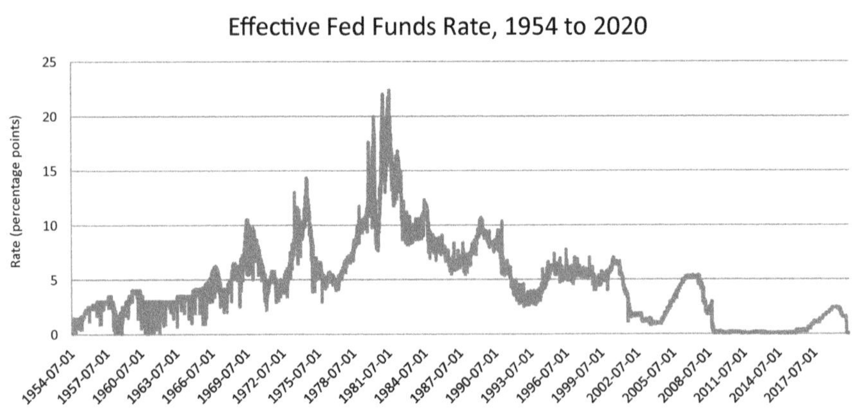


**Fig. 7.3** The discount rate lever is not particularly operational with rates near 0 (*Source* FRED)

expansion is possible. The Fed is effectively encouraging other banks to "pump" on its behalf. In general, US banks can extend $10 of credit for every $1 of reserves. Assuming that they decide to lend the entire $10, bank deposits will increase by $10, theoretically allowing other agents to lend up to $100. As the cycle continues, credit can grow geometrically in the absence of other constraints. This is the basis of fractional reserve banking, which underpins the modern, credit-fueled economy.

The Fed's swapping of cash for assets adds liquidity to the market. This brings us to a definition of "liquidity", in the context of the banking system. (Note that liquidity also refers to price impact of executing an order in the market, but we are not concerned about that specific use of the word here.) Quoting directly from the US Federal Reserve Bank's FAQs.

(https://www.federalreserve.gov/faqs/cat_21427.htm#:~:text=Liquidity%20is%20a%20measure%20of,term%20business%20and%20financial%20obligations.&text=Liquid%20assets%20are%20cash%20and,needed%20to%20meet%20financial%20obligations).

In the current context, liquidity is a measure of the cash and related assets banks have available to quickly pay bills and meet short-term business and financial obligations.

As the Fed's balance sheet increases, banks have a larger capacity to lend. This does not imply that these agents will automatically decide to do so. During high volatility "risk off" regimes, they may decide to constrain their lending activities for the time being. Unless other agents step in, the added liquidity supply will not flow through the network to investors and real economic borrowers. However, when Fed assets accelerate, capital markets usually do benefit over the medium term. Easing might operate with a lag, but it does tend to improve median outcomes.

In order to justify this claim, we need to identify times when the Fed is easing more aggressively than usual and estimate what its impact might be. The next figure shows the trend in the Fed's balance sheet from the roaring 1920s to the present (Figs. 7.4 and 7.5).

Our trend indicator tracks the 12 month rolling percentage change in Fed assets over time. We have focused on percentage rather than absolute changes to account for the fact that Fed assets have increased by several orders of magnitude over the past century.

The trend indicator is usually positive, based on the natural course of inflation and other factors. For example, the Fed has been increasing the supply of physical currency according to a predictable schedule over time. This is evident in the following Fig. 7.6. We observe a steepening trend in the wake of the Global Financial Crisis, but the path is reasonably smooth throughout

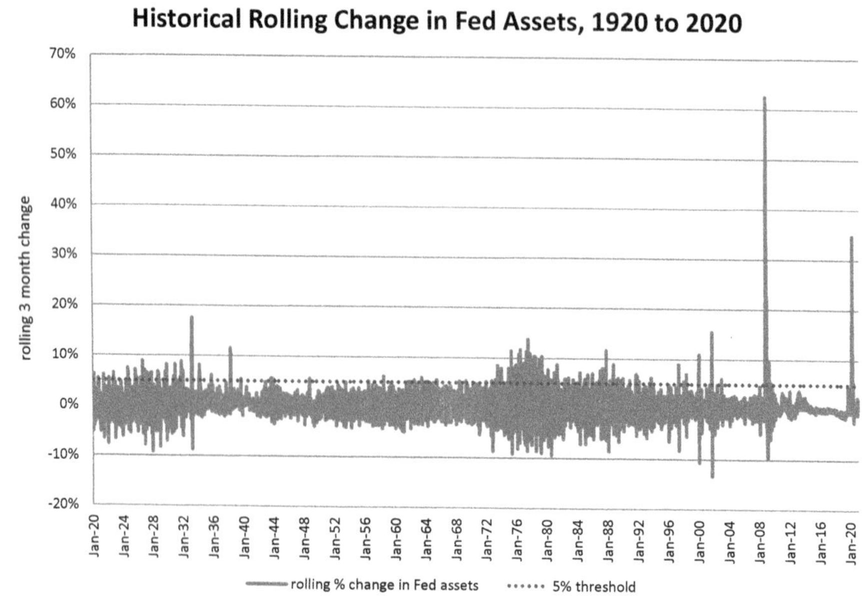


**Fig. 7.4** The Fed is always large, but becomes a Dominant Agent based on how it acts relative to the recent past (*Source* Center for Financial Stability)

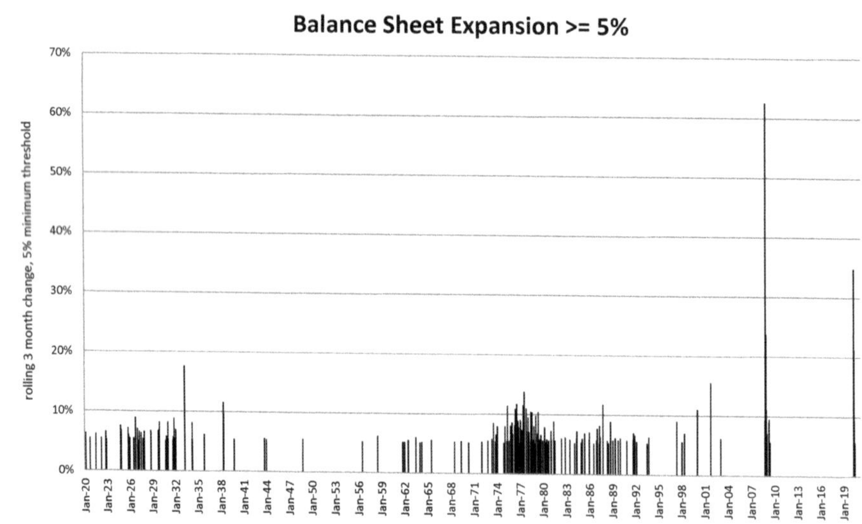


**Fig. 7.5** Times when the Fed has acted fairly strongly at the margins (*Source* Center for Financial Stability)

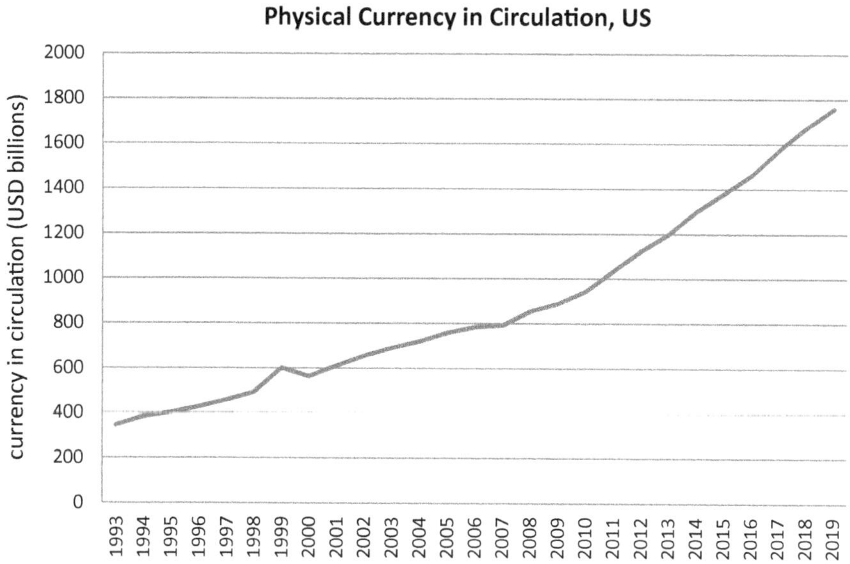


**Fig. 7.6** The amount of physical currency in circulation increases quite predictably over time (*Source* FRED)

Referring back to Fig. 7.5, we can identify periods of sharp balance sheet expansion, where the trend in Fed assets is above some threshold. In the next graph, we have isolated times where the trend was above +10%. For each a bubble or spike in the graph, the Fed was expanding at a significantly higher rate than usual. To varying degrees, it was engaging in something we might call "QE" today. As a point of reference, the average 12 month rolling change in Fed assets was +1.80% from 1920 to February 2021.

As we can see in the Fig. 7.7, the Fed has increased its willingness to experiment since 2008. As of this writing, the genie has been out of the bottle for well over a decade. However, we do observe material increases in balance sheet trend on several occasions. The 1930s (Great Depression era), 1970s (Stagflation era) and the aftermath of the.com bubble are notable. This is significant, as it allows us to analyze the impact of unconventional Fed policy in a wider number of instances. To repeat, the graph above gives us a larger number of instances where we can analyze the impact of above trend Fed asset growth. In each case of quantitative easing ("QE"), they paid for securities by adding the appropriate amount to bank reserve accounts held at the Fed. This is effectively money printing, as the cash required to pay for the securities did not exist before the Fed decided to add them to its balance sheet.

To summarize, QE has three main objectives.

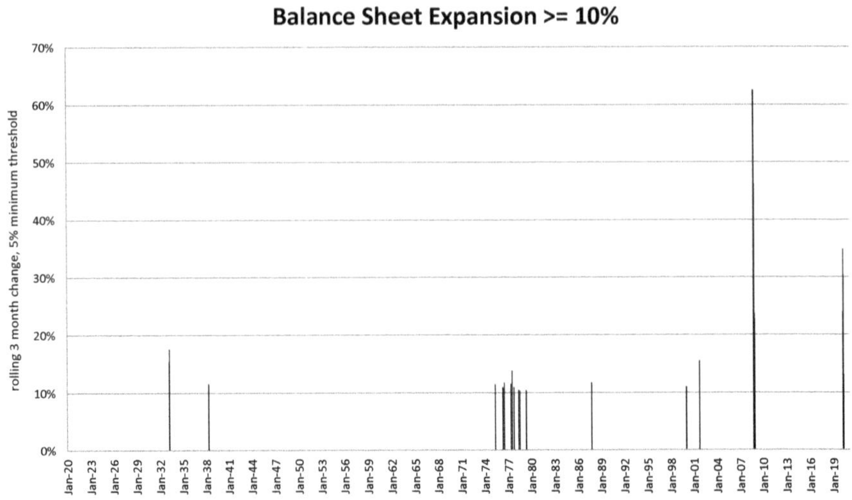


**Fig. 7.7** Times when the Fed has acted very strongly at the margins

- By swapping reserves for securities, it improves bank solvency and hence the ability of banks to lend to other financial agents. However, balance sheet expansion does not automatically increase the velocity of money. If banks decide that the risk-adjusted return on new loans is too low, they may decide to sit on their hands.
- QE can also support asset prices during a credit event, by creating artificial demand for distressed securities until market conditions stabilize. This was the case in 2008, when the Fed hoovered up mortgage-linked debt and in 2020, when it bought a range of corporate bond ETFs.
- Finally, QE can keep Treasury rates low when the government wants to borrow in scale. This reduces debt financing costs for the government (though, of course, financing costs are not a direct problem for governments that print their own currency). Recall that borrowing automatically translates to an increase in GDP once the money is spent.

It is important to realize that, while distressed asset purchases can act as a "get out of jail free" card, they impede the normal functioning of financial markets in the long term. In particular, QE can cause excessive risk-taking, misallocation of capital to non-productive activities and potentially, uncontrolled inflation. We need only look at post-World War I Germany and 2007–2009 Zimbabwe for examples of hyperinflation.

At this point, we will not engage in a long discourse about the potential unintended consequences of QE. This is a highly contentious topic, with advocates of Modern Monetary Theory and Austrian Economics generally on the opposite ends of the spectrum. According to Central Bank orthodoxy, the Fed has the power to dampen oscillations in the credit cycle by controlling the cost and quantity of funds over time. By contrast, agents who think of the network as a complex non-linear system do not believe that the economy can be optimized, nor that Central Bank levers generate predictable results. On the contrary, they worry that Central Bank intervention can be highly destabilizing in the long term.

Emerging from this rabbit hole, we want to see how QE and changes to the Fed Funds rate impact corporate credit spreads after a risk event. Our working hypothesis is that, when Central Banks act as Dominant Agents, they have the power to improve median outcomes in the credit markets. We will test this hypothesis in the next section.

## The Fed's Historical Reaction Function

Our first study is based upon monthly data from July 1954 to December 2020. (Our credit spread data only goes back to 1954. This effectively defines the starting point of our window.) Here, we want to address the following question: How have rate cuts and QE affected credit spreads historically? In particular, we want to see whether Fed policy was effective after an initial widening in credit spreads. We took the series of steps below.

- First, we created a trend indicator for the Moody's BAA corporate spread over Treasuries. Recall that this spread measures the cost of debt financing for low investment grade companies relative to a piece of US government debt with equivalent duration.
- Our trend indicator took the difference between the spread at the end of a given month and the average spread over the trailing 12 months.
- When the trend indicator was more than 1 standard deviation above its historical average, we flagged this as a credit event. A 1 standard deviation move corresponded to a widening of around 0.41% in a given month, relative to the average over the past 12 months.
- We then gave the Fed 3 months to act. If it cut rates by at least 1% over the 3 month action window, we classified this as a rate cut event. Similarly, if the Fed increased its balance sheet by at least 5% over the window, we categorized its actions as a QE event. (Note that these round number thresholds are somewhat arbitrary. However, we emphasize that they were not optimized in any way.)

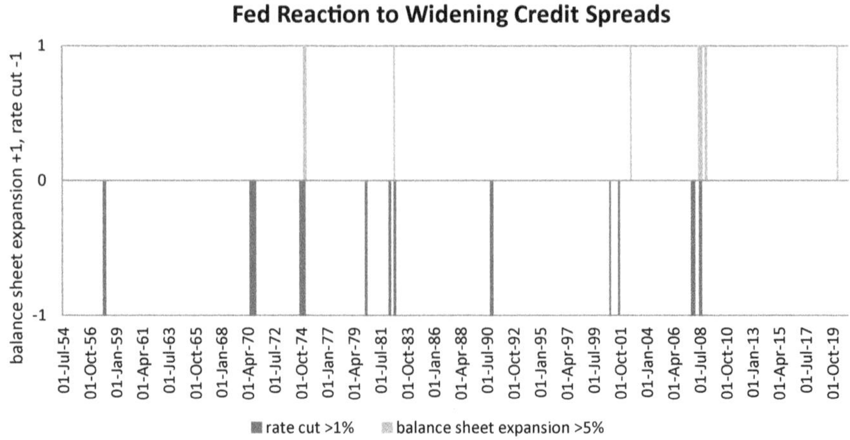


**Fig. 7.8** The Fed's historical response to widening BAA credit spreads (*Source* FRED)

- Finally, we tabulated the 6 month forward change in BAA spreads in each case, i.e., when the Fed cut rates, engaged in QE or did nothing.

In the Fig. 7.8, we can see what how the Fed historically reacted to widening BAA spreads, when it did react, according to our 1 and 5% thresholds above.

Over the 1954–2020 window, the trend in BAA spreads was at least 1 standard deviation above normal in 92 months. Over the subsequent 3 months, the Fed cut rates by at least 1% on 33 occasions, engaged in balance sheet expansion of at least 5% in 12 and did nothing on 53. (Note that the Fed both cut rates *and* increased its balance sheet 6 times in response to a credit event.)

## Typical Impact of Rate Cuts and QE

Given the Fed's variable response function, we want to see what actually happened to credit spreads over the next 6 months. 6 months is a reasonable amount of time for funds to flow through the system to real economic borrowers in the private sector.

The next Fig. 7.9 tabulates the historical outcomes of the Fed's action and inaction, respectively.

On average, credit spreads declined more sharply when the Fed did almost nothing, compared with a rate cut of at least 1%. This implies that the natural

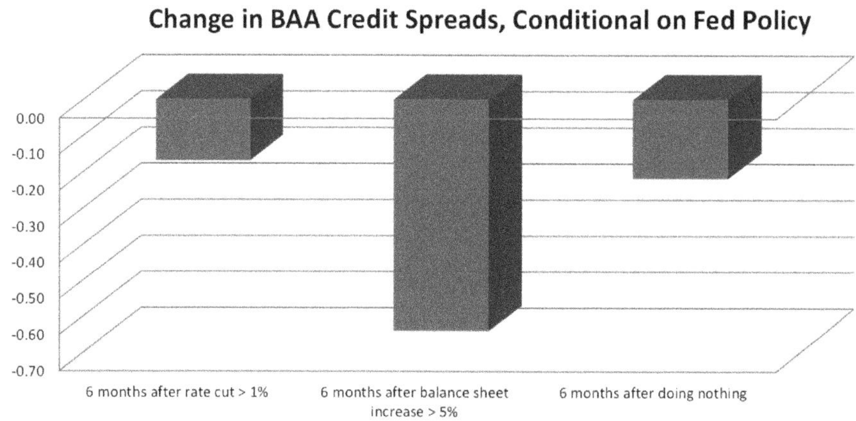


**Fig. 7.9** 6 month forward impact of Fed policy on BAA credit spreads (*Source* FRED)

force of mean reversion in spreads was stronger than the impact of orchestrated lower interbank lending rates. (We accept that, on average, the Fed has managed to engineer a steeper yield curve through its various rate cuts. This has historically increased profitability for the commercial banking system.) We might draw the conclusion that no action was superior to a sharp rate cut in stabilizing the credit markets.

We cannot completely discount the possibility that the Fed, in its infinite wisdom, only acted when credit spreads were unlikely to normalize. Otherwise, they let the system self-correct. It may be that other economic indicators gave them a much better read on market stability than risk spreads alone. Still, the figure above does not offer a ringing endorsement for rate cuts as a stabilizing market force.

Using the bar chart as a guide, we observe that QE did work when the Fed decided to unleash it. The middle bar shows an average decrease of 64 basis points in BAA when Fed assets grew by at least 5% in the previous 3 months. This compares with a 22 basis point decline when the Fed did nothing and a 17 basis point decline after a cumulative 1% rate cut.

## Multi-factor Regression Results

While provocative, the study above is not sufficient to conclude that QE always works. We can gain more insight into the problem by regressing 6 month forward changes in BAA spreads against a set of relevant factors.

**Table 7.1** Multivariate regression results

| | Coeffixients | Standard error | *T* Statistic |
|---|---|---|---|
| Intercept | 0.12 | 0.01 | 8.80 |
| Lagged spread | −0.16 | 0.04 | −4.16 |
| Fed assets, % change | −1.21 | 0.05 | −22.05 |
| Fed funds rate trend | −0.09 | 0.02 | −5.68 |

- We used weekly data from 1986 to 2020 in our regression, based on available credit spread history (at weekly frequency) from the FRED website.
- Our input variables were: the 6 month trailing change in BAA spreads, the 12 month percentage change in Fed assets and the Fed Funds rate, relative to its 12 month moving average. The last variable is a trend indicator for Fed Funds, as in the previous section.
- These variables were used to predict the 6 month forward change in BAA spreads.

The Table 7.1 summarizes the results of our regression.

As in the previous section, Fed balance sheet expansion had the greatest impact on changes in forward BAA spreads, with a hefty *T* Statistic of around – 22. Since our regression is based on overlapping data, we accept that this statistic is upwardly biased. Still, in relative terms, Fed assets have significantly more explanatory power than trailing BAA spreads and the recent trend in rates.

The *R* squared of our regression is 0.22, which is significant. In the next figure, we can see how our predicted changes in forward BAA spreads compare to the realized ones, collected in sample (Fig. 7.10).

The regression line is sensitive to a relatively small collection of points at the extreme of the lower left quadrant. BAA credit spreads decreased sharply from a high level in the aftermath of the COVID-19 and Great Financial Crisis. On both occasions, the Fed expanded its balance sheet by an unprecedented amount.

It is true that, in 57 different weeks, both the predicted and realized 6 month forward change in BAA spreads was less than 0.5. On the surface, it might seem as though there is enough data to draw strong conclusions about the impact of QE. However, all of these weeks clustered within one of two ranges: November 2008–July 2009 and April 2020–August 2020. The 57 weeks have considerable overlap. What we are really seeing is that the Fed went two for two in its radical experiments with monetary policy. This does

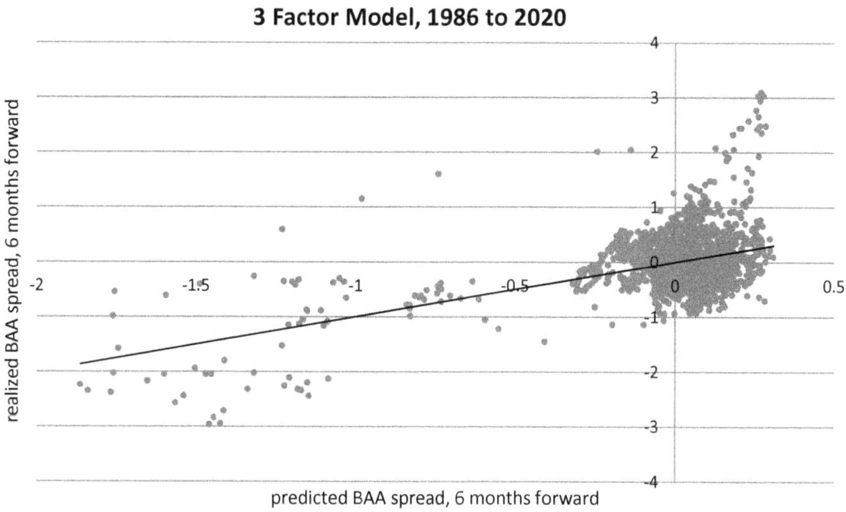


**Fig. 7.10** Quality of 3-factor forecasting model (*Source* FRED)

not constitute strong evidence that QE will always be successful in stabilizing the credit markets.

Indeed, if we focus only on the interval from 1986 to 2006, the Fed impact function looks starkly different. This leaves out the intervals that dominate our regression from 1986 to 2020, without having to deal with any discontinuities in the data. We wind up with markedly different regression coefficients and predictive power (Table 7.2).

Here, the lagged spread variable has *more* predictive power than Fed balance sheet expansion or variations in the Fed Funds rate. We observe that this variable does not have any direct dependence on Central Bank activity. The regression coefficient for the lagged spread is negative, for a simple reason: credit spreads have a natural tendency to mean revert over time.

In other words, until the Great Financial Crisis, mean reversion was a more powerful force than Fed policy. We remark that conditions were not always calm from 1986 to 2006. There were several bouts of extreme volatility in this interval, including Black Monday in 1987, the Asian Financial Crisis in

**Table 7.2** Regression results before the great financial crisis

| | Coefficients | Standard error | *T* stat |
|---|---|---|---|
| Intercept | 0.04 | 0.03 | 1.64 |
| Lagged spread | −0.36 | 0.05 | −6.85 |
| Balance sheet% change | −1.11 | 0.35 | −3.14 |
| Fed funds rate change | 0.03 | 0.01 | 2.60 |

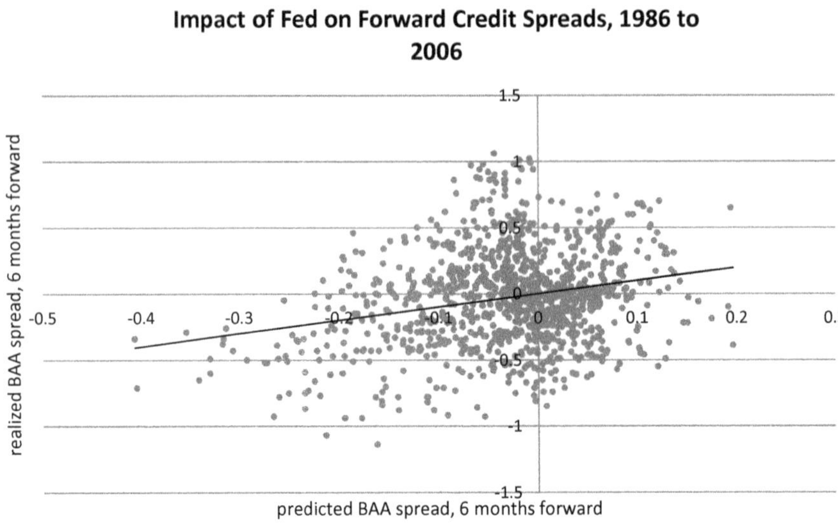


**Fig. 7.11** Impact of Fed policy is cloudy in advance of the GFC (*Source* FRED)

1997, and the collapse of the tech bubble from 2000 to 2002. The following Fig. 7.11 restricts our 3-factor regression to the period from 1986 to 2006. Without many extreme values for the regression to latch onto, we wind up with a relatively modest *R* squared of 0.06.

In conclusion, we can say that extreme QE has worked on the two occasions that the Fed has tried it. However, we have insufficient evidence to draw any strong conclusions about the *range* of possible outcomes when the Fed increases its balance sheet aggressively. In the next section, we will turn our attention from credit to the US stock market. Readers should not come away thinking that the Fed put offers an ironclad guarantee that US credit and equity markets will never collapse.

In the next section, we will turn our attention from the Fed to the banking system at large. Our goal is to establish a connection between the quantity of debt in the network and long-term equity returns.

## Part 2: The Single Greatest Predictor of Long-Term Equity Returns

The material in Part 2 draws heavily from.
http://www.philosophicaleconomics.com/2013/12/the-single-greatest-predictor-of-future-stock-market-returns/

To our knowledge, this article was the first to establish a statistical link between Central Bank QE and forward equity returns. We should also emphasize that its aims were more general than that.

We have several objectives here.

- First, we will describe the mechanism that converts an increase in the supply of credit into higher long-term equity returns.
- In other words, indebtedness is actually bullish for equities, at least in the expansionary phases of the credit cycle. In general, risky assets benefit as funds flow through the banking system.
- Again following the article above, we then demonstrate that equity ownership (measured in dollars) relative to bonds and deposits is a better indicator of long-term forward S&P 500 returns than a standard metric such as the Shiller CAPE index.
- Moreover, the degree of outperformance increases as we shrink the forecast horizon. Over a 2 year horizon, the predictive power of equity ownership is roughly twice as large as Shiller CAPE.
- Finally, we will discuss how relative equity ownership accounts for quantitative easing ("QE") in a way that balance sheet ratios cannot. By comparing the supply of debt and equities over time, it is supportive of high valuations in periods of rapid credit expansion.

Our methodology will involve repeating the study in the paper above, with minor modifications. First, we will update the results to December 2020, using nearly identical inputs. Since 10 years is an unacceptably long horizon for many investors, we will also examine the quality of forecasts over shorter horizons. In Mean Field terms, we can think of the problem as one where banks modify the distribution of equity returns as they change the cost and availability of funds. After periods of unusual credit expansion, equities tend to outperform. Conversely, when a large number of agents settle their debt or do not roll it over, forward equity returns typically decline.

The "Fed model", which compares Treasury yields to the average dividend yield on the S&P 500, encapsulates a similar idea. Stocks are valued on a cross-asset class basis, rather than simply relative to the past. In this paradigm, equities become more attractive as yields decline. On a relative basis, the income component of S&P returns is higher than it was before. By contrast, after a sustained rise in yields, the potential upside in Treasuries eventually lures investors back into bonds.

However, the Fed model does not solve the valuation problem entirely. It is not able to cope with Central Bank balance sheet expansion or an increase in the flow of funds through the network. The Fed model restricts itself to the cost of funds, with no direct reference to the quantity of credit available.

## Institutional Strategic Asset Allocation Templates

In order to make sense of stock and bond valuations, we first need to understand how institutions typically structure their portfolios. While banks are the Dominant Agents on the supply side, sovereign wealth funds, endowments, pension funds and insurance companies account for the majority of demand. They are the primary consumers of products created by the financial system. Many of these entities rely upon Strategic Asset Allocation ("SAA") templates when they allocate capital to various sectors, countries and asset classes. These templates also serve as a roadmap for many retail and high net worth accounts managed by financial advisors.

SAA weights are typically based on the long-term expected returns (on a risk-adjusted basis) for various asset classes. An SAA template neatly breaks the problem of building a multi-asset class portfolio into distinct parts, as in the following Fig. 7.12.

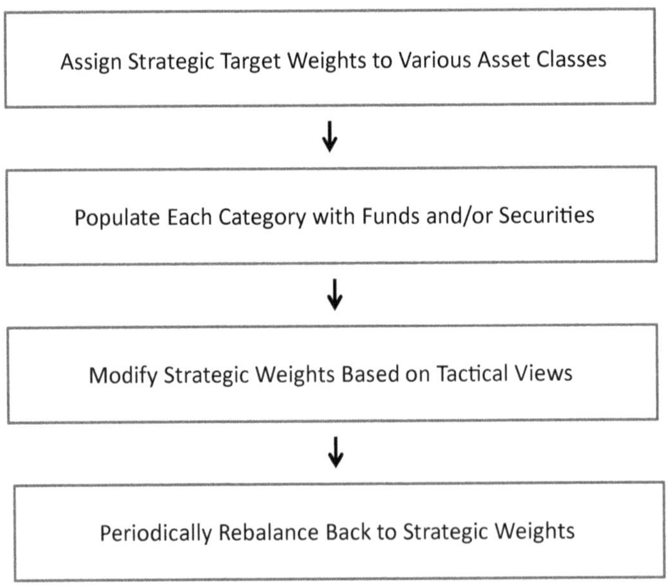


**Fig. 7.12** Components of the investment problem in a Strategic Asset Allocation framework

Dividing the problem in this way leaves some alpha on the table. Risk-adjusted returns are lower than they might be with a coordinated investment strategy. Vital synergies between top-down and bottom-up portfolio construction are lost. Fund managers who are not restricted to a single asset class have a larger opportunity set to work with. They do not have to invest with one hand tied behind their backs. This is one reason why global macro-funds (i.e., funds that have the flexibility to allocate freely across asset classes) have been able to attract some of the best money management talent over the years.

Still, SAA templates can be advantageous from an operational standpoint. When separate teams are responsible for portfolio construction, manager selection and formulating tactical views, performance evaluation is easier. In addition, parts of the investment process can be outsourced to external asset managers.

SAA weights represent medium to long-term target allocations to stocks, bonds and various other asset classes. A typical horizon might be 3–5 years. An investment committee can veer away from these weights over shorter horizons, based on tactical views or risk considerations. However, the expectation is that they will eventually rebalance back to the weights specified in the SAA template. The next question is how SAA weights are decided. Typically, they are based on longer-term return projections for various asset classes, subject to risk tolerance and other constraints. These projections might be a function of current valuations or a simple extrapolation from the past. More cynically, SAA weights are also a product of groupthink. This is understandable, as investment committees seek validation for the decisions they make. They rely on published studies to defend their process and do not want performance to diverge too widely from their peers, especially on the downside.

A simplified template might target 50% in equities, 30% in bonds, 10% in real assets and 10% in alternative investments, such as hedge funds and private equity. Stocks and private equity are included to meet longer-term return targets, hedge funds for diversification and bonds for income generation, duration management and risk mitigation. (We will ignore the relatively recent and perverse phenomenon of investing in stocks for income and bonds for capital appreciation.) Cash and short duration government bonds, such as T-bills, fall in the capital preservation category, while longer maturity and corporate bonds typically offer more income in exchange for higher risk. Restricting ourselves to stocks and bonds and industry SAA standard allocates 60% of capital to equities and 40% to bonds. This is known as a "60/40" portfolio and is dictated more by convention than its real performance characteristics. Note that other schemes, such as equal weighting, are also common. Risk parity portfolios, which allocate to stocks and bonds based on their historical volatility, assign a higher relative weight to bonds. These have gained quite a bit of traction in the industry. They are controversial from the standpoint of market stability, given that equities have to be sold after a spike in volatility. A dangerous feedback loop can arise, with strategies that target a fixed level of risk amplifying the size of market sell offs. However, we will not focus on risk parity for now, as it distracts from the main narrative thread in this section.

Even in the absence of tactical views, SAA requires periodic rebalancing. For example, suppose that equities outperform bonds over some time period and issuance remains fixed. Then, in dollar terms, their weight will drift above 60%. An allocator with a 60/40 mandate will eventually have to sell stocks and invest the proceeds back into bonds to re-establish the target allocation. This should exert downward pressure on stock returns, while supporting bond returns.

Collectively, there is a set of weights representing the composite target allocation to stocks and bonds. This is an asset-weighted average across all agents who rely on SAA. Admittedly, we do not know what these combined SAA weights are. Still, we can say the following: if the weights move by a large amount, allocators will eventually rebalance back to the target. This induces some mean reversion in the dollar value of stocks and bonds available to investors. Significantly, mean reversion in supply does not force the spread in stock and bond performance to be mean reverting. A simple example serves to illustrate this point. If the face value of all marketable bonds doubles over some period, say, bond prices do not need to go up for the dollar supply of bonds to increase. In this scenario, stock returns can outpace bonds for quite some time without violating the market's aggregate SAA portfolio. We will investigate this crucial idea in the next section.

## Bond Supply Varies as a Function of Yields and Issuance

Equity and bond supply have very different characteristics.

In the equity markets, new issuance tends to be a very small percentage of total market capitalization. This is apparent in the next Fig. 7.13. We can see that rolling 1 year issuance ranges from roughly −0.65 to 0%. Over the entire historical data set, share buybacks actually outpace share dilution. In other words, net supply (measured in number of shares) has reliably contracted, though at a glacial rate.

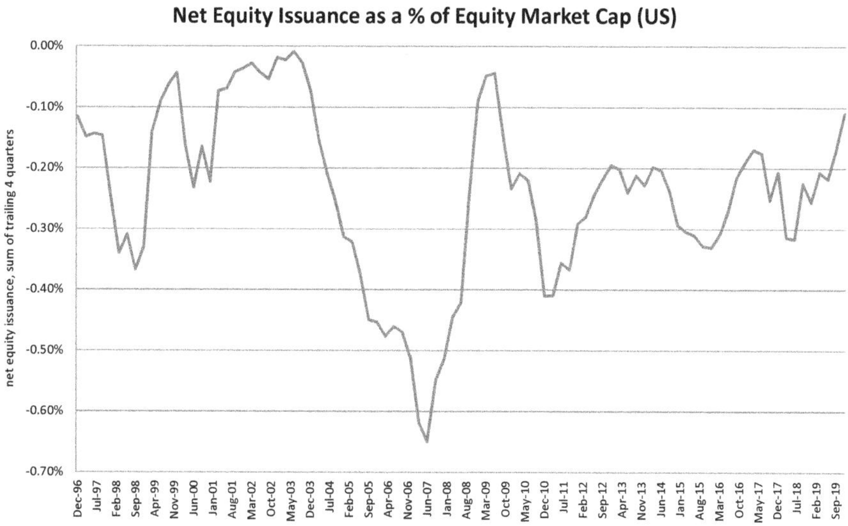


**Fig. 7.13** The dollar quantity of equities has not been very sensitive to new issuance (*Source* FRED)

Stickiness in the number of shares available has an important implication for allocators. In particular, the dollar supply of equities is largely dependent on *performance*. When the broad equity market is trending higher, supply increases. Stock market capitalization goes up, without an attendant increase in the number of shares available. Conversely, during a bear market, the total dollar value of equities declines. We can conclude that if the supply of bonds remained constant, allocators would have to buy equity dips and sell rallies to stay close to their SAA targets. Relative stock and bond performance would be mean reverting.

However, bond supply is categorically NOT constant. It tends to increase steadily over time, with larger increases during expansionary phases of the credit cycle. As a rule, the quantity of deposits and securitized bonds goes up from one year to year. Modern economies have simply become more indebted as time passes.

In this context, it is important to understand that every $1 of liabilities for one agent corresponds to $1 of bonds or deposits for some other agent. (Note that we are not distinguishing between physical cash and money in a bank account for the purposes of this discussion.) If a customer borrows $10,000 to buy something, the funds will appear as a $10,000 deposit in the seller's account at the point of payment.

In credit-fueled modern economies, total liabilities and hence the sum of bonds and deposits are nearly always going up. The following Fig. 7.14 shows

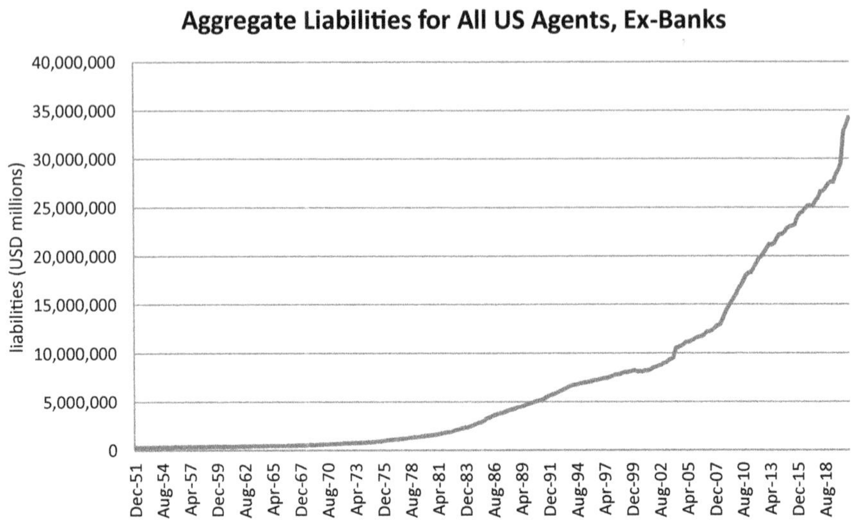


**Fig. 7.14** The US credit supercycle since 1951 (*Source* FRED)

an inexorable increase in credit supply over time. Note that this graph does not give a complete description of leverage within the financial network. The true exposure to equity ratio is much higher. For example, many institutions include swaps, forwards and futures in their portfolio. These contracts can have notional values that are several orders of magnitude higher than the initial margin required to support them. However, aggregate liabilities accurately reflect the supply of physical bonds and cash that investors can allocate to

The steady increase in bond and deposit supply has an important implication. For equities to keep up with bonds and cash as a percentage of the US asset pie, they need to increase in *price* over time. Since net equity share issuance is mildly negative, that is the only reliable path to growth in dollar terms.

A vital insight in the Philosophical Economist article is that increasing bond supply offers an alternative explanation for the equity risk premium. Equities do not have a higher expected return than bonds simply because they are relatively risky, offering fewer protections to investors. The capital structure argument is only part of the story. Rather, large institutions bid up the prices of stocks to maintain their SAA weights over time, given an increase in the available supply of bonds. The cult of equities is a function of rebalancing between stocks and bonds. Interestingly, most agents are probably unaware that they are the source of the equity risk premium.

It may be that valuation is merely a secondary concern to target positioning. Suppose that every institution targeted a 60%/40% allocation to stocks and bonds and net bond issuance were 10% in a given year. Then, equities would have to return +10% for the 60/40 allocation to be preserved. This operates under the conservative assumption that bonds were flat for the year.

In the next section, we will apply the simple accounting argument that every liability is someone else's asset when tracking bond supply over time.

## Estimating the Quantity of (Bonds + Cash) Over Time

At first glance, tracking the supply of bonds and deposits would seem to be an arduous task. The brute force approach involves tracking every new bond issue, pricing every outstanding issue, adjusting for bonds that have recently matured and adding some broad measure of money supply. Thankfully, so long as we do not distinguish between securitized debt and deposits, we can indirectly estimate the dollar supply of bonds and cash in the financial network. This requires an understanding of how funds flow through the network, with banks acting as crucial intermediaries when they add to the amount of credit in the system. Once again, the basic idea is developed in the Philosophical Economist article referenced above.

Banks act as intermediaries in the loan markets, issuing new loans and changing the mix of assets held by investors. They have a vital impact on the amount of credit available. However, the composition of their balance sheets does not have much effect on the total quantity of bonds and cash in the system. For example, suppose that a bank has bought $10,000,000 of bonds. From an accounting standpoint, it has taken $10,000,000 of assets out of the market and replaced them with $10,000,000 of cash deposits. The total dollar supply of cash and bonds owned by real money investors remains constant.

The real economic borrowers in the financial network are households, non-financial companies and the domestic government. When a company wants to borrow money, it can either source a loan from a bank or issue some bonds. In the second case, investment banks are typically involved in the debt offering. Borrowing acts a source of funds, increasing the company's ability to invest in new projects or in the capital markets. As we have already stated, every $1 of borrowed money appears as $1 of assets on another agent's account. For example, a loan used to pay for raw materials becomes a deposit on the commodity producer's checking account at the time of payment. Similarly, buyers of a bond IPO receive an asset in exchange for cash.

Households are also real economic borrowers, but differ from non-financial corporations in an important way. They can take out loans, but do not have the ability to issue bonds to finance their activities. In this respect, governments are at the other end of the spectrum. A country that issues its own currency will generally issue various forms of debt, but does not really have to do so. Debt issuance at specific maturities is a form of yield curve control. Treasury issuance also plays a major role as collateral in the global banking system. Given that the major currencies are currently not backed by gold, Treasury departments can print as much money as required to finance their activities. Strictly speaking, local currency debt can never default. However, uncontrolled printing can lead to uncontrolled inflation and asset bubbles, where money flows into highly speculative and non-productive areas of the economy. It can also lead to a run on the currency, severely compromising a country's position in the global economy.

To repeat, the dollar quantity of liabilities equals the dollar quantity of bonds and deposits held by households, non-financial corporations and the government. The equivalence between liabilities and the supply of bonds and deposits has important practical consequences. Once we know the total amount of borrowed money in the system, we also know the amount of bonds and deposits that real money investors hold. Non-financial liability data is readily available from the FRED (Federal Reserve Bank of St. Louis) database. This relieves us from the burden of having to monitor new issuance and deposits over time. We emphasize that bank liabilities should not be included in this calculation. Banks certainly do buy and sell assets to finance their activities. However, their primary function is to match borrowers and savers, while capturing a spread.

In their trading activities, banks are transformers, turning bonds to cash or vice versa, without changing the sum of bonds and cash in the system. Restricting to non-financial liabilities avoids double counting. Credit grows through bond issuance or the extension of new loans, rather than open market operations. When the Fed purchases assets, commercial bank balance sheets do not immediately increase. Banks simply wind up with higher reserve balances, allowing them to lend more if they choose to do so. Other transactions cancel out at the network level. If one agent decides to withdraw money from a checking account and buy something, the deposit simply transfers from one beneficial owner to another. There is no change in aggregate deposits.

Banks occasionally do issue bonds to finance acquisitions of other banks. Again, this does not constitute new credit creation, but swaps cash for bonds in the hands of investors. The average duration of investor portfolios has increased, without any change to the quantity of bonds and deposits held.

Since the Fed does not have fractional reserve constraints, there are no hard limits on the size of its balance sheet. This is a topic of great discussion nowadays. When the government issues Treasuries to fund its various activities, the Fed can buy them by simply changing a few entries in its accounts. Cash is passed to the Treasury in exchange for government bonds. The Fed's balance sheet might have grown, but assets still match liabilities. They functionally have to.

## Specifying the Equity Supply Indicator Variable

Calculating the dollar supply of US equities does not require any fancy contortions. We can simply track the market capitalization of the broad US equity market over time. While a broad index, such as the Wilshire 5000, will do, the FRED database provides this information directly. In particular, the unwieldy handle "BOGZ1LM893064105Q" measures the dollar value of all US corporate equities, at quarterly frequency.

Meanwhile, "DNSLAL" estimates the total dollar level of domestic liabilities, across all non-financial sectors. It is the sum of nominal government, state/municipal, corporate and household liabilities and released in quarterly intervals. Based on the equivalence between liabilities, bonds and deposits, DNSLAL indirectly tracks the total quantity of bonds and deposits available to investors.

We now have access to all the terms necessary to define our equity supply indicator variable. Namely, we can track the dollar quantity of equities relative to the dollar quantity of equities, bonds and deposits over time. $\frac{\$\ supply\ of\ US\ equities}{\$\ supply\ of\ US\ equities,\ bonds\ and\ deposits}$ is the variable we will use to predict forward equity returns. This ratio restricts the Strategic Asset Allocation decision to a choice between stocks, bonds and cash, but turns out to be surprisingly effective.

Based on the formula, equity supply has to be bounded between 0 and 100%. The long-term average turns out to be around 50%, as we can see in the following Fig. 7.15. The average dollar allocation of end investors to stocks has been roughly equal to the average allocation to bonds and deposits. This is not quite a 60/40 split and hinges on the fact that certain pensions and other liability-driven strategies are required to hold a large percentage of

**Fig. 7.15** The historical dollar supply of equities relative to (equities + bonds + cash) (*Source* FRED)

bonds. As we will see, equity ownership above 60% has historically signaled danger ahead.

Stocks have historically been expensive when the indicator approaches 60%, for the following mechanical reason. When relative equity supply is high, many agents have to sell stocks to meet their SAA objectives. This adds to their cash balances, which can then be deployed into bonds. The selling pressure associated with rebalancing has a negative impact on equity returns until aggregate target weights are hit. Conversely, when equity supply is low (e.g., during a period of credit expansion), investors need to bid up the prices of stocks until they reach their SAA target weights. It is important to understand that this phenomenon has no direct dependence upon typical equity valuation metrics, such as price to earnings or price to book value.

## Empirical Results

Now that we have constructed our equity supply indicator, we need to put it to the test. How well does it predict forward US equity returns, compared with standard metrics? For the purposes of illustration, our equity benchmark will be the S&P 500. The S&P 500 has several desirable characteristics, namely breadth, a long history and mass recognition. The following Fig. 7.16 relates our supply variable to 10 year forward returns for the S&P 500. We observe that 10–12 years is a standard forecast horizon for equity valuation indicators, such as those proposed by Hussman (2019).

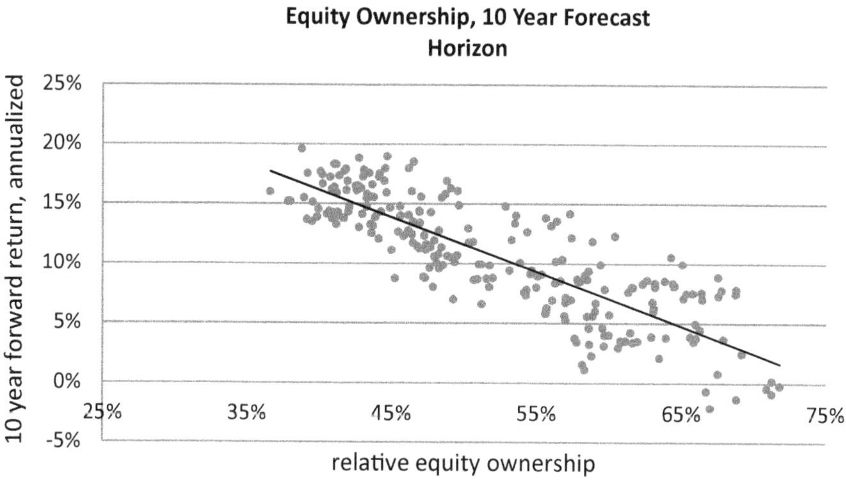


**Fig. 7.16** Equity supply forecasting results, 10 year forward horizon (*Source* FRED)

The results are encouraging. Using quarterly data from 1951 to 2020, we wind up with an R-squared of nearly 0.72. Since our forecast horizon is 10 years in this example, our supply indicator only extends to 2010. As we have already stated, equity supply does not incorporate any information about corporate earnings, sales, revenues or book value. Balance sheet ratios for individual companies do not play a direct role.

It turns out that equity supply is simpler and yet more powerful than the ratios typically used by financial analysts. By comparison, the next chart uses the widely quoted Shiller CAPE ratio to forecast 10 year S&P 500 forward returns. CAPE is essentially a smoothed version of the standard price-to-earnings ratio, using a trailing 10 year average of inflation-adjusted earnings in the denominator (Fig. 7.17).

Over the same historical window, Shiller CAPE generates an R-squared of around 0.66. Succinctly, equity supply trumps price to earnings over long range horizons. This is true at least for the widely quoted US equity markets.

When we shrink the forecast window to 5 years, the difference in predictive power is even more glaring. In particular, relative equity supply retains 90% of its signal, with an R-squared of around 0.63 from 1986 to the present. CAPE still acts as a decent signal. However, it suffers a larger drop in performance, with an R-squared of 0.41. This is evident from the following two Figs. 7.18 and 7.19.

In some sense, the difference in 2 year forecasts is even more revealing. Significantly, there is less overlap in 2 year forward S&P returns from one quarter to the next. There are effectively more degrees of freedom in our

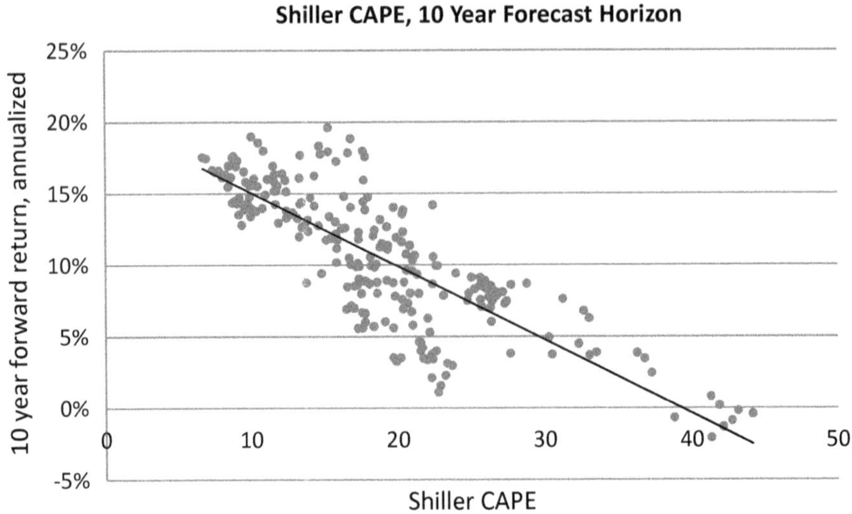


**Fig. 7.17** Shiller CAPE forecasting results, 10 year forward horizon (*Source* Online Data, Robert Shiller [http://www.econ.yale.edu/~shiller/data.htm])

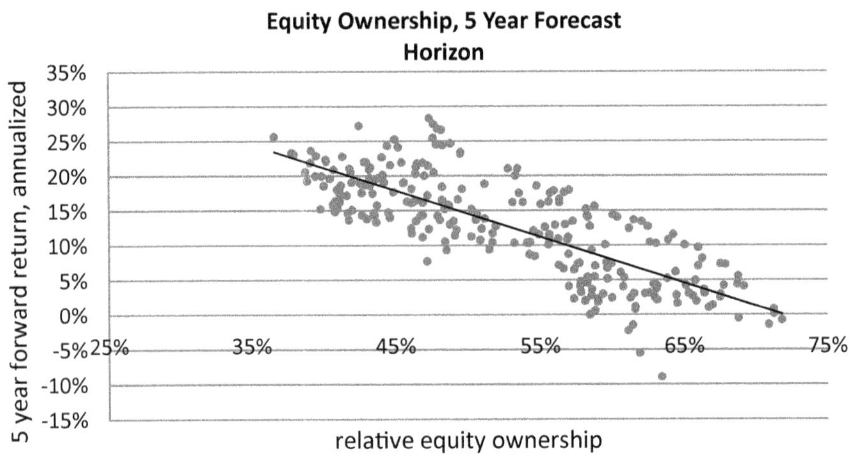


**Fig. 7.18** Equity supply forecasting results, 5 year forward horizon (*Source* FRED)

regression, improving the quality of our statistical results. Here, equity ownership has an R-squared of 0.28, nearly twice as large as CAPE. As before, the following scatter plots tell the story (Figs. 7.20 and 7.21).

We emphasize that Shiller CAPE has historically outperformed other fundamental forecasting variables, such as nominal price to earnings ratios.

In summary, relative equity ownership has outperformed CAPE over 2, 5 and 10 year horizons, with the largest relative pickup over a 2 year forward

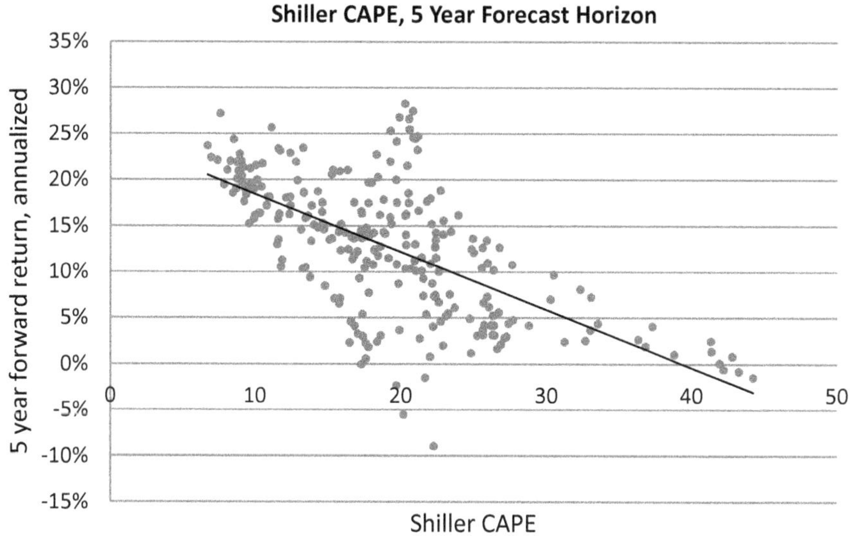


**Fig. 7.19** Relative deterioration in the power of Shiller CAPE, 5 year forecast horizon (*Source* Online Data, Robert Shiller [http://www.econ.yale.edu/~shiller/data.htm])

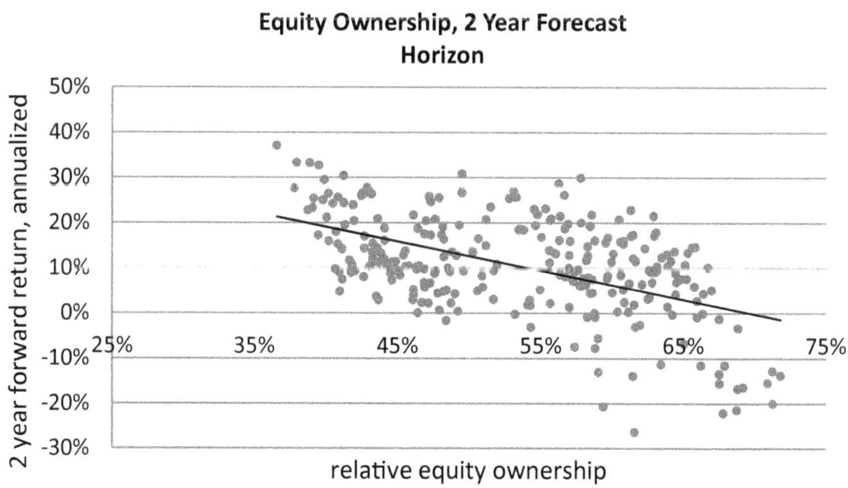


**Fig. 7.20** Equity supply indicator results, 2 year forecast horizon (*Source* FRED)

horizon. As we will see in the next section, it also has the unique capacity to make sense of valuations in a world of extreme Central Bank intervention (Fig. 7.22).

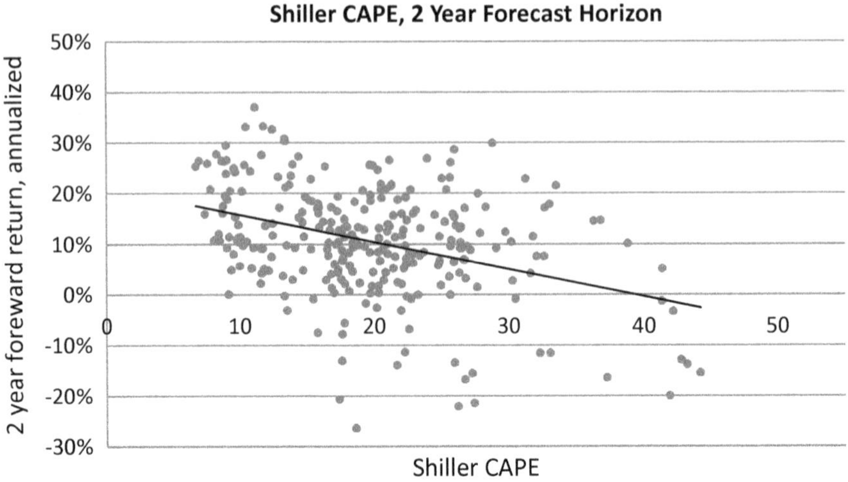


**Fig. 7.21** Shiller CAPE forecasting results, 2 year forward horizon (*Source* Online Data, Robert Shiller [http://www.econ.yale.edu/~shiller/data.htm])

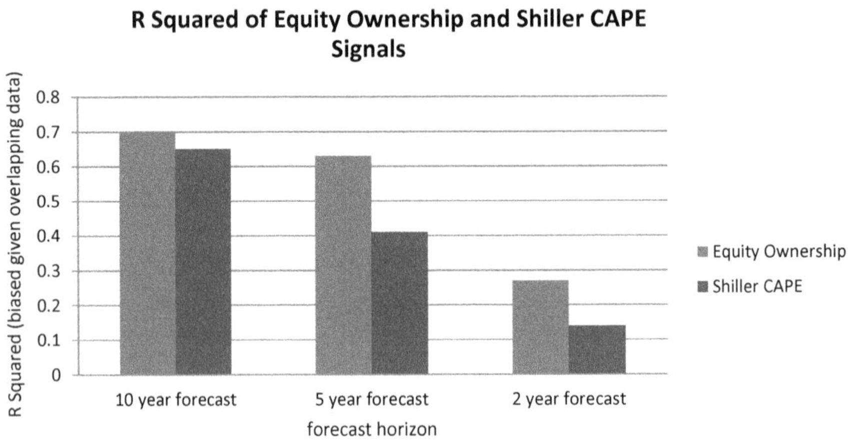


**Fig. 7.22** Summary of results (*Source* FRED, Robert Shiller [http://www.econ.yale.edu/~shiller/data.htm])

## A Comparison of Post-GFC Valuations

As it turns out, the equity supply variable is particularly well suited to the current QE dominated environment. It allows for higher equity valuations when

- government borrowing is increasing rapidly

- large corporations are taking advantage of an increase in prices to borrow even more and
- companies ambivalent about long-term growth prospects are engaging in net share buybacks. This simultaneously increases the supply of debt and decreases the quantity of equity shares available.

These factors all serve to justify price increases in the S&P 500 in a Goldilocks environment characterized by modest growth and an accommodative Fed. The ratio of US GDP to equity market capitalization, reportedly favored by Warren Buffett, is based on a similar idea. Here, the government can increase GDP (at least for a while) by borrowing money and engaging in large infrastructure projects. In this way, the quantity of debt and GDP are functionally related. However, relative equity supply incorporates new credit creation more directly than GDP. For example, consumer consumption can increase without an increase in credit for the household sector. GDP might go up, but fewer deposits are available for investment in the future. In other words, GDP does not give a clear picture of the quantity of funds available to real money investors.

We can now return to a functional comparison of relative equity supply and CAPE. CAPE shows a relatively large increase in equity valuations in the post-GFC landscape. An agent relying on CAPE would have been inclined to be more defensive than an equity supply investor. This would have led to significant underperformance from 2013 to the present. This is observable in the following Fig. 7.23. We do accept that both indicators would categorize

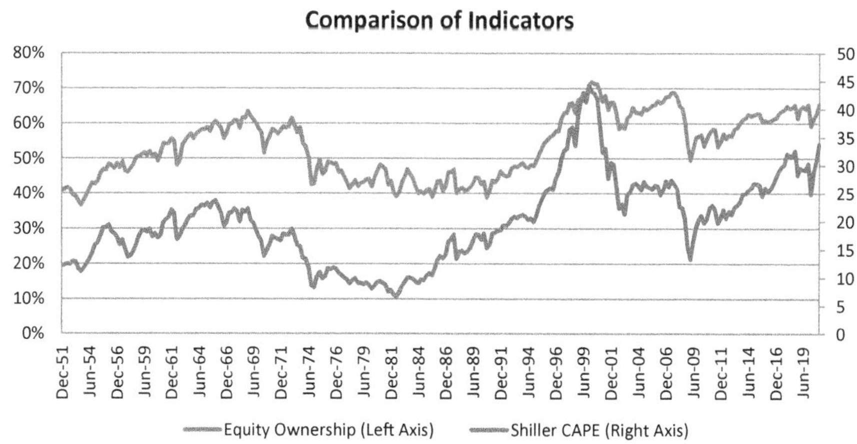


**Fig. 7.23** Historical time series for each indicator (*Source* FRED, Robert Shiller [http://www.econ.yale.edu/~shiller/data.htm])

stocks as expensive as of this writing.

Assuming that the equity supply paradigm is correct, we can make a strong conclusion. The extended bull market in equities has at least been partially enabled by an unprecedented increase in credit creation. If equities have been in a bubble, so have bonds, based on declining yields and record issuance.

## Concluding Thoughts

In this chapter, we have shown that credit expansion tends to contract spreads over reasonable horizons. Equities also tend to benefit, generally with a lag. This is not without consequences, as excess credit creation and untempered bullish sentiment has a tendency to borrow returns from the future. In other words, an abundance of liquidity can smooth things over for now, but may increase the severity of the next crisis. When aggregate leverage is high, markets are particularly vulnerable to random external shocks. The network is in a state of overload.

There is another way to think of the problem, in a more formal way. We can divide the credit cycle into four states, as in the following table.

| State | Description |
|---|---|
| 1 | Leverage low, decreasing |
| 2 | Leverage low, increasing |
| 3 | Leverage high, increasing |
| 4 | Leverage high, decreasing |

State 4 is the clear danger zone. Investors and the banking system at large have overextended themselves and are losing their access to funds. This is where the tremors across all capital markets are most meaningful. Realized volatility might be low, but if the value of risky assets drops enough, a chain reaction is likely to occur. Risk systems will turn red, prime brokers will raise their margin requirements and investors will be forced to liquidate more positions. Simultaneously, banks may lose access to cheap revolving lines of credit, restricting the flow of funds through the system.

All of this is consistent with Minsky's (2021) analysis of the business cycle. Minsky argued that the business cycle, with its exaggerated peaks and troughs, was a direct byproduct of a credit-fueled economy. Abundant credit might extend the bullish phase of the cycle, but comes at a cost. The subsequent crash would be much harder. In summary, leverage is a crucial parameter in the financial network, with banks acting as Dominant Agents in the creation and destruction of it.

# 8

# Playing Defense and Attack in the Presence of a Dominant Agent

> In the good mystery there is nothing wasted, no sentence, no word that is not significant. And even if it is not significant, it has the potential to be so—which amounts to the same thing.
>
> Paul Auster, City of Glass

The case studies we have presented in this book fall directly into the "Grey Swan" category. These are events that do not occur very often and cannot be timed exactly, but are the inevitable outcome of excess leverage and overzealous positioning. They do not come out of nowhere. In certain cases, we have been able to identify pre-conditions for liquidations and extended sell offs. We have pulled events from the extreme tails of the historical distribution and assigned higher probabilities to them, converting inaccurately labeled "Black Swans" into gray ones. In these cases, the historical distribution of returns does not characterize forward looking risk. In this sense, our book is highly complementary to Taleb (2007).

More specifically, we have focused on four main categories of Dominant Agents

- market makers, especially those that deal in options
- flow desks that hedge provider exposure in exchange-traded products
- dealers that support the pricing mechanism for various exchange-traded funds
- Central Banks, who vary the amount of cash and credit available to support the capital markets and indirectly, the economy at large.


H. P. Krishnan and A. Bennington, *Market Tremors*,
https://doi.org/10.1007/978-3-030-79253-4_8

We emphasize that this list is by no means exhaustive. For example, large institutions, such as pension and endowment funds, can also act as Dominant Agents. We alluded to their importance in Chapter 7. In particular, during periods of monetary expansion, these agents can push equity prices higher as they rebalance back to a set of target portfolio weights. Leveraged hedge funds (increasingly under the guise of family offices) also have the power to disrupt markets when forced to liquidate positions. The LTCM collapse, described by Lowenstein (2000) among others, falls directly into this category.

We have also glossed over the impact of various systematic strategies on the markets they trade. For example, trend following programs not only benefit from large directional moves in a given futures contract, but can also serve to amplify them. While other "risk targeting" strategies, such as volatility control funds, do not directly focus on trend, their behavior has a large overlap. When equity indices such as the S&P 500 rally, volatility tends to decline. In this regime, volatility control funds mechanically add to their equity exposure, implicitly following the trend. Positions are scaled inversely to volatility. By contrast, during a correction, these funds reduce risk by selling into an established downtrend.

The reasons for restricting our focus are not very complex. Decent risk estimates require good data. Whereas we can only estimate the size of a given structured product or strategy, we have direct access to (1) options open interest, (2) the market capitalization of an ETN or ETF and (3) the quantity of assets on a Central Bank's balance sheet. Accurate size estimates remove one layer of uncertainty from our Mean Field–Dominant Agent risk estimates.

## Sizing Positions Sensibly

As we have already mentioned, Market Tremors does not offer a catalog of trading strategies. Rather, it tries to incorporate credit and positioning into an overall assessment of risk, using a coherent methodology. However, we thought it might be useful to give some general guidelines about how the ideas in this book might be applied.

The simplest takeaway from the book would be something like this:

*do not size positions as* $\frac{1}{volatility}$ *when realized volatility is very low.*

Investors who ignore this premise do so at their own peril. They wind up with bloated allocations to pegged currencies, illiquid assets and crowded strategies that have a short volatility profile. When too many investors pile into a strategy that has low recent realized volatility, danger may be lurking below the surface. Various hedge funds have suffered permanent losses by taking volatility at face value, parking excess cash in risky money market accounts or relatively illiquid debt. The Treasury function of a bank or hedge fund should not be its main alpha generator.

A slightly more sophisticated version of this rule would be:

*do not consider sizing positions as* $\frac{1}{volatility}$ *unless you are able to adjust for positioning, credit and liquidity risk.*

In Chapter 5, we created a price impact adjusted risk estimate for VIX futures. Our more conservative estimate, while not exact, would have discouraged investors from shorting too many VIX futures in advance of the Volmageddon.

Focusing on Central Banks for a moment, we can set another guideline:

*take some exposure to credit and equity risk when CB balance sheet size increases, while maintaining a sturdy downside hedge.*

We find ourselves in this regime as of this writing. In Chapter 7, we observed that **median** outcomes for equities and corporate bonds improve after a bout of QE. However, we cannot say anything definitive about **extreme** outcomes. There is no certainty that the "Fed put" places a hard floor under equity or credit indices. There is no reason to expect intervention in the initial phases of a crash or during a garden variety bear market where markets are continuing to function properly. In fact, the scenario may be one where Federal Reserve assets stagnate or drop after a period of unusually strong growth may be as risky as any. Most shocks in recent memory have been deflationary, allowing Central Banks to pump money into the system without too much concern about yield expansion. However, in a world where inflationary shocks are becoming increasingly likely, options hedges offer the most reliable protection against a risk event in either direction. Long volatility is the final bastion of safety. Hedging has a broad meaning in this context, combining downside equity and credit structures with currency strategies that protect against monetary inflation.

## Identifying Pressure Points in the Market

Our focus on positioning risk indirectly puts technical analysis on a firmer footing. Market commentators have long focused on key support and resistance levels, along with signals such as the "golden cross". This signal is based on the difference between the 50 and 200 day trailing average for a broad equity index, such as the S&P 500. When the 50-day average crosses the 200 from below, the signal is considered bullish or "golden". Conversely, when it crosses from above, we are faced with the dreaded "death cross", where a cascade of selling may follow.

A question then arises. Why should round numbers (e.g., the S&P 500 at 4000) or arbitrary though widely quoted trend signals carry any value? Traditionally, many financial economists, including Fischer Black, considered these notions to be nothing more than superstition and wished to root them out of the financial lexicon. Other practitioners have suggested that technical signals retain value only because they encourage investment discipline. Given the same inputs, the same decisions will be made every time, without emotional intervention.

However, there is another way to think about the problem, one that has been gaining currency over time. Specific price levels, technical signals and volatility sizing inputs have significance precisely because they are **indicators of agent positioning**. If enough investors use the same decision rules, those rules will impact market prices. For example, options open interest for S&P E-mini futures options tends to congregate at round numbers. There are likely to be more open contracts at a 3500 strike than a 3530 one, say. It follows that if dealers are short these puts, they will have to rebalance their hedges more aggressively near 3500 than 3530. 3500 then becomes a key support level, as there will be excess selling pressure as the futures approach the strike.

Similarly, the death cross has significance because longer-term trend followers use similar inputs in their models. Near the death cross, a trend follower is likely to increase its short position, at least on a risk-adjusted basis. By extension, the difference between trailing 1 month and 12 month equity index volatility carries meaning, given that volatility control funds use this spread as a rebalancing mechanism.

We are now ready to issue the following advice.

1. *Take key support and resistance levels seriously, but* ***verify*** *where they are on your own.*

2. *Build your own DIY ("Do It Yourself") trend following, volatility control and risk parity models. Calibrate them to track the performance of individual funds or benchmark indices. Pay particular attention to levels where the model signal changes from BUY to SELL,* or vice versa. *These are your key levels.*
3. *Check the options markets in the assets you trade for large open interest at specific strikes. Infer whether dealers are likely to be long or short. When dealers are short, expect volatility expansion in a wide range around the strike.*
4. *When volatility expansion is nearby (even if it has not been realized yet), reduce exposure or hedge extreme downside scenarios with options. In the absence of an existing long position, consider going on the attack by setting STOP SELL orders above key support levels.*

## Exploiting Products with Fragile Design Features

In Chapters 4–6, we took aim at leveraged exchange-traded products, whose rebalancing requirements exceed what the underlying market can support. We also directed our attention at ETPs that try to convert a basket of illiquid securities into a single security that trades like a liquid stock.

More broadly, the rise of ETFs and "passively" managed mutual funds has altered the distribution of equity returns. Following Mike Green (personal correspondence), we can issue the following advice:

> *expect stronger positive trends during the virtuous cycle where inflows lead to mechanical buying and more performance-chasing inflows. Also prepare for sudden liquidations, often from a low volatility base.*

Many of the hedging strategies outlined in Krishnan (2017) are useful for protecting against extreme downside shocks with low premium outlay.

If we focus on specific exchange-traded products, the problems range from chronic underperformance to toxic leakage into the underlying market. They give rise to the following suggestions.

1. *Avoid buying and holding levered products when the reference index is mean reverting over daily horizons. You will constantly get topped and tailed, leading to underperformance over longer horizons.*
2. *For levered products, estimate the percentage of open interest or daily volume that will have to be bought or sold to rebalance at the close after a fixed size shock. For unlevered products, estimate the price impact of rebalancing in response to outflows. Adjust position sizes to account for the price impact of*

*these trades. More informally, keep an eye on flows into structured products that have strict rebalancing requirements.*

3. *Hold a smaller amount in ETFs that track an illiquid reference index than seems mathematically optimal. Do not automatically assume that an ETF trading at a severe discount offers good value, as the arbitrage mechanism between the ETF and NAV may be broken.*

We have included a spreadsheet at the end of this chapter that summarizes these ideas concisely. We are delighted that you, the reader, have made it this far, to the conclusion of Market Tremors.

| Dominant Agent Category | Sub-Category | What To Look For | How To Attack, Defend or Hedge |
|---|---|---|---|
| Market Makers | | | |
| source: www.squeezemetrics.com (DIX index) | Automated Market Makers in Equities | large short interest in a given security | buy, assuming demand from end investors, until dealers cover |
| **Chapter 6** | Options Market Makers in S&P 500 and other Equity Indices | large open interest at specific put strikes | set STOP sell orders above strikes with high open interest. Alternatively, buy wide put spreads around strikes to bet on follow through. |
| Systematic Strategies | | | |
| personal correspondance with Mark Serafini and others | Trend Following Strategies | breakouts that will cause a "typical" strategy to trade in the direction of the trend | build your own trend following model that tracks the performance of large funds, products or indices. trade in advance of model BUYS and SELLS, in the same direction. |
| source: Chandumont, "The Volatility Regime" and others | Volatility Control Strategies | jumps in equity volatility relative to a medium-term trailing average | DIY replication of publicly available strategies, anticipate rebalancing based on AUM, changes in estimated volatility and rebalancing schedule |
| source: Inker, "The Hidden Risk of Risk Parity Strategies" and others | Risk Parity Strategies | dislocations in stock, bond volatility | same as above |

| Dominant Agent Category | Sub-Category | What To Look For | How To Attack, Defend or Hedge |
|---|---|---|---|
| Exchange-Traded Products | | | |
| **Chapter 3** | Passive Equity ETFs | AUMs and trading volumes that approach or exceed actively managed portfolios | trade momentum based on flow-performance feedback, with left tail hedges to protect against cascading sales |
| **Chapter 3 Postscript and Chapter 4** | Leveraged Products | AUMs that damage underlying market given rebalancing requirements after a random shock | buy longer-dated puts or put spreads on strategies that mean revert over 1 day horizons. underallocate relative to historical volatility as AUMs increase. buy shorter-dated puts at strikes where market impact of rebalancing will be unusually large. |
| **Chapter 5** | Products With An Illiquid Benchmark | AUMs that break arbitrage mechanism if ETF trades at a persistent discount to NAV | underallocate relative to historical volatility in calm regimes |
| Mutual Funds | | | |
| **Chapter 5** | Passive Equity Mutual Funds | AUMs and trading volumes that approach or exceed actively managed portfolios | trade momentum based on flow-performance feedback, with left tail hedges to protect against cascading sales |
| **Chapter 5** | Corporate Bond Funds | recent underperformance, leading to redemptions from first movers | exit early and also try to be an early investor after a significant drop |
| Central Banks | | | |
| **Chapter 7** | Domestic (US Fed For $ Based Investors) | sharp changes in balance sheet size | sharp increases: reinvest in carry strategies cautiously; sharp decreases, relative to trend: sell equities and buy government bonds |
| source: www.crossborder.com | Foreign Central Banks | balance sheet changes that are out of sync with domestic CB | sell foreign currency if foreign CB is relatively dovish |

# References


Angelidis, Timotheos, and Alexandros Benos. 2006. Liquidity Adjusted Value-at-Risk Based on Components of the Bid-Ask Spread. *Applied Financial Economics* 16 (11): 835–851.

Avellaneda, Marco, and Michael Lipkin. 2003. A Market-Induced Mechanism for Stock Pinning. *Quantitative Finance* 3: 417–425.

Bank of International Settlements 2014. Market-Making and Proprietary Trading: Industry Trends, Drivers and Policy Implications. CFGS Papers, 52.

Bartolini, Matthew. 2019. ETF Mythbusting: High Yield ETFs are not Distorting the Bond Market. *ETF Strategy*, July 23.

Bao, Jack, Jun Pan, and Jiang Wang. 2011. The Illiquidity of Corporate Bonds. *The Journal of Finance* 66 (3): 911–946.

Bensoussan, Alain, Michael Chau, and Phillip Yam. 2014. Mean Field Games with a Dominating Player. *Applied Mathematics & Optimization* 74 (1): 91–128.

Bollerslev, Tim. 1986. Generalized Autoregressive Conditional Heteroskedasticity. *Journal of Econometrics* 31 (3): 307–327.

Bookstaber, Richard. 2017. *The End of Theory: Financial Crises, the Failure of Economics, and the Sweep of Human Interaction.* Princeton: Princeton University Press.

Bouchaud, Jean-Phillippe. 2009. Price Impact. *ResearchGate*. https://www.researchgate.net/publication/46462472_Price_Impact. Accessed 21 May 2021.

Capponi, Agostino, Paul Glasserman, and Marko Weber. 2018. Swing Pricing for Mutual Funds: Breaking the Feedback Loop between Fire Sales and Bond Runs. Office of Financial Research, US Department of Treasury Working Paper 18–04.

Carmona, Rene, and Francois Delarue. 2013. Probabilistic Analysis of Mean-Field Games. *SIAM Journal on Control and Optimization* 51 (4): 2705–2734.




H. P. Krishnan and A. Bennington, *Market Tremors*,
https://doi.org/10.1007/978-3-030-79253-4

Carmona, Rene, and Xiuneng Zhu. 2016. A Probabilistic Approach to Mean Field Games with Major and Minor Players. *The Annals of Applied Probability* 26 (3): 1535–1580.

Chandumont, Marie-Laure. 2015. The Volatility Regime: Why Managed Volatility Funds Exacerbate Equity Markets Correction. *The Actuary* 13 (1): 36–42.

Chen, Qi, Itay Goldstein, and Wei Jiang. 2010. Payoff Complementarities and Financial Fragility: Evidence from Mutual Fund Outflows? *The Journal of Financial Economics* 97 (2): 239–262.

Derman, Emanuel. 2003. The Boy's Guide to Pricing and Hedging. RISK January.

Einhorn, David. 2008. Private Profits and Socialized Risk. https://www.tilsonfunds.com/Einhorn-4-08.pdf. Accessed 21 May 2021.

Ellis, Katrina, Roni Michaely, and Maureen O'Hara. 2000. The Accuracy of Trade Classification Rules: Evidence from Nasdaq. *The Journal of Financial and Quantitative Analysis.* 35 (4): 529–551.

Engle, Robert. 1982. Autoregressive Conditional Heteroscedasticity with Estimates of the Variance of United Kingdom Inflation. *Econometrica* 50 (4): 987–1007.

Feigenbaum, J, and P. G. Freund. 1998. Discrete Scale Invariance and the "Second Black Monday". *Modern Physics Letters B* 12: 57–60.

Goldstein, Itay, Hao Jiang, and David Ng. 2017. Investor Flows and Fragility in Corporate Bond Ffunds. *Journal of Financial Economics* 126 (3): 592–613.

Gopikrishnan, P., V. Plerou, L. A. Nunes Amaral, M. Meyer, and H. E. Stanley. Scaling of the Distribution of Fluctuations of Financial Market Indices. *Physical Review E* 60: 5305–5316.

Haldane, Andrew G., and Arthur E. Turrell. 2019. Drawing on different disciplines: Macroeconomic agent-based models. *Journal of Evolutionary Economics* 29 (1): 39–66.

Hotchkis, Wiley. 2017. The Pitfalls of High Yield ETFs. September.

Huskaj, Bujar, and Nordén, Lars L. 2014. Two Order Books Are Better Than One? Trading at Settlement (TAS) in VIX Futures SSRN. https://ssrn.com/abstract=2437114. Accessed 21 May 2021.

Hussman, John. 2019. The Meaning of Valuation. https://www.hussmanfunds.com/comment/mc191203/. Accessed 21 May 2021.

Janeway, W.H. 2018. *Doing Capitalism in the Innovation Economy: Markets, Speculation and the State*, 2nd ed. Cambridge: Cambridge University Press.

Johansen, Anders, Olivier Ledoit, and Didier Sornette. 1999. Predicting Financial Crashes using Discrete Scale Invariance. *Journal of Risk* 1 (4): 5–32.

Johansen, Anders, Olivier Ledoit, and Didier Sornette. 2000. Crashes as Critical Points. *International Journal of Theoretical and Applied Finance* 3: 219–255.

Krishnan, Hari, and Izzy Nelken. 2001. The Effect of Stock Pinning on Option Prices, RISK, December.

Krishnan, Hari. 2017. *The Second Leg Down: Strategies for Profiting After a Market Sell Off*. Chichester: John Wiley and Sons.

Kyle, Albert S., and Anna A. Obizhaeva. 2017. Dimensional Analysis, Leverage Neutrality, and Market Microstructure Invariance. https://www.econ.ucdavis.edu/events/papers/1010Kyle.pdf. Accessed 21 May 2021.

Lahart, Justing. 2007. In Time of Tumult Obscure Economist Gains Currency—Mr. Minksy Long Argued Markets Were Crisis Prone: His "Moment Has Arrived". *Wall Street Journal*, August 18.

Lasry, Jean-Michel, and Pierre-Louis. Lions. 2007. Mean Field Games. *Japanese Journal of Mathematics* 2: 229–260.

Lee, Charles M.C., and Mark J. Ready. 1991. Inferring Trade Direction from Intraday Data. *The Journal of Finance* 46 (2): 733–746.

Lee, Tim, Jamie Lee, and Kevin Coldiron. 2019. *The Rise of Carry: The Dangerous Consequences of Volatility Suppression and the New Financial Order of Decaying Growth and Recurring Crisis*. New York: McGraw-Hill.

Lowenstein, Roger. 2000. *When Genius Failed: The Rise and Fall of Long-Term Capital Management*. New York: Random House.

Markowitz, Harry. 1952. Portfolio Selection. *The Journal of Finance* 7 (1): 77–91.

Mehrling, Perry. 2005. *Fischer Black and the Revolutionary Idea of Finance*. Hoboken, NJ: John Wiley and Sons.

Minski, Jill. 2021. Market Cap to GDP: An Updated Look at the Buffett Valuation Indicator. Advisor Perspectives, February 4.

Napach, Bernice. 2019. U.S. Passive Fund Assets Now Top Their Active Counterparts. ThinkAdvisor, October 29.

Nasdaq. 2020. Limit Up-Limit Down: Frequently Asked Questions. https://www.nasdaqtrader.com/content/MarketRegulation/LULD_FAQ.pdf. Accessed 21 May 2021.

Ni, Sophie Xiaoyan, Neil D. Pearson, and Allen M. Poteshman. 2005. Stock Price Clustering on Option Expiration Dates? *The Journal of Financial Economics* 78 (1): 49–87.

O'Hara, Maureen. 1999. *Market Microstructure Theory*, 1st ed. Malden, MA: Blackwell.

Gopikrishnan, P., V. Plerou, L.A.N. Amaral, M. Meyer, and H.E. Stanley. 1999. Scaling of the Distributions of Fluctuations of Financial Market Indices. *Physical Review E* 60: 5305–5316.

Perotta, Anthony J. and Colby Jenkins. 2016. Bond Liquidity Metrics: Reading between the Lines. https://research.tabbgroup.com/report/v14-007-bond-liquidity-metrics-reading-between-lines. Accessed 21 May 2021.

The Philosophical Economist. (2013). The Single Greatest Predictor of Future Stock Market Returns. *Phillosophical Economics*. https://www.philosophicaleconomics.com/2013/12/the-single-greatest-predictor-of-future-stock-market-returns/. Accessed 19 August 2021.

Pohl, Mathias, Alexander Ristig, Walther Schachermeyer, and Ludovic Tangpi. 2017. The Amazing Power of Dimensional Analysis: Quantifying Market Impact. *Market Microstructure and Liquidity* 3 (4): 03n4.

Scoblic, J. Peter, and Philip E. Tetlock. 2020. A Better Crystal Ball: The Right Way to Think About the Future. Foreign Affairs November/December 1.

Sharpe, William. 1964. Capital Asset Prices: A Theory of Market Equilibrium Under Conditions of Risk. *The Journal of Finance* 19 (3): 425–442.

Silber, William. 1991. Discounts on Rrestricted Stock: The Impact of Illiquidity on Stock Prices. *Financial Analysts Journal* 47 (4): 60–64.

Sornette, Didier, Anders Johansen, and Jean-Philippe. Bouchaud. 1996. Stock Market Crashes, Precursors and Replicas. *Journal de Physique* 1 (6): 167–175.

Sushko, Vladyslav, and Grant Turner. 2018. The Implications of Passive Investing for Securities Markets. *BIS Quarterly Review* March 2018: 113–131.

Taleb, Nassim. 1997. The Jorion-Taleb Debate. Derivatives Strategy, April.

Taleb, Nassim. 2007. *The Black Swan: The Impact of the Highly Improbable*. New York: Random House.

Thurner, Stefan, J. Doyne Farmer, and John Geanakoplos. 2012. Leverage Causes Fat Tails and Clustered Volatility. *Quantitative Finance* 12 (5), 695–707. https://doi.org/10.1080/14697688.2012.674301.

Vasicek, Oldrich. 1977. An Equilibrium Characterization of the Term Structure. *Journal of Financial Economics* 5 (2): 177–188.

Yates, Chrisotpher. 2021. The Consequences of Passive Investing. Seeking Alpha, January 28.

Zarinelli, Elia, Michele Treccani, J. Doyne Farmer, and Fabrizio Lillo. 2015. Beyond the Square Root: Evidence for Logarithmic Dependence of Market Impact on Size and Participation Rate. *Market Microstructure and Liquidity* 1 (2).

Zou, Joseph, and Emanuel Derman. 1999. Strike-Adjusted Spread: A New Metric for Estimating the Value of Equity Options. SSRN. https://ssrn.com/abstract=170629. Accessed 21 May 2021.

# Index

A

algorithmic trading 10, 28
arbitrage 66–70, 122, 123, 127, 131, 133, 136, 141, 154, 184
authorized participants ("APs") 67, 69

B

the Black-Scholes Formula 182
broker/dealers 2, 39, 51, 62, 63, 66–69, 73, 76, 78, 97, 98, 103, 108, 121–127, 130, 133–141, 145, 146, 152, 154, 155, 163, 167–171, 176, 179, 182, 186–195, 198, 232, 233, 236
buy-write strategy 188

C

Center for Research in Securities Prices (CRSP) 147, 150
Central Banks (CBs) 2, 4–7, 9, 11, 17, 19, 20, 22, 40, 51, 53–56, 94, 163, 202, 203, 205, 206, 211, 215, 217, 229, 233–235
circuit breakers 80, 131–133, 154
commercial bank assets 204
Commodity Trading Advisors (CTAs) 46–48
convertible arbitrage fund 141
convexity 30, 142–144
counterparty risk 9, 19
Covid lockdown 153
credit cycle 2, 4, 69, 140, 211, 217, 221, 232
credit expansion 2, 217, 226, 232

D

The Dark Index (DIX) 173, 174
delta hedge 52, 94, 165–167, 169, 172, 174, 185, 192, 198
diffusion equation 33
Dominant Agent 27, 40–51, 53, 56–59, 62, 72, 73, 80, 84, 85, 104, 107, 114, 115, 118, 119, 122, 123, 130, 141, 168, 171,


H. P. Krishnan and A. Bennington, *Market Tremors*,
https://doi.org/10.1007/978-3-030-79253-4

172, 185, 191, 198, 201, 202, 205, 208, 211, 218, 232–234
downside deviation 32

E

Economic Nowcasts 160
endogenous risk 9, 17, 18, 20, 38
endowment funds 234
equity risk premium 165, 222
Exchange-Traded Funds (ETFs) 22, 25, 39, 50–52, 61–72, 74–80, 121–136, 141, 146, 147, 149–152, 154–156, 199, 201, 210, 233, 234, 237
Exchange-Traded Notes (ETNs) 50, 61, 63, 70–72, 74–77, 79, 80, 85, 90, 91, 97–101, 103, 104, 107, 112, 115, 117–119, 121
Exchange-Traded Products (ETPs) 22, 41, 50, 51, 62, 63, 65, 66, 72–75, 78, 85, 233, 237
exogenous risk 9, 194
expected shortfall 32, 47, 114, 119

F

Fed balance sheet 214, 215
Federal Reserve System (Fed) 36, 54–56
feedback loop 3, 17, 18, 27, 40, 70, 85, 99, 115, 122, 128, 143, 146, 155, 157, 163, 171, 193, 202, 205, 220
the Fed "Put" 2, 7, 22, 137, 155, 157, 202–218, 225
Feigenbaum and Freund Model 56
financial agent 14, 210
fire sale 27, 38, 44, 105, 111, 123, 135, 149
flash crash 28, 51, 95, 150
flow desk 71, 104, 119, 233
fractional reserve banking 38, 207
futures and options 18, 25

G

Gamestop (Ticker: GME) 53, 98
gamma, gamma hedging 29, 53
Gamma Index (GEX) 53, 159, 173–186, 193, 198, 199
GARCH 34
the GJN Model (Goldstein, Jiang and Ng) 142, 157
Global Financial Crisis (GFC) 2, 11, 12, 19, 37, 38, 85, 137, 207, 216

H

high frequency traders (HFTs) 11, 51, 52, 104
hostile takeover 44, 114, 119
HYG 125–129, 131–136, 146, 149, 151, 154–156, 158

I

index collars (options strategy) 163, 165, 194
indistinguishability 34–37, 39, 40
insurance companies 4, 18, 124, 139, 145, 218
inverse VIX ETPs 22, 78

J

JLS Model (Johansen, Ledoit and Sornette) 56
JNK 126, 127, 132–136, 146, 149, 154–156, 158

L

leveraged products 73–75, 77
levered VIX ETPs 51
liquidity providers and takers 52
liquidity risk 6, 69, 145, 235
long volatility 87, 97
"LPPL" or Log Periodic Power Law Model 57

LQD ETF 155

M

margin 2, 3, 27, 36, 38, 52, 78, 117, 119, 122, 141, 167, 204, 208, 222, 232
market makers 10, 22, 29, 36, 40, 49, 51–53, 66, 67, 91, 121, 130, 133, 165–174, 176, 179, 180, 182, 183, 185, 187–194, 198, 201, 233
max (maximum) drawdown 4, 20, 74, 85, 92, 176
Mean Field 21, 26, 27, 32–36, 40–43, 46, 48, 52, 56, 57, 59, 62, 84, 85, 114, 118, 122, 123, 128, 130, 168, 171, 205, 217, 234
Mean Field Theory (MFT) 21, 25, 30, 44
Mexican Peso Crisis 58
Moody's BAA corporate spread 211
mutual fund 61, 64, 65, 124, 130, 141–147, 152, 154–157, 237

N

Nash equilibrium 59
Net Asset Value (NAV) 63, 66–68, 72, 81, 98, 122, 125–128, 130, 131, 133, 136, 141, 143, 154, 155
node 10, 11, 19, 36–39

O

open market operations 205, 206, 224
options open interest 53, 168, 170, 172, 191, 234, 236
options straddles 187

P

the pain trade 12
parameter stability 45, 48
passive strategies 76
path dependency 32, 73, 79, 80, 107
pension funds 7, 39, 124, 139, 145, 164, 218
portfolio theory 14–17, 21, 25, 27, 32
positioning risk 9, 13, 14, 27, 30, 38, 40, 41, 56, 168, 181
price impact function 105, 113, 114, 121, 123
primary dealers 36, 55, 136, 137, 206
primary market transactions 126, 127, 135

Q

Quantitative easing (QE) 7, 23, 202, 204, 209–217, 230, 235

R

risk on/risk off=risk seeking/risk averse 28, 67, 100, 126, 130, 149, 170, 207

S

shadow banks 204
Shiller CAPE index 217, 227–230
short volatility 4, 6, 59, 73, 98, 104, 115, 118, 163, 188, 235
60/40 portfolio 219, 220
the S&P 500 Volatility Index, or VIX 4, 5, 22, 39, 50, 66, 71–73, 80, 83–105, 107, 109, 110, 112–119, 121, 127, 131, 133, 144, 145, 149, 156, 163, 164, 180–183, 199, 201, 235
stock pinning 192, 194

Strategic Asset Allocation (SAA) Template 6, 218–222, 225, 226
SVXY 97–99, 117, 118

T

takeover premium 44, 112, 113, 134
TAS (Trade at Settlement) Order Book 103, 104
tender offer 111, 112, 114
TRACE database 140

U

utility function 21, 38, 59

V

Value-at-Risk (VAR) 46–48
Vanguard Total Bond Index 147, 150
VCIT ETF 155
velocity of money 204, 210
volatility control strategies 180, 234
Volmageddon=Volpocalypse 22, 58, 71, 83, 85, 92, 98, 100, 101, 105, 107, 108, 110, 113–119, 123, 127, 201, 235
Volume-Weighted Average Price (VWAP) 106

W

WTI (West Texas Intermediate) Crude Oil Futures 109

X

XIV 83, 97–99, 116–118

GPSR Compliance
The European Union's (EU) General Product Safety Regulation (GPSR) is a set of rules that requires consumer products to be safe and our obligations to ensure this.

If you have any concerns about our products, you can contact us on

ProductSafety@springernature.com

In case Publisher is established outside the EU, the EU authorized representative is:

Springer Nature Customer Service Center GmbH
Europaplatz 3
69115 Heidelberg, Germany

www.ingramcontent.com/pod-product-compliance
Ingram Content Group UK Ltd.
Pitfield, Milton Keynes, MK11 3LW, UK
UKHW020729041026
15590UKWH00002B/970
* 9 7 8 3 0 3 0 7 9 2 5 2 7 *